Daydream Believers

Daydream Believers

How a Few Grand Ideas Wrecked American Power

Fred Kaplan

John Wiley & Sons, Inc.

Published by John Wiley & Sons, Inc., Hoboken, New Jersey
Published simultaneously in Canada

For general information about our other products and services, please contact our Customer Care Department within the United States at (800) 762-2974, outside the United States at (317) 572-3993 or fax (317) 572-4002.

Wiley also publishes its books in a variety of electronic formats. Some content that appears in print may not be available in electronic books. For more information about Wiley products, visit our web site at www.wiley.com.

Library of Congress Cataloging-in-Publication Data:

Kaplan, Fred M.
   Daydream believers : how a few grand ideas wrecked American
power / Fred Kaplan.
      p. cm.
   Includes bibliographical references and index.
   ISBN 978-0-470-12118-4 (cloth)
   1. United States—Foreign relations—2001– 2. United States—Military policy.
3. Power (Social sciences)—United States—History—21st century. 4. Strategy—
History—21st century.   I. Title.
   JZ1480.K38 2008
   327.73—dc22

                                                                2007044576

Printed in the United States of America

10 9 8 7 6 5 4 3 2 1

To Brooke, Maxine, and Sophie

All men dream: but not equally. Those who dream by night in the dusty recesses of their minds wake in the day to find that it was vanity. But the dreamers of the day are dangerous men, for they may act their dream with open eyes, to make it possible.

—T. E. Lawrence, *Seven Pillars of Wisdom*

Contents

Introduction

Nearly all of America's blunders in war and peace these past few years stem from a single grand misconception: that the world changed after September 11, when in fact it didn't.

Certainly things about the world changed, not least Americans' sudden awareness that they were vulnerable. But the way the world works—the nature of power, warfare, and politics among nations—remained essentially the same.

A real change, a seismic shift in global politics, had taken place a decade earlier, with the collapse of the Soviet Union and the end of the Cold War. Yet America's political leaders at the start of the twenty-first century misunderstood this shift—and in a way that their misreading of 9/11 would exacerbate.

George W. Bush and his top aides in the White House and the Pentagon came to office believing that the United States had emerged from its Cold War victory as the world's "sole super-power" and that they could therefore do pretty much as they pleased: issue orders and expect obeisance, topple rogue regimes at will, honor alliances and treaties when they were useful, and disregard them when they weren't.

But in fact, the end of the Cold War made America weaker, less capable of exerting its will on others. And its leaders' failure to recognize this, their inclination to devise policies based on the premise of omnipotence, made America weaker still.

For all its rigidities and horrors, the Cold War was a system of international order and security. Most nations fell into one of two camps: the American-led West or the Soviet-controlled East. In exchange for their loyalty or submission, these countries received guarantees of protection. The collapse of the Soviet Union at the end of 1991 meant the collapse of this system—and the evaporation of the threat whose very existence had bolstered America's power and influence.

As long as there were two superpowers, the countries in between often felt compelled to pay fealty to their protector's interests, even when those interests collided with their own. Now, in a world with just one superpower, there was no fulcrum of pressure, no common looming enemy, to keep the bloc in line. Many of America's allies remained allied, whether out of inertia, shared values, shared interests, or a continuing desire for security. But they were also free to go their own way, pursue their own interests, form their own alliances of convenience, without much regard to Washington's thoughts about the matter.

There were two traditional courses a president might have taken to preserve American influence in this geopolitical setting. One was to don the mantle of explicit empire: build up vast armies, deploy them worldwide, and not hesitate to unleash them when necessary. But there was neither the money nor the manpower for a truly imperial army; nor did the American people have the stomach for prolonged engagement in brutal, distant wars.

The other course was to revitalize alliances, renovating the old ones, cultivating new ones, forging as many links around as many issues and interests as possible. A president could have taken this course for purely pragmatic reasons. Powerful nations, especially powerful democracies, have always needed allies, if not to get a job done, then to get it done with shared burdens and legitimacy—to get it done and keep it done. And in a world with no opposing superpower to cement its alliances by default, the United States would need allies more than ever and would have to work harder at diplomacy to lure—and keep—them on board.

Few in high office recognized this paradox of power. To President George W. Bush and most of his aides (as well as the Republican-controlled Congress, many editorial-page writers, and a growing number of Democrats), American power seemed not merely undiminished but nearly absolute. It was a new era, time to devise new ways of seeing and dealing with the world—new strategies that would take full advantage of what they saw as their unbridled supremacy.

The traditional paths to influence were waved off as the figments of "old thinking." Multinational diplomacy was unnecessary; the United States could go it alone. Fine if allies wanted to come along; even better—less constraining—if they didn't. Nor were massive armies any longer a prerequisite to dominance. New American-made technologies made possible lightning victories on the battlefield with far fewer troops and much lighter armaments. The mere demonstration of these weapons, of how quickly they can crush an enemy's army and destroy its regime, would compel other foes to change their ways and fall into our orbit or else face the same doom. Other new technologies, it was believed, would soon allow us to shoot down an enemy's nuclear missiles, ending the twentieth century's most harrowing nightmare and nullifying the one grave threat that hostile regimes might still pose.

These ideas had been developed and debated all through the 1990s by foreign policy intellectuals, many of them former mid-level officials in the Republican administrations of Ronald Reagan and George H. W. Bush. Exiled to think tanks during the Democratic reign of Bill Clinton, they were now ushered back to power by the election of Bush's son—and eager to translate their ideas into reality.

In the opening months of George W. Bush's presidency, they met the resistance that new ideas usually spark from bureaucracies. Then came September 11. The attacks on the World Trade Center and the Pentagon weren't quite unprecedented in the annals of history, but they were new to American soil, and top officials quickly agreed that they demanded a new kind of response—a new strategy for dealing not just with the attackers but with the entire range of threats in the post–Cold War world.

These policy intellectuals—some called themselves "vulcans" or "neoconservatives"—had a new strategy set to go. And nobody else did, at least nobody so highly placed or committed. Their strategy, which converged neatly with Bush's and his top officials' own predilections, would serve as the framework for how to look at the world and what to do next.

America would go to war against this new kind of foe; the intellectuals had a strategy for a new kind of war. The old rostrums of stability, deterrence, and containment were deemed irrelevant (after all, they hadn't prevented 9/11); the new strategists called for regime change, preemption, and victory. And their concept of victory was expansive, to include not only defeating an enemy in battle or "making the world safe for democracy" but—in an ambitious twist on that age-old ideal—remaking the world *into* a democracy.

Yet this new strategy was not as new as it seemed. Pieces of it had been around for decades, had been tried before, and had proved illusory. Some of them, this time out, appeared to hold more promise. Technology had improved; the political climate was more receptive. But the world hadn't become so pliable. The laws of physics remained intact. Military and political power still had their limits.

Bombs could now hit targets with uncanny precision, and armies could maneuver across landscapes with impressive speed. But winning battles didn't mean achieving the objectives of a war. Toppling a rogue regime was one thing, and not always easy; but propping up a new government to replace it was another thing entirely, and creating the conditions for democracy was something else still.

There were some appealing ideas in the new strategy. But its champions—once in high office, keen to carve out new policies— started to tout and embrace the ideas as if they were elixirs, not merely useful tools. They grew entranced by the new kinds of power—the new kind of world—that these ideas might bring into being. The ideas morphed into a vision, the vision into a dream. After September 11, they took their dream into the real world— acted it with open eyes—and saw it dissolve into a nightmare.

1

The Mirage of Instant Victory

Two weeks after George W. Bush took office, his secretary of defense, Donald Rumsfeld, invited an old friend named Andrew Marshall to lunch.

Rumsfeld had held this job once before, in 1975, during the final year of Gerald Ford's brief presidency. He was just forty-two back then, the youngest defense secretary in history. Now, at sixty-eight, he was the oldest, though still vigorous. In the quarter-century between the two appointments, he had done well in the private sector, most notably as chief executive officer of G. D. Searle Pharmaceuticals. By the time Bush was elected, Rumsfeld was eager to return to power, but only if he had a mandate to shake things up. Bush gave him that mandate.

Near the start of his presidential campaign, Bush had given a speech at The Citadel—the historic military college in Charleston, South Carolina—spelling out his top priorities for a new defense policy. He would deploy antiballistic missiles "at the earliest possible date," even if doing so meant withdrawing from the ABM Treaty, the long-standing centerpiece of Russian-American arms control accords. And he would transform the United States military. A "revolution in the technology of war" was in the works, he declared. Battles of the future would be won not by an army's "mass or size," but by its "mobility and swiftness," and vital new roles would be played by information networks and by highly accurate missiles and bombs.

If taken seriously, this was a truly dramatic pronouncement. It would mean a new concept of nuclear deterrence, an overhaul of the Army, a new look for war and peace.

As president, Bush said, he would order his secretary of defense to conduct "an immediate, comprehensive review of our military—the structure of its forces, the state of its strategy, the priorities of its procurement." The secretary would have "a broad mandate—to challenge the status quo and envision a new architecture of American defense for decades to come." Now that he was president, he told Rumsfeld to carry out that comprehensive review.

That's why Rumsfeld asked Andy Marshall to come have lunch. Marshall had done more than any single person to foment this revolution. He had been a central figure in spelling out its elements and implications. He had directly influenced dozens of defense officials and analysts, in and out of government. Bush's Citadel speech was based in large measure, on ideas that Marshall had long propagated.

Marshall was just short of eighty years old when Rumsfeld called him. He'd been working in the Pentagon for the last twenty-eight of those years, uninterrupted, through six—now, with Bush, seven—presidents. His title all those years was Director of the Office of Net Assessment. James Schlesinger had appointed him to the job when he was defense secretary back in 1973, during Richard Nixon's administration. Schlesinger and Marshall had been friends and colleagues at the RAND Corporation, the U.S. Air Force–sponsored think tank in Santa Monica that fostered some of the early thinking about nuclear war and nuclear deterrence in the 1950s.

Marshall had started work at RAND in 1949, among the very first of those thinkers. Some of his associates would write books, or give lectures to vast audiences, or take jobs in Washington. But Marshall had no craving for the limelight or for visible power. When he did finally go to work in the nation's capital—at first, briefly, as a consultant at the National Security Council before moving over to the Pentagon—his office was obscure by design, mandated to report only to his immediate boss, not to Congress or the public, and that suited him fine. He was a gnomic operator who never put his name on an article and rarely said a word at meetings. His furtiveness spawned a mystique, which amused him. After the movie *The Empire Strikes Back* came out, some referred to him as "Yoda." He had stayed at his job for so long (longer than anyone else at a policy level in all of Washington) for two reasons. First, he tried, as much as possible, to stay out of the fights over budgets and weapons systems, which stirred so many rivalries and frayed so many tempers. Second, he built a far-flung network of acolytes and loyalists: officers whose unconventional projects he had encouraged and helped to fund; analysts whose work he had sponsored and whose ideas he had helped form; and high-ranking officials, as well as committee chairmen on Capitol Hill, who simply valued having a man of ideas so high up in the Pentagon.

When Bill Cohen, the third of President Clinton's three secretaries of defense, tried to eliminate Marshall's office as a cost-cutting measure, dozens of powerhouses from all over Washington urged—in some cases threatened—Cohen to back off. He did.

Marshall figured the lunch with Rumsfeld would be a perfunctory get-together, the two of them in the secretary's office, discussing what roles the Office of Net Assessment might play this time around. But he was told the lunch would take place in the Gold Room—the ornate private dining hall near the secretary's office on the Pentagon's third floor, where the waiters have security clearances, so that classified matters can be discussed without restraint—and that a few other officials, including Rumsfeld's new deputy secretary, Paul Wolfowitz, would also attend.

As soon as everyone sat down, Rumsfeld came to the point. He wanted Marshall to write a paper on a new strategy, a guide on how to look at the new world and how the U.S. military should adapt to it.

Marshall was almost excited. His office had no institutional power; it was influential only to the extent that a secretary of defense wanted it to be, and the last couple of secretaries hadn't been keen about the notion. He had known and liked Rumsfeld for many years. The first time Rumsfeld was secretary, he frequently marked up the margins of Marshall's reports with notes and questions. In recent years, when Rumsfeld chaired panels on military issues—to prepare for a return to power—he had always asked Marshall to present a briefing.

Rumsfeld wanted the strategy paper done within six weeks. Marshall wrote a first draft in just a few days. A paper like this had been swirling around in his head for years. The events and inventions that served as its foundation had been evolving and coalescing for three decades, and he had been tracking them all closely, in some cases helping to push them along. Maybe now something would really happen; maybe someone would translate his ideas into policy.

• • •

In 1973, the year Marshall came to the Pentagon, two big things were happening in the realm of defense policy. First, the Vietnam War, clearly a disaster, was winding down. Second, attention was shifting back to the military balance in Europe, and it didn't look good. Along the border of East and West Germany, the troops of the Soviet Union and the Warsaw Pact had long outnumbered those of the United States and the North Atlantic Treaty Organization. NATO's qualitative superiority had always compensated for the Warsaw Pact's numerical edge. Now it seemed that the Soviets were catching up on quality.

The Yom Kippur War erupted in October, one month before Marshall went to work for Schlesinger. Israel beat back the Arab armies through superior tactics and firepower, but some of the Arabs' Soviet-made weapons performed better than expected. The war also revealed how intense and fast-paced modern battles could be. Guided missiles, especially antiarmor and antiair missiles, played a bigger role than they had in previous wars. Forces advanced and retreated on the battlefield with remarkable speed.

Officers who considered the possibility of a NATO–Warsaw Pact war had assumed the United States would have time to mobilize reinforcements if the Soviets ever invaded. Now it seemed that the first battle might be decisive. And it was widely accepted that the United States couldn't use nuclear weapons to beat back the Soviet army; the Soviets had attained nuclear parity with America by this point; if the U.S. fired nukes, the U.S.S.R. could fire back.

That year, the Advanced Research Projects Agency, a high-tech think tank inside the Pentagon, commissioned a secret study that carried a deliberately vague title: "The Long Range Research and Development Planning Program." Its purpose was "to identify and characterize" new military technologies that might give the president "a variety of response options"—including "alternatives to massive nuclear destruction"—if the Soviets invaded Western Europe.

ARPA set up three working panels to conduct the study. One, the Strategic Alternatives Panel, was chaired by a defense analyst named Albert Wohlstetter. At the time, Wohlstetter was a professor at the University of Chicago. But through the 1950s and into the early '60s, he had been one of the top nuclear strategists at the RAND Corporation. Wohlstetter was Andy Marshall's chief mentor in his RAND days; he was the chief mentor to most of the analysts who thought about deterring and fighting nuclear wars.

Wohlstetter was intensely charismatic. He grew up in New York City, studied mathematical logic and philosophy at City College, knew about good wine, food, modern design, and architecture. His wife, Roberta, wrote a seminal book on why U.S. intelligence didn't detect signs of the attack on Pearl Harbor. (Titled *Pearl Harbor: Warning and Decision*, it was written at RAND under Andy Marshall's supervision.) She was also a gourmet cook. Albert's acolytes would gather for dinner at the Wohlstetters' home in the Hollywood hills and discuss the finer things in life as well as the deadliest. It was a heady experience for men who spent their workdays calculating bomb-damage probabilities on slide rules.

In the early '50s, Wohlstetter had led RAND's most famous study, a quantitative analysis concluding that the U.S. Strategic Air Command's massive fleet of nuclear bombers was vulnerable to a

Soviet sneak attack. There were vast gaps in SAC's early-warning radar systems. The bombers themselves were sitting out on runways, unprotected and, for the most part, unarmed. They lacked the range to fly nonstop from the United States to Russia, so, in order to launch a retaliatory attack, they would first have to fly to "staging bases," where they would be armed and refueled. The problem, in Wohlstetter's analysis, was that the equation worked both ways. The staging bases were close enough to hit Russia, but that meant Russian bombers were close enough to hit the bases. The Soviets could bomb the bases and render them useless before American commanders could even get their own strike under way.

Wohlstetter was a showman. He took his top-secret study to Washington and briefed it to officers and officials—in the Pentagon, the State Department, and the White House—ninety-two times. A few years later, he wrote a follow-up study that revealed vulnerabilities in the Air Force's deployment plan for intercontinental ballistic missiles. He wrote an unclassified version of the study and published it in the January 1959 issue of *Foreign Affairs* under the title "The Delicate Balance of Terror." Everyone in the foreign policy establishment read the article. Everyone was stunned by it. Washington was in the grip of fear over a "missile gap." The intelligence branch of the Air Force and its allies in Congress were charging that the United States was perilously behind the Soviet Union in long-range missiles. Wohlstetter considered the charge oversimplified, but his article fed the fears and lent them intellectual credibility.

Though he didn't know it, Wohlstetter's conclusions were based on faulty intelligence (it turned out that the Soviet Union was way *behind* the United States in long-range missiles and had *no* ability to launch a disarming first strike). His analysis had useful consequences, in any case. The Air Force dispersed its bomber fleet and put the planes on alert. When ICBMs came along, they too were dispersed and encased in underground, blast-resistant silos.

Inside the community of defense intellectuals, Wohlstetter's study influenced the way all such subsequent studies would be conducted. His method of quantitative "systems analysis" gave the strategists a niche. The military establishment at the time had no training in this sort of analysis. Civilians like Wohlstetter and his colleagues could brief their studies in Washington—and possibly have an impact. And Wohlstetter emerged from the exercise a sort of demigod; in certain circles, anything he said would be taken very seriously.

•   •   •

When Wohlstetter was appointed to the Strategic Alternatives Panel, he talked frequently with Marshall about the study. ARPA had a number of intriguing technologies on the drawing board. One implicit purpose of this study was to make a case that these projects should be given more money. Thinking about the lessons of the Yom Kippur War and the growing parity in the European balance of power, Wohlstetter figured out at least a theoretical role for some of those projects, especially those involving highly accurate bombs and missiles.

"Based on the analysis," Wohlstetter wrote in the classified report, which was finished in February 1975, "it appears that non-nuclear weapons with near-zero miss may be technically feasible and militarily effective."

A bomb's ability to destroy a target depends on two things: its explosive power and its accuracy. There's a trade-off: the bigger the blast, the less need for an accurate weapon; the more accurate the weapon, the less need for a big blast. If small, non-nuclear weapons really could be guided to within a few feet of their targets ("near-zero miss," as Wohlstetter put it), they would have the same destructive power—the same ability to destroy a specific target—as a much larger nuclear bomb.

Wohlstetter was also intrigued by another set of ARPA programs called remotely piloted vehicles, or RPVs—small, unmanned aircraft, guided by remote control and loaded with a small bomb and a camera.

The idea was the brainchild of John Foster, a former Los Alamos physicist and at the time director of the Pentagon's research and engineering division. Foster got the idea from his enthusiasm for model airplanes. When Wohlstetter was writing his report, two RPVs, called Praerie and Calere, were in the early stages of development. Each vehicle weighed seventy-five pounds, was powered by a modified lawn mower engine, and could stay aloft for two hours while carrying a twenty-eight-pound payload.

Wohlstetter envisioned a way to link all these technologies—the RPVs, the highly accurate munitions, and a few other devices, some still hypothetical—into a single weapons system or a network of systems. A camera inside an RPV, he wrote, would scan the ground along its flight path and transmit the images back to base, where a commander would steer the vehicle to the target by remote control. The RPV would also carry an accurate bomb or missile, which the commander could fire—again, by remote control—when the plane came within range of the target. Both the vehicle and the bomb could be guided by radio, microwaves, or—in the more distant future—the signals from satellites using the Global Positioning System, the first of which were about to be launched while Wohlstetter was writing his paper. With GPS guidance, he calculated, bombs could land "less than 10 feet" from their targets.

The project's assignment had been to identify technologies that could give the president a variety of non-nuclear "strategic response options" to a Soviet invasion of Western Europe. Here was such an option.

If the Soviets invaded West Germany, these accurate, long-range bombs and missiles could destroy targets well behind enemy lines—knocking out air bases, supply depots, follow-on echelons of Soviet tank formations, and so forth—and could thus disrupt and delay the Soviet offensive, giving NATO a chance to regroup and fight back.

In 1976, as a direct result of this study, ARPA began to develop a program called Assault Breaker, designed to launch "precision strikes" against moving targets deep behind enemy lines. The weapon system consisted of several components: "precision-guided" missiles, radar that could track enemy tanks and guide the missiles to their locations, as well as a data-transmission network that linked the weapons and the radar together. Bundled together, this "system of systems," as ARPA described it, matched Wohlstetter's concept almost exactly.

• • •

In 1978, ARPA and the U.S. Army started conducting tests to demonstrate the Assault Breaker's technical feasibility. One year later, Andrew Marshall started noticing signs that the Russians were in a panic. One major task of his Office of Net Assessment was to monitor the writings of Soviet military officers. In their classified journal, *Military Thought*, then in a series of articles by Marshal Nikolai Ogarkov in their army's newspaper, *Red Star*, Soviet commanders were depicting the Assault Breaker as a huge threat to their strategy on the European front.

The Russians tended to view history as a force propelled by revolutions. In the twentieth century, military revolutions—technological advances that triggered whole new strategies of warfare—had included the armored tank, aerial bombardment, radio, radar, and nuclear weapons. Ogarkov in particular saw the Assault Breaker as the harbinger of another "military-technical revolution," as he called it, which could give the United States a decisive edge on the battlefield.

Andy Marshall didn't quite know what to make of these writings. The Assault Breaker was still new; the early technical tests were uneven, at best. It was unclear whether the system would ever work. But the Russians were taking it very seriously, and that was important. If *they* thought that these weapons not only worked but revolutionized warfare, the Pentagon should buy lots of them, to reinforce the Russians' perception, to persuade them that they couldn't win a war in Europe and that, therefore, they shouldn't start one.

By the mid-1980s, as microprocessing technologies advanced, the various branches of the U.S. military developed a host of new weapons that fell into this category—laser-guided bombs, radar-guided missiles, high-resolution surveillance gear, and high-speed communications networks that could link them together.

In the summer of 1986, Wohlstetter and another former RAND analyst named Fred Iklé chaired a panel called the Commission on Integrated Long-Term Strategy. Marshall and a RAND economist named Charles Wolf ran one of the commission's working groups, which focused on likely changes in the "security environment" over the next twenty years. Two of the predictions by Marshall and Wolf were especially pertinent. One was that Ogarkov would be proved right—the new weapons systems really would change the face of warfare. The other was that the Soviet economy was in worse shape than the CIA was estimating. The implication of the two predictions together was that the high-tech weapons might give America a profound advantage—and that the Soviet Union might not have the resources to compete. Marshall, in describing this phenomenon, didn't want to use the Russian term—"military-technical revolution." So he called it a "revolution in military affairs." The term caught on in certain circles and was widely referred to by its initials, RMA.

The final report, finished in August 1988 and titled *Discriminate Deterrence*, was an elaboration of the ideas that Wohlstetter, Marshall, and a few others had been mulling for the past decade. But unlike the earlier reports, this one was issued to the public, replete with a Pentagon press conference featuring the coauthors. Several Western European governments reacted furiously. They took any suggestion that America might not protect them with nuclear weapons as a sign of abandonment, a ripping apart of the transatlantic alliance. (The Cold War's final decade was a strangely abstract time.)

But the report's more enduring impact was that it put the RMA concept on the table—with official backing—just at the moment when many of the weapons systems it envisioned were going into production and assuming high profiles in the Pentagon budget.

These weapons included not just the Assault Breaker, which had been taken over by the U.S. Army, but a new generation of laser-guided bombs in the arsenals of the Air Force. And the new secretary of the Air Force, appointed after George H. W. Bush took over the White House in January 1989, was Donald Rice, a man as sympathetic to these new weapons as anyone could be.

• • •

Through most of the 1970s and '80s, Don Rice was president of the RAND Corporation. He kept in touch with Marshall and Wohlstetter during those years, and he knew about their reports on accurate weapons. Marshall and Wohlstetter had left Santa Monica many years earlier, but they had stayed in touch with several RAND analysts who were engrossed in similar studies on how the laser-guided bombs could boost the Air Force's fortunes.

These weapons had achieved one spectacular success toward the end of the Vietnam War—the bombing of the Thanh Hoa Bridge, a 540-foot-long span of steel across the Song Ma River, seventy miles south of Hanoi. Most of the North Vietnamese Army's supplies were sent across this bridge. In the mid-to-late 1960s, U.S. Air Force and Navy pilots flew hundreds of sorties, dropping thousands of bombs in an attempt to destroy it. These were "dumb bombs," not much different from those used in World War II. Dropped from an airplane's bomb bay, they fell by the force of gravity and, on their way down to Earth, were thrown off target by the wind. The North Vietnamese had surrounded the bridge with a ring of air defenses—three hundred antiair artillery guns, eighty-five surface-to-air missile sites, and a wing of MiG fighter jets at a nearby base. Eleven U.S. planes were shot down trying to get at the bridge. As a result, American pilots had to fly at higher altitudes to avoid the air defenses, which made their bombs drift still farther away from the target. Overhead photos showed so many bomb craters around the bridge that some nicknamed the area the "valley of the moon."

On May 13, 1972, the Air Force had another go at the bridge, its first in four and a half years, this time flying a mere fourteen F-4 fighter bombers, some of them loaded with two dozen two-thousand- to three-thousand-pound versions of the new laser-guided bombs. They looked like any other bombs, except that the nose cone contained a laser-seeker. A crewman aimed a laser beam down at the target; the bomb's laser-seeker followed the beam. Several of these bombs scored direct hits, putting the bridge out of commission for the rest of the year (though, since the Viet Cong found alternative supply routes, they didn't profoundly affect the war).

For the rest of the decade, and into the 1980s, the Pentagon's research-and-development departments kept modifying these bombs, and Congress kept funding them, but most Air Force generals weren't enthusiastic, didn't believe that the new weapons justified big changes to their budgets or to their war plans.

There were two reasons for the generals' skepticism. First, they were pilots. Those who had risen through the ranks flying nuclear bombers for the Strategic Air Command didn't think much about conventional warfare generally. Those who had flown tactical fighter planes didn't warm to the idea of "smart bombs," as the weapons came to be called. To these officers, air combat meant fast, maneuverable planes swooping in low, underneath the range of enemy radar, so low you could practically plant the bombs on the target; to do that, you needed skilled pilots and maneuverable planes; the only thing the bombs had to do was explode.

Second, the new bombs had a technical flaw. Laser beams are obstructed or deflected when they hit dust, smoke, or rain. Dust and smoke are common on the battlefield; rain is commonplace in northern Europe, where, in the wake of Vietnam, the generals were turning their attention. In short, if there was a war in Europe, these new wonder weapons might be duds.

When Don Rice came into the Pentagon, he knew that service secretaries rarely had power; they were, in the main, civilian figureheads in a building run by uniformed officers. But Rice knew the Air Force well from his days at RAND. He was determined not only to be an exceptional secretary but also to override the officers' resistance to the new technology—to make sure the smart bombs were given a higher priority in the budget and a central place in a more expansive Air Force strategy. The Wohlstetter-Iklé report had been out for several months. Rice had an ally in Marshall, who had connections higher up. Inside the Air Force itself, Rice sought out the smartest young officers and appointed them to a special "Secretary's Staff Group."

One of the most ambitious of these officers was a lieutenant colonel named Dave Deptula. The previous year, Deptula had worked with an even harder-driving colonel—some hailed him as a visionary, others dismissed him as a crank—named John Warden. All Air Force officers knew the tale of Billy Mitchell, the aviator of the First World War who believed that future wars would be won by air power alone and that ground armies, with their brute skirmishes, would be rendered obsolete. Nobody quite believed that anymore, but many dreamed of a day when air power would at least dominate the other aspects of warfare—that is, when the Air Force would dominate the Army and the Navy.

The ideas that Warden was talking about, combined with the new technologies, suggested to some that their day was near.

• • •

On November 9, 1989, the Berlin Wall fell. Five days later, Don Rice called a meeting of his staff group. The world was on the verge of a dramatic shift. The U.S. military was geared to fight a war in Europe. That was where most of its troops and bases were. Yet the great division in Europe was on the verge of mending. What was the new world going to look like? What threats would the United States face? Most important, what would be the role of the U.S. Air Force?

After several weeks of intense discussions, Rice assigned Deptula to write a paper answering these questions, especially the last one. It would be, remarkably, the first official statement of the Air Force's role since 1947, the year it became an independent branch of the armed services. (Before then, it was the air wing of the Army.) The paper was completed in June 1990 and titled "Global Reach—Global Power." It argued that as the Cold War wound down, new threats would emerge from as-yet-unknown quarters; that the United States might have to respond to these threats on short notice but with massive force; and that the modern Air Force uniquely possessed the traits that America would need in this new era—"speed, range, flexibility, precision, and lethality."

To Rice, Deptula, and the rest of the small study group, the new guided bombs—the instruments of "precision and lethality"— were central to this vision of reinvigorated Air Force supremacy.

As recently as 1986, when Ronald Reagan ordered an air raid on Libya, the job had taken 119 aircraft and 20 warships. Now, Deptula calculated, the same job could be done with the laser-guided bombs on board only 6 B-2 Stealth bombers. And the B-2s wouldn't need access to remote foreign bases. They had the range to fly, fully loaded, from American territory to almost anywhere on Earth.

Don Rice distributed Deptula's paper to every senator and congressman and to all the major media. The Air Force public affairs office adopted the title "Global Reach—Global Power" as the service's new slogan. Air commanders scheduled a large military exercise for August to demonstrate their new power.

They were preempted in their plans. On August 2, 1990, Saddam Hussein, the president of Iraq, invaded Kuwait. President George H. W. Bush decided to push back. The Air Force demonstration would be a real war.

• • •

In the week following Iraq's invasion, Warden and Deptula drew up a plan for a U.S. air attack. Warden, who ran a special office on air doctrine in the Pentagon's basement, had devised a concept of air warfare that he called the "five-rings" strategy. He likened the modern battlefield to the rings on a dartboard. In the bull's-eye were the enemy's political and military leaders, along with their networks of command, control, and communication. The next ring consisted of the nation's infrastructure—electrical grids, power plants, and military factories. The third ring was its transportation—roads, bridges, airfields, and ports. The fourth was the population. The fifth and most outward ring was the enemy's army.

In Warden's scheme, the first ring—the enemy's leadership and communications network—was the prime target. Obliterate that ring, and the enemy will collapse. The enemy's troops, tanks, and other frontline weapons were the *least* important targets, hardly worth an air campaign's attention. It was the exact reverse of the conventional view of air warfare, which put the highest priority on destroying the enemy's army in the field.

The attack plan drawn up by Warden and Deptula applied the five-ring strategy to Iraq. Though President Bush's goal was to push the Iraqi troops out of Kuwait, Warden and Deptula argued that the best way to do that was to launch air strikes against dozens of key targets in the Iraqi capital, Baghdad. They called the plan Instant Thunder, by way of contrasting it with Rolling Thunder, the Vietnam War's bombing plan, which had called for rolling out a gradual escalation of air strikes over a period of months. Instant Thunder, as they envisioned it, would last six days. The plan even listed the specific targets—eighty-four of them—that corresponded to the innermost rings, the key "nodes" that held together Saddam's military command. Destroy those nodes, and the regime collapses like the proverbial house of cards.

Don Rice, who had encouraged Warden to push his plan, told Secretary of Defense Dick Cheney that the air strikes *alone* would defeat Iraq. No ground war would be needed afterward. Cut off from their commanders, the Iraqi troops in Kuwait would be so isolated and debilitated that the Arab armies, which had joined the American-led coalition mainly for political reasons, could push them out and reoccupy Kuwait by themselves. The American troops, he said, could stand by, like a "cocked fist," waiting to pounce if needed, but they would probably not be needed.

Few outside Rice's inner circle believed that air power alone could do the job: not Cheney, not even most Air Force officers, certainly not the top military leaders of the war effort—General Colin Powell, chairman of the Joint Chiefs of Staff, and General Norman Schwarzkopf, commander of U.S. Central Command—both of whom were Army officers.

Still, Deptula was sent to Riyadh, Saudi Arabia, to run the air campaign's operations. The strategy that he and Warden had devised back in the Pentagon was heavily watered down—most would say realigned with reality—but much of its basic concept survived, especially the emphasis on bombing early and repeatedly the bull's-eye targets in Baghdad.

The accuracy of the laser-guided bombs made this concept at least feasible. Warden drew up a chart showing how many bombs had been required to destroy a basic target—say, a factory—in various wars over time. In WWII, when the average "dumb bomb" missed its target by more than a half-mile, a B-17 had to drop 9,000 of them to score a direct hit. In Korea and Vietnam, when primitive guided bombs first entered the arsenal, an F-104 or F-105 still had to drop 176 bombs to hit a single specific target. In Desert Storm, the official name for the first war against Iraq, Warden predicted that an F-16 would have to drop a mere 30 bombs—and that the brand-new F-117 Stealth fighter-bomber would need to drop just 1.

In the era of dumb bombs, it would have been impossible to contemplate attacking targets in a large city like Baghdad. Thousands, tens of thousands, of bombs would miss their targets and therefore kill vast numbers of civilians. (It was one thing to kill lots of Germans and Japanese in the course of a world war, quite another thing to kill so many Iraqis for the limited goal of pushing Saddam's occupation army out of Kuwait.) In the era of smart bombs, though, you could think about hitting specific targets within a city. Maybe you could pull it off.

• • •

As it turned out, the war didn't quite go as the air-power champions had hoped. In some respects, the results were stunning. On the attack's first night, F-117A Stealth planes crept into Iraqi skies and bombed crucial air-defense batteries. Other fighters and bombers followed over the next few days in waves, dropping hundreds of bombs on communications centers, command posts, microwave relays, and leadership bunkers. The campaign harked back to the attack on the Thanh Hoa Bridge, but repeated many times over, and more precisely still. In particularly dramatic strikes, laser-guided bombs scored direct hits on a bridge, a specific building, even a specific chimney pipe. Video footage shot from bomb-bay cameras was broadcast to the world on CNN, over and over.

But the five-rings theory wasn't vindicated. The opening days' air strikes, against the key nodes, were supposed to cut Saddam off from his troops—maybe, if things went really well, cut him off from his officer corps, who might feel compelled to mount a coup. But the U.S. Air Force's own official history of the war concluded that Saddam's network of command, control, and communication never collapsed. The study noted that despite "the lethality and precision of the attacks," this network "turned out to be more redundant and more able to reconstitute itself than first thought. Fiber-optic networks and computerized switching systems proved particularly tough to put out of action."

Nor was the overall air campaign as revolutionary as the videotapes suggested. Smart bombs were still new, expensive, and in short supply. Of the thousands of bombs dropped during America's thirty-day air campaign, just 9 percent were smart bombs—and many of them weren't so smart. The technical flaw, which had been noted by many officers a decade earlier in the wake of the Vietnam War, had not yet been corrected. A lot of laser-guided bombs went astray, as their beams were deflected by dust and smoke. After the first week, most of the air strikes consisted of B-52s laying down hundreds of dumb bombs on Iraqi bunkers and A-10 attack planes swooping in low and firing hundreds of armor-piercing rounds at Iraqi tanks. It was old-fashioned bombing and strafing of troops in the field—the sort of bombing that, according to Warden's five-rings theory, would not be necessary.

Ultimately, the war didn't end until Saddam Hussein's elite Republican Guards were killed and pushed back in a still more old-fashioned way—by American troops on the ground, a half million of them. The endgame seemed to vindicate the traditional Army view, which was spelled out by General Powell and thus became known as the "Powell doctrine"—that a nation should not go to war, and could not attain victory, without "overwhelming force."

Still, the Gulf War did mark a shift in the relationship between air and ground forces on the battlefield. Before, air forces were seen as supporting ground forces. Now their positions seemed reversed.

• • •

On January 24, 1991, eight days after the air war started, Andy Marshall called a staff meeting. He was wondering whether the "revolution in military affairs" was now a reality, whether the opening air strikes of the Gulf War—their speed, accuracy, concentration, and the types of targets they were hitting—marked a fundamental change in the nature of warfare, similar to the Germans' "blitzkrieg" tactics at the start of World War II.

It was an unforeseen twist. Nearly twenty years earlier, Marshall and Wohlstetter had thought that these new weapons would restore parity to the Soviet-American military balance in Europe. Now that the Soviet Union was gone, it seemed that they might secure American military preeminence worldwide.

Marshall asked his military assistant, Andrew Krepinevich, to write a paper exploring the question. Krepinevich was an Army lieutenant colonel who, five years earlier, had written a book called *The Army and Vietnam*, which argued that the United States lost the war, in part, because the Army commanders fought it as a conventional battle, similar to Korea or World War II, with heavy firepower and large-scale units—when in fact it was a guerrilla war, which required more flexible, small-scale tactics.

His paper for Marshall concluded that the revolution had indeed begun. "Quality is becoming far more important than quantity, revolutionizing the nature of warfare," Krepinevich wrote. It would soon be possible, he continued, to identify an enemy's "center of gravity," its "jugular" or "central nervous system"—the small number of targets that, if successfully hit, would destroy its ability to resist. The new precision weapons made it possible to hit these nerve centers with a small number of bombs or missiles. The 1991 Gulf War was a "sequential war"—thirty days of air strikes, followed by four days of fighting on the ground. The new weapons would make possible "near-simultaneous operations" in the air and on land, against enemy targets across the battlefield from front to rear. The strikes on targets deep in enemy territory would be the "tip of the spear" that opened the way for "more 'traditional' forms of military power." These strikes might be so successful that the traditional forms would not be needed.

The key weapons systems in this new kind of warfare, Krepine-vich continued, would be unmanned aircraft, high-speed com-puters, and precision-guided munitions. Weapons such as tanks, short-range fighter planes, and large surface ships—weapons that can't be mobilized quickly, can't easily be integrated into this net-work, and can't be used at all without large, vulnerable supply lines—would "likely become progressively less central to military operations."

Those "less central" weapons, of course, were the core assets of the U.S. Army, Air Force, and Navy.

The paper was finished in July 1992. To those in the know, it was the culmination, synthesis, and extension of all the reports done on the subject—most of them classified—over the previous seventeen years by Marshall, Wohlstetter, Deptula, and others. But this paper advanced the agenda in two ways. First, it provided a context in which to view the recent Gulf War. Second, though also classified, it circulated widely among those with security clear-ances. In those circles, it became *the* topic of conversation—the centerpiece of a debate over what wars might look like, and how defense strategies and budgets should be reshaped, in a world without the Cold War or the Soviet Union.

Nonetheless, in political circles, including the Pentagon's upper corridors, the report seemed dead in the water. The Cold War was over, and the United States had won it. The military estab-lishment saw no need for a revolution. Why change anything when you're by far the most powerful fighting force in the world?

In the wider political world, the public wanted a "peace divi-dend." The budget-slashing started not with Bill Clinton but with George H. W. Bush. In his State of the Union address in January 1992, Bush announced the cancellation of several high-profile weapons systems—MX missiles, B-2 bombers, Advanced Cruise

Missiles. In budget hearings the same month, Secretary of Defense Dick Cheney—who at first resisted any arms reductions but finally followed the president's orders—testified that he was cutting the five-year defense plan by $300 billion, with another $50 billion of cuts to come. "You've directed me to buy more M-1s, F-14s, and F-16s—all great systems," Cheney told the Senate Armed Services Committee, "but we have enough of them." At the same hearing, General Powell testified about plans to cut Army divisions by one-third, Navy aircraft carriers by one-fifth, and active-duty troops by a half-million men and women, to say nothing of "major reductions" in Air Force fighter wings and strategic bombers.

By coincidence, the kinds of weapons that were cut—expensive items that yielded big savings—were precisely the kinds of weapons that Krepinevich had advocated cutting. They were artifacts of old-style warfare—tanks, big ships, short-range fighter aircraft—that would only bog down a revolutionary style of fighting.

But advancing the revolution would require spending more money for the new weapons—and overhauling military strategy, tactics, and training. Few officials paid much attention to these matters, either in the final year of George H. W. Bush's presidency or in the first few years of Bill Clinton's. Andy Marshall briefed some high-ranking Pentagon officials on the issues. In August 1993 he wrote a memorandum titled "Some Thoughts on Military Revolutions," a politely toned-down summary of Krepinevich's paper. But it stimulated little interest. And the Pentagon's top generals—who, by and large, still consisted of men who had risen through the ranks as Army tank officers, Air Force fighter pilots, or Navy aircraft-carrier commanders—had no interest in pursuing these ideas at all.

• • •

By the mid-1990s, several members of the Senate Armed Services Committee, many of whom had known Marshall for years, were growing concerned that his ideas weren't being taken seriously enough. In 1996, Joe Lieberman, Democrat of Connecticut, and Dan Coats, Republican of Indiana, coauthored a bill to create a National Defense Panel, which they envisioned as a forum for advancing the "revolution in military affairs."

The panel had nine members. Seven were selected by the Defense Department, one by the committee's Republicans, and one by its Democrats. The Republicans picked an ex-Marine and former Pentagon official named Richard Armitage. The Democrats picked Andrew Krepinevich. One of the panel's staff members was Dave Deptula, who was now a full colonel.

The secretary of defense, Bill Cohen, wasn't enthusiastic about this panel. He thought it should suggest ways to make the military more efficient. Armitage and Krepinevich saw their mission as making the military more *effective*, and they struck up an alliance to keep the panel on that track.

Most of the panelists had a more political and diplomatic focus than Armitage and Krepinevich did. But much of the final report reflected Marshall's thesis. "We are on the cusp of a military revolution," the report stated up front, "stimulated by rapid advances in information . . . technologies."

While preparing the report, Krepinevich coined the term that would enter the public lexicon. Marshall's phrase, the "revolution in military affairs," *described* the new era. Krepinevich mulled over a slogan that would prescribe what to *do* about it. He finally hit on it: "military transformation." The panel released its report in December 1997. The title: *Transforming Defense*.

Not long after, Armitage went to work on the presidential campaign of the Republican governor of Texas, George W. Bush. On September 23, 1999, Bush gave his speech at The Citadel, the speech in which he heralded a "revolution in the technology of war," an era when battles would be won not by "mass or size" but by "mobility and swiftness." Armitage wrote the first draft of that speech. He took much of its language straight out of the National Defense Panel report.

• • •

Donald Rumsfeld took special note of that speech. Two days earlier, he had chaired a panel assembled by a former Pentagon official and weapons physicist named James Wade. When Rumsfeld was briefly secretary of defense in the mid-'70s, Wade was chief of his policy planning staff. The two kept in touch over the years.

Wade was heavily influenced by Andy Marshall's thinking. Marshall was the bookish intellectual; Wade was the sharp-elbows operator. Through the 1980s, when Wade was the assistant secretary of defense for research and development, he put Marshall's ideas in motion, pressuring the Pentagon's top civilians and the reluctant military chiefs to boost spending on the new precision-guided weapons and advanced radar systems. Now, like many advocates, he feared the revolution had stalled, and he set out to do his own bit of jump-starting.

He formed the panel to discuss—and thereby promote—a book that he had recently coauthored called *Shock and Awe: Achieving Rapid Dominance*, which was essentially his own take on Marshall's "revolution in military affairs," with an emphasis on the primacy of speed. The aim of shock-and-awe warfare was, as he put it, "to stun, and then rapidly defeat the enemy through a series of carefully orchestrated land, sea, air, and special operations forces strikes that take place nearly simultaneously across a wide battle space," with the aim of throwing the enemy into "immediate paralysis" and "capitulation."

Marshall was a member of Wade's panel. So were Johnny Foster, the former Pentagon R&D chief and model-airplane enthusiast who dreamed up the modern remotely piloted vehicle, and Newt Gingrich, the former House Speaker whose views on military matters still carried weight in Republican circles.

When Rumsfeld read Bush's Citadel speech, he knew exactly where its ideas came from. He realized how central they now were in the mainstream Republican agenda—and how big a role they might play in his own reentry into high office.

(Three years later, as Rumsfeld geared up for the invasion of Iraq, he sent a copy of Wade's book to the U.S. commander, General Tommy Franks. As the war began, Franks publicly said the point of the bombing campaign was to "shock and awe" the enemy.)

After Bush won the 2000 election, his policy advisers wanted Dan Coats, the congressman who had set up the National Defense Panel, to become secretary of defense and Rich Armitage to be his deputy. But Coats did poorly in his interview with the president-elect; he came across as uninformed and as tepid about reviving a missile-defense program, which Bush considered his top priority.

Dick Cheney, Bush's vice president, suggested Rumsfeld as an alternative. Thirty years earlier, Rumsfeld had tapped Cheney to come work for him in Richard Nixon's White House. The two had been friends and political allies ever since. Now it was time for Cheney to return the favor. The original plan was that Rumsfeld would be director of the Central Intelligence Agency. But he was more interested in returning to the Pentagon. He had spent the past two years as chairman to three defense panels—not just Wade's one-day session, but also a six-month-long panel to investigate the threat from hostile nations' ballistic missiles and another panel, which was just wrapping up, on the vulnerability of America's military systems in outer space. Rumsfeld scored well with Bush; he seemed so energetic, and he knew so much. He got the job.

One result of this switch was that Armitage was out. Bush had selected Colin Powell as secretary of state. Everyone knew that Armitage was Powell's best friend. Rumsfeld didn't want a State Department spy in his midst. When he met with Armitage at the transition headquarters, Rumsfeld told him, "You have less than a 50–50 chance of being my deputy."

Armitage, husky, profane, and able to match Rumsfeld's brusqueness, replied, "No, I have a *zero* chance." The meeting didn't last long.

Meanwhile, Paul Wolfowitz, one of Bush's top foreign policy advisers during the campaign, had his own bad interview with Powell. Wolfowitz wanted to be deputy secretary of state, but Powell wasn't keen on that notion. In his exile during the Clinton years, Wolfowitz had been one of the leading "neoconservatives," the group of ex-Reagan officials who, in the 1970s, rebelled against Nixon-Kissinger Realpolitik with its emphasis on vital security interests and a stable balance of international power. The neocons, and Wolfowitz in particular, denounced Kissinger's school of thinking as immoral because it tolerated Soviet Communism's oppression and human-rights violations for the sake of détente and arms-control treaties. Now the neocons were advocating the forcible overthrow of various other dictators, especially in the Middle East, above all Saddam Hussein. Powell proudly regarded himself as a Realist and was leery of the neocons' rush to arms. Wolfowitz, however, had performed professionally as ambassador to Thailand, so Powell offered him the job of ambassador to the United Nations. Wolfowitz had no interest in that.

Instead, Rumsfeld took on Wolfowitz as deputy secretary of defense. Armitage went to Foggy Bottom to serve as his friend Powell's deputy. And so the power equation of the next four years was set—the hard-driven Rumsfeld at the Pentagon and his protégé Cheney in the White House, squeezing the pinstriped diplomats at State in a pincer hold.

Rumsfeld had no intention of merely presiding over a federal agency. He was determined to shake it up. He was looking for levers, and Marshall's concepts—their very labels, "revolution," "transformation"—seemed the model of a shake-up in waiting. And so he invited his old friend Andy Marshall to lunch and asked him to write *the* paper on a new military strategy.

• • •

As expected, the military chiefs resisted Rumsfeld's call for transformation. The quarrel centered not so much on Marshall's paper, which was written for Rumsfeld's eyes, but on a larger, more institutional follow-on document called the Quadrennial Defense Review—a congressionally mandated report, to be put out by the Pentagon every four years, outlining the official strategy and how it relates to the military's budget and programs. The next QDR was due in September 2001. Krepinevich was brought back as a consultant to write much of it. Deptula, now a two-star general, contributed sections, too.

It was a wide-ranging document, full of boilerplate and interservice compromises. But the key themes stood out clearly. These were "the ongoing revolution in military affairs," which "could change the conduct of military operations"; the beginning of an "ambitious transformation of U.S. military forces," including a "transition to network-centric warfare," to exploit this revolution; and the need to focus more on "long-range precision strike" munitions and "rapidly deployable" forces, which could deal with threats "swiftly wherever they might arise."

The military services resisted, especially the Army, whose generals understood that "rapidly deployable" was a synonym for "smaller and lighter"—meaning fewer big and heavy armored vehicles, such as the M-1 Abrams tank, the U.S. Army's mainstay. The QDR referred to such weapons as "legacy systems." Legacies are about the past, not the present, much less the future. Army officers had good reason to conclude that Rumsfeld meant to put them out to pasture.

In his first six months, Rumsfeld managed to kill just two Army weapons systems: the Cheyenne helicopter, which many Army officers realized was a dog in any case, and the Crusader artillery cannon, which was deemed too large and heavy for a transformational military. But on all other fronts, the Army—and much of the Air Force and Navy, which saw their beloved fighter planes and aircraft carriers threatened—put up a huge struggle.

Rumsfeld got into so many quarrels with the brass and grew so frustrated by their obstacles that Pentagon reporters were predicting he would be the first casualty of Bush's cabinet.

On September 10, 2001, Rumsfeld delivered a "town hall" speech to the Pentagon's employees. "The topic today," he began, "is an adversary that poses a threat, a serious threat, to the security of the United States of America. This adversary is one of the world's last bastions of central planning. . . . With brutal consistency, it stifles free thought and crushes new ideas. It disrupts the defense of the United States and places the lives of men and women in uniform at risk. Perhaps this adversary sounds like the former Soviet Union, but that enemy is gone." The new foe, he said, is "more subtle and implacable. . . . It's the Pentagon bureaucracy."

The next morning, a group of al-Qaeda jihadists crashed passenger jetliners into the Pentagon and the World Trade Center's Twin Towers, killing nearly three thousand Americans. In retrospect, Rumsfeld's speech of the day before seemed churlish. But to some, not least Rumsfeld himself, it was galvanizing. Over the next month, the Bush administration planned for war against al-Qaeda's harbor and sponsor, the Taliban regime of Afghanistan. The war would be a test of what the Pentagon could do. It would be a test of transformation.

• • •

In a sense, Afghanistan was precisely the sort of post–Cold War battleground that Marshall and the other transformation theorists foresaw—remote, landlocked, with no secure or friendly nearby bases and no easy access routes for American ground troops. Long-range planes carrying accurate bombs seemed the best way to punch in. But Afghanistan also seemed to defy transformation's premises. It was a preindustrial society. What "nerve centers" could the smart bombs attack? Did it *have* nerve centers? Did the concept make any sense? American air power could get to Afghanistan, but what would it do once it got there? In planning meetings, Rumsfeld complained about the country's lack of good targets.

The breakthrough idea came not from the Pentagon but from the Central Intelligence Agency. CIA director George Tenet suggested sending in several twelve-man teams of special-operations forces. Helicopters could fly them into Afghanistan from secret bases in nearby Uzbekistan. The special-ops teams could link up with anti-Taliban warlords, with whom the CIA had relations from the days when they jointly beat back the Soviet Union's occupation.

Bush approved the plan, but nobody—not Bush, Rumsfeld, Tenet, and certainly not Tommy Franks, the hidebound Army general who rose through the ranks as an artillery officer and was now commander of U.S. Central Command—believed it would be enough to defeat the Taliban.

Franks and his staff worked up a war plan that involved two Army divisions invading Afghanistan through Pakistan. He regarded the combination of special-ops forces and air power as a prelude—a useful way of distracting the Taliban, keeping them off balance—while the "decisive" stage of the battle was prepared, a process that Franks calculated would take nine months.

Dave Deptula, now the head of the Air Force Combat Command, was sent to Prince Sultan Air Force Base, in Al Kharj, Saudi Arabia, to run the war's Air Operations Center. But even he knew that there was no systematic plan and no way, really, to lay one out in any detail. The operation was made up as they went along.

However, in the decade since Desert Storm, without much notice, two major advances had been made in the technology of air warfare—both fulfilling the visions in Albert Wohlstetter's ARPA study of the mid-1970s.

• • •

One of these advances was an unmanned aerial vehicle called Predator, the realization of Johnny Foster's epiphany about model airplanes and military reconnaissance. Predator could fly for twenty-four hours straight, at an altitude of 25,000 feet, carrying a 450-pound payload, which initially consisted of communications gear and a camera focused on the ground below. The digital images taken by this camera were beamed to a satellite, then transmitted to a ground station hundreds or thousands of miles away (theoretically, anywhere on Earth), where an operator, who controlled Predator's flight path with a joystick, could watch its video stream on a monitor in real time.

The second big advance was a new kind of smart bomb, which the Air Force and Navy developed together, called the Joint Direct Attack Munition or JDAM. The JDAM project was put in motion by Don Rice in the weeks following the 1991 Gulf War. Looking at the postwar aerial photos, he saw a lot of empty craters in the sand, the result of laser-guided bombs that missed their targets because the lasers had been deflected by smoke or dust. Rice ordered a technical review of alternative technologies that might guide bombs accurately in all kinds of weather and conditions. Air Force scientists quickly hit upon satellite guidance by the Global Positioning System. Wohlstetter, in his paper fifteen years earlier, had mentioned the GPS as one of "various accuracy-improvement programs" on the drawing board. At that time, it was barely a vision in a handful of R&D labs.

Its significance was threefold. First, with GPS guidance, a smart bomb could not be thrown off course by bad weather, smoke, or camouflage. The ground operator would punch a target's coordinates into a computer and upload the instruction to a satellite, which would beam the data to the JDAM's GPS receiver. The JDAM wouldn't follow a laser beam; rather, it would plunge to a specific point on the earth—a designated latitude and longitude—and explode precisely on target.

Second, JDAMs were cheap, so the Pentagon could buy a lot of them. The laser-guided bombs used in Desert Storm cost over $250,000 each. A JDAM cost just $20,000. They were kits, consisting of the GPS receiver and other electronic gear, which could be attached to the tail of almost any bomb in the U.S. Air Force or Navy's inventory. In other words, JDAMs would turn dumb bombs into smart bombs for almost no money.

Third, they could be carried inside nearly any plane with a bomb bay. The plane didn't have to be at all sophisticated; it wouldn't have to be more than an airbus, dropping off JDAMs from a very high altitude, above the range of antiaircraft fire. No crew member, laser, or radar inside the plane needed to guide the weapon to its target; the weapon would do that by itself.

Both new weapons, Predator and the JDAM, were first used during Clinton's presidency, in the war to defend Kosovo against Serbian dictator Slobodan Milosevic. The programs had moved slowly through the Pentagon bureaucracy. Predator's first test flight took place in 1994; JDAM entered production a year later.

But by the time of Kosovo, in 1999, fewer than one hundred of each were available for use.

In Clinton's final year, the Pentagon and the CIA developed a modified version of Predator that carried not only a camera but a laser-seeker and a Hellfire antitank missile, which could be fired by the same sort of joystick that steered Predator. It was successfully tested in January 2001, just before Clinton left office. The Air Force mission statement noted that the Hellfire-armed Predator would be ideal for hitting "fleeting and perishable" targets—a phrase that could mean tanks on the battlefield or cars carrying terrorists. Richard Clarke, the White House counterterrorism chief, sent a memo to Condoleezza Rice, President-elect Bush's incoming national security adviser, recommending "going forward" with new missions that exploited this new feature.

The armed Predator was due for deployment on September 1, 2001. Technical flaws delayed it, but after September 11, the first units were shipped to Afghanistan anyway. So were the JDAMs. On October 7, the bombing began.

Early on, the JDAMs—dropped by B-1, B-2, and B-52 bombers, and by F-14 and F-18 fighter-bombers launched from nearby aircraft carriers—destroyed the Taliban's handful of bases and runways, putting the regime's air force out of commission. But for the next two weeks, the bombing had little effect. As Rumsfeld had fretted, Afghanistan had no industry, no centralized command facilities, few paved roads—no "high-payoff targets." Combat planes bombed and strafed Taliban troops, but the troops could hide—and reemerge to fight.

Not until October 15 did U.S. special-operations soldiers meet up with warlords of the Northern Alliance, the main anti-Taliban insurgency. Then, toward the end of the month, something remarkable happened.

●　●　●

A few miles outside the village of Mazar-i-Sharif, Afghanistan's second-largest city, an American special-ops officer, wearing native garb and a thick beard, rode along a rocky trail on horseback. Through his night-vision binoculars, he spotted a regiment of Taliban fighters a few hundred yards away. He pulled out a laptop computer, typed out the regiment's coordinates, and pushed the Send button. A Predator drone, hovering twenty thousand feet overhead, received the message and beamed it to Deptula's headquarters at Sultan Air Base in Saudi Arabia. An Air Force officer at the base sent back a signal to the Predator, directing it to fly over the regiment. A video camera on the drone's belly scanned the terrain and streamed the imagery back to the base in real time. The officer then ordered a B-52 bomber pilot, who was patrolling the skies, to attack the target. En route, the pilot punched the target's coordinates into the GPS receiver of one of his JDAMs. He flew to the area and fired the JDAM, which darted toward the regiment, exploded, and killed the Taliban.

The total time that elapsed—from the officer punching in the data to the pilot dropping his bomb—was *nineteen minutes*. Just a decade earlier, in Desert Storm, the sequence would have taken three *days*. A few years before then, it could not have taken place at all; it could not have been imagined.

Over the next few weeks, the incident at Mazar was replicated, with variations, all across Afghanistan—phenomenally accurate air strikes by American bombers, followed by offensives on the ground by anti-Taliban insurgents, along with small teams of soldiers, Marines, Green Berets, and CIA advisers. In mid-November, just five weeks after the war began, the Taliban were driven out of Kabul, the country's capital; commanders of the Northern Alliance, the main U.S.-backed insurgency, moved in. A month after that, U.S. Marines secured the airport in Kandahar in a battle that became known as the "Taliban's last stand." Osama bin Laden and al-Qaeda no longer had a base of operations. On December 22, a new interim government, led by Hamid Karzai and backed by a vast international coalition, took office.

On January 31, Donald Rumsfeld delivered a triumphant speech at the National Defense University in Washington, D.C., recounting the air strikes on Mazar-i-Sharif as the turning point of the war—and as Exhibit A in the case for transformation.

"This is precisely what transformation is about," Rumsfeld exclaimed to his audience of officers and students. "Here we are in the year 2002, fighting the first war of the twenty-first century, and the horse cavalry was back . . . being used in previously unimaginable ways. It showed that a revolution in military affairs"—Marshall's phrase—"is about more than building new high-tech weapons, though that is certainly part of it. It's also about new ways of thinking and new ways of fighting."

In World War II, he said, taking another page from Marshall and Krepinevich, the German army's blitzkrieg "revolutionized warfare," with its "small, high-quality, mobile shock forces"—coordinated with dive bombers and mobilized infantry and artillery—all concentrated on one part of the front line. "In a similar way," he said, "the battle for Mazar was a transformational battle. Coalition forces took existing military capabilities, from the most advanced laser-guided weapons to antique, forty-year-old B-52s . . . to the most rudimentary—a man on horseback. And they used them together in unprecedented ways, with devastating effect on enemy positions, on enemy morale, and this time, on the cause of evil in the world."

Rumsfeld was overstating his case. American air power and the new precise weapons made a big difference, but not all the difference; they didn't produce the battlefield victory by themselves. Air strikes had no effect on the Taliban's hold until ground troops were in place to follow through. Even then, the Americans and Afghan rebels met fierce resistance from Taliban and al-Qaeda fighters.

In the early clashes, the Taliban forces did little to disguise their presence or take cover. However, by the end of October, they had begun to adapt to U.S. tactics and technology. They smeared mud on their vehicles, so the cameras in the sky wouldn't spot them. They camouflaged their movements and took cover along the mountainous terrain. In November and December, in battles at Bai Beche and Sayd Slim Kalay, north of Kandahar, they mastered cover and concealment so well that U.S. special-ops forces couldn't find them and thus couldn't beam their positions to the Predators overhead.

The new technology had proved very effective at killing people and destroying targets, but—even when it was combined with a small number of ground forces—it didn't bring capitulation; it didn't win the war. The world hadn't quite yet changed that much.

When Rumsfeld gave his victory speech at the National Defense University, Kabul had fallen, but the Taliban and al-Qaeda were still fighting. The biggest battle of all wouldn't be fought until March. It was called Operation Anaconda, and its aim was to root out the al-Qaeda holdouts in the Shah-i-kot Valley. If Rumsfeld hadn't already drawn his conclusions—not just about the Afghan war, but about the nature of modern warfare generally—Anaconda might have compelled him to draw different ones.

Before the operation began, Predators and spy satellites took aerial photos of the entire prospective battlefield—a fairly confined space of less than fifty square miles—in order to locate every al-Qaeda position. Yet postwar analyses determined that fewer than half of these positions were detected before the battle began—and most of the fire came from positions that the aerial cameras hadn't detected.

At the start of Anaconda, U.S. infantry troops dismounted from their assault helicopters and found themselves almost on top of dug-in al-Qaeda troops. The American soldiers were pinned down for most of the day, and had to be airlifted out that night. For the next week, U.S. bombers pounded al-Qaeda's positions. Yet by the time the American soldiers fought their way back, they were again met with al-Qaeda fire.

American forces won the battle—but only after overrunning and killing al-Qaeda forces on the ground. And doing that was harder than it might have been because, after Kabul fell, Rumsfeld—thinking the war was over and the theory of transformation had been proved—put sharp limits on how many American troops could be mobilized. No units—not even individual soldiers or Marines—could be sent to Afghanistan without Rumsfeld's explicit permission.

Meanwhile, air power couldn't stop Osama bin Laden from escaping into the mountains of Tora Bora along the Pakistani border.

And the American and British hadn't deployed enough troops to surround the area on the ground. Instead, they assigned the task to Afghan warlords, who—whether due to loyalty, indifference, incompetence, or bribes—let bin Laden slip through.

Finally, the Taliban fighters themselves were not defeated. They maintained their armed resistance against Karzai's government and stepped it up, gradually, then fiercely, after Bush and Rumsfeld—basking in apparent victory—moved on to the next war, in Iraq.

It wasn't that the United States won the war but lost the peace, as many critics later charged. Rather, the United States won the battle but left the war unfinished. The Taliban were ousted from power, for the moment, but they remained a powerful force, which returned to fight a few years later. And Osama bin Laden, President Bush's number-one dead-or-alive target, wasn't caught for even a moment.

•   •   •

When Rumsfeld proclaimed in late January that the theory of transformation had been vindicated, it was not yet obvious that the war remained unfinished. Two things about the Afghan war, up to that point, bolstered his confidence. First, the brutal ground clashes notwithstanding, air power—and, specifically, the new, amazingly accurate air munitions—played an indisputably prominent role and crushed Taliban defenses more rapidly than any other weapons could have.

Second, the senior officers of the U.S. Army and Central Command turned out to be wrong about everything. General Franks, the CentCom commander, had told Rumsfeld at the outset that the decisive phase of combat wouldn't take place until the following summer, the earliest time when two armored divisions could be mobilized for combat. Franks approved the air operations with their unorthodox pairing of special-ops forces and high-tech bombs. He thought they might keep the Taliban preoccupied while CentCom prepared for the *real* battle ahead. He never expected—nor did many of the air-combat planners working with General Deptula—that they *were* the real battle.

War plans are broken down into four phases. Phase I: Set the conditions; Phase II: Initial operations; Phase III: Decisive operations; and Phase IV: Postconflict stability. By the time Kabul fell in November 2001, General Franks's planners at CentCom thought the war was still in Phase II.

Rumsfeld kept this misjudgment constantly in mind over the next year, as he and the generals argued about how many troops would be needed for the invasion of Iraq. When the generals said they needed three hundred thousand troops, Rumsfeld would remember that they had vastly overstated the numbers they needed in Afghanistan. They were wrong then, and it seemed a logical inference that they were just as wrong now.

He had been at odds with the generals, openly and brusquely, ever since the start of Bush's term—over the new strategy, over the Quadrennial Defense Review, over decisions to cut weapons systems. Their drastic misreading of the war in Afghanistan hardened his belief that they were wrong as a matter of course and that their wrongheadedness stemmed from their failure to grasp the "revolution in military affairs," which, to Rumsfeld's mind, had transformed the nature of warfare.

His disdain toward the Army was reinforced by his frequent dealings with Tommy Franks, the general he had come to know best. Franks, by no means a strategist, was widely regarded as a dim bulb, even by fellow officers. Rumsfeld, by nature impatient with people who weren't smart, despised Franks and wanted to get rid of him after the Afghanistan war. But over the Christmas holidays, Bush invited Franks out to his ranch in Crawford, Texas. Franks was a tall, salty, plain-speaking, profane Texan—he had gone to the same high school as Bush's wife, Laura—and he and the president got along like gangbusters. Bush called Rumsfeld and said, "Tommy Franks is a hell of a guy!" Rumsfeld realized that Franks would have to stay.

Confident that the Army was stuck in an outdated mind-set and frustrated at having to deal with the likes of Franks as the top commander, Rumsfeld tore into CentCom's war plans on Iraq. He would ask questions. Franks couldn't answer them satisfactorily. So Rumsfeld would slash. He'd slice out not only whole combat units but elements within the units. Why did the brigades need so much heavy artillery, when smart bombs dropped from the air could smash up enemy defenses just as well? In transformational warfare, ground forces should be light, lithe, and fast. Artillery cannons and the long supply lines that went with them were heavy, cumbersome, and slow.

On one level, Rumsfeld was right and the officers were wrong. The Army, it turned out, did not need a few hundred thousand troops to crush the Iraqi military and topple Saddam's regime. Nor did its brigades need so much artillery; precision bombing and shelling blasted and scattered Iraqi defenses, so that American armored vehicles could punch on through.

But on another level, Rumsfeld profoundly misunderstood what was happening on the battlefield, what constituted victory, and what war—this war, as well as war in general—was all about.

The first thing that Rumsfeld missed was that, Tommy Franks aside, the Army wasn't entirely clueless. Just as bright young Air Force officers had rethought their service's roles and strategies in the wake of Vietnam, bright young Army officers had done so, too. One of the brightest was a colonel named Huba Wass de Czege.

• • •

Wass de Czege was born in Transylvania in 1941, the son of prominent Hungarian novelist Albert Wass de Czege, who fought briefly in the Hungarian army on the western front during World War II before escaping with his family across the border to Bavaria. When Huba was ten, they emigrated to America, where his father taught French and German at universities. The first English-language book that Huba read was about West Point. He dreamed of going there when he grew older, and he did.

After graduation, he served two tours of duty in Vietnam, his second, in 1968, as a company commander with the 173rd Airborne

Brigade. Brash and confident, he would tell his men that the Army's way of fighting, with its emphasis on large-scale units and static set pieces, was doomed. Deployed to the Highlands, not far from the North Vietnamese border, Wass de Czege formed his own small-scale unit—just him, his first sergeant, a radio operator, and a forward observer for calling in artillery support. Most teams of this sort stayed hunkered down, waiting for Viet Cong to come to them; Wass de Czege's team went out on raids every night, scoping the terrain, avoiding the major trails, and ambushing the enemy from behind. Wass de Czege's four-man operation, according to a postwar memoir by one of his men, "killed and wounded more enemy than the entire rest of the battalion."

His superiors didn't go for his unorthodox methods. But after the war ended in disaster, a few Army generals were on the lookout for reformers, and Wass de Czege—who, after his tour, went to Harvard's John F. Kennedy School of Government and then back to West Point for a graduate degree in social sciences—seemed a likely candidate.

Like their Air Force counterparts, the Army's strategists were turning their gaze back to Europe and noticing a more intense bat-tlefield and a more serious Soviet threat. In 1982, they called on Wass de Czege to rewrite the Army's field manual on operations, FM 100-5. This was no academic exercise. FM 100-5 was the book that laid down the principles of Army strategy, tactics, and training.

The edition in use at the time had been written in 1976 by Gen-eral William DePuy, a highly decorated veteran of World War II and a deputy chief of staff at headquarters in Vietnam. DePuy and his aides—nicknamed the "Boathouse Gang" for the retreat on the Virginia coast where they went to write the field manual—shifted doctrine back toward large-scale, close-range armored combat on the plains of Germany. But they viewed warfare as mechanistic, al-most abstract, a static clash of firepower and attrition; and they as-sumed that the Soviet army would mount frontal assaults against NATO's reinforced strongpoints. It was, in short, a regurgitation, on a larger and deadlier scale, of everything that was wrong about American tactics in Vietnam.

Wass de Czege's revision of FM 100-5 took a wholly different path, emphasizing speed, maneuver, flexibility, and taking the initiative with offensive thrusts that enveloped the enemy from the flanks and the rear. It was an elaboration of his own company's tactics in Vietnam.

He was promoted to brigadier general and placed in charge of a new one-year postgraduate program at the Army's Command and General Staff College in Fort Leavenworth, Kansas. It was called the School of Advanced Military Studies, or SAMS, and its purpose was to instill these ideas in the elite echelon of the future officer corps.

While preparing to write the new field manual, Wass de Czege read the classics of military strategy—Sun Tzu's *The Art of War*, Karl von Clausewitz's *On Strategy*, J. C. C. Fuller's *The Conduct of War*, and B. H. Liddell Hart's *Strategy: The Indirect Approach*. Their ideas resonated with his own combat experience, with its emphases on surprise, shock, and maneuver. At one point, he looked up the 1940 edition of FM 100-5, written on the eve of the Second World War, and found that it stressed the same principles; clearly, its authors had also gone back and read the classics. Yet Wass de Czege hadn't been exposed to any of these works at West Point, nor was anyone teaching them at Fort Leavenworth before he started SAMS. The Army, he realized, had forgotten history—had forgotten how to fight wars.

SAMS began in the summer of 1983, with twelve students attending classes in a converted gymnasium. The next year, enrollment doubled to twenty-four (eight of whom would go on to become generals) and increased gradually each year after. During the course of a school year, each student read one hundred fifty books and wrote two monographs, one on tactics, one on operations. "We need to begin a program of deeper and broader education in the science and art of how to prepare for, and conduct, war," Wass de Czege wrote at the time. The aim of so much reading was to distill "enduring principles and insights," which will make officers "adaptive and innovative," to teach them not so much what to think, but *how* to think, about military affairs.

The basic ideas weren't so different from the strategies circulating inside the Air Force around this time—the premium on speed, surprise, and going on the offensive, not only on the front lines but also deep behind those lines—except that in the Army's case, there was no pretense that one service could fight and win by itself. Wass de Czege acknowledged that air power would be needed to attack the deep targets and to protect the flanks while ground forces advanced. A few years later, he wrote a revision of his field manual to emphasize this idea of joint warfare, which he called *AirLand Battle*.

By then, he had trained three years' worth of acolytes, who called themselves the "Jedi Knights," after the maneuver warriors in the movie *Star Wars: Return of the Jedi*, which came out in 1983, the year that Wass de Czege came to Leavenworth.

During the Gulf War of 1990–91, the commander of U.S. forces, General Norman Schwarzkopf, recruited four Jedi Knights, headed by a lieutenant colonel named Joseph Purvis, to write a plan for the ground-war phase of Desert Storm. What they devised was a reflection of Wass de Czege's thinking—a feint up the middle to lock the Iraqi Army in place, and a simultaneous thrust of American forces from way to the west, enveloping the Iraqis from the flanks and the rear, and destroying them from all sides.

The U.S. Marines were on the same page of maneuver warfare, owing to the influence of another, more maverick, officer named John Boyd. A former Air Force fighter pilot, he was known as "Forty-Second Boyd" because, at the fighter-pilot training school where he taught in the 1960s, he had a standing bet—which he never lost—that he could "shoot down" anybody in forty seconds or less.

Boyd's background was very different from Wass de Czege's. He grew up impoverished in Erie, Pennsylvania. His household wasn't bookish, nor were his manners refined. But when a puzzle intrigued him, he immersed himself in it. He had an uncanny creative spark; he grasped concepts quickly and saw the links that connected them in ways that more educated specialists missed.

He had become a pilot toward the end of the Korean War and, during that time, devised a formula for successful air-to-air combat.

It had to do with outmaneuvering the other pilot, anticipating his next move, and reacting to it preemptively—"getting inside the other guy's decision loop," as Boyd put it. Over the next few years, he worked his observations into a lecture called "The Aerial Attack Study," which soon became a textbook for fighter-pilot tactics, not only in the United States but, by emulation, almost everywhere.

Around the time Wass de Czege was staging ambushes in the Vietnamese Highlands, Boyd started seriously studying military history—Sun Tzu, Nazi blitzkriegs, and everything in between. He came to realize that the secret he discovered for successful aerial combat was also the secret of successful warfare generally, from battalion tactics to grand strategy. The key ingredients were speed, maneuver, deception, and multiple thrusts deep behind enemy lines, siring confusion and disorder among the enemy ranks and disorienting them into surrender. It was like "shock and awe," but on the ground, and it was directed not against theoretical "nerve centers" in the enemy's capital, but against the enemy's military and command structure.

Over the next two decades, Boyd worked on a study that he called "Patterns of Conflict." It evolved into a massive briefing, twelve hours long in its final stage, which he delivered with tireless devotion—over a thousand times, by his estimate—to any officer, official, scholar, journalist, or legislator who cared to listen.

Wass de Czege, too, had long conversations with Boyd during the time he was writing FM 100-5, and he invited Boyd to deliver guest lectures at SAMS.

Boyd made a deeper impression still on the U.S. Marines. In the early 1980s, a colonel named Mike Wyly, vice president of the Marine Corps University at Quantico, wrote a revision of the Marines' field manual, called FMFM-1, based explicitly on Boyd's study. Wyly met with far less institutional resistance than Wass de Czege did. The Army's main weapon was the heavy tank; the Marine Corps's was the light-armored vehicle. Under the old strategy of firepower and attrition, the Marines were regarded as the Army's little cousin. Under a strategy of maneuver warfare, with its emphasis on litheness and speed, the Marines could be regarded as equal, maybe even superior. The Marine Corps commandant at the time of Desert Storm, General Alfred Gray, was an avowed Boyd disciple. When the Marines led the assault up the middle into Kuwait, Gray ordered them to avoid direct frontal attacks and instead to maneuver around the Iraqi defenses, bypassing them, then enveloping them from behind or ambushing their flanks.

Before the Army and Marines could take advantage of the technology that emerged in the 1990s—the smart bombs and the computerized radar that let commanders see the battlefield in real time and adjust their tactics and positions accordingly—they had to know how to fight with speed, maneuver, and flexibility. They learned how to do that from Wass de Czege and Boyd.

Wass de Czege saw the war in Afghanistan as marking not a revolution but an evolution in military affairs. Especially as the fighting wore on, and the Taliban adapted to American tactics, it looked more and more like a classic "combined-arms" campaign, in which commanders call in heavy fire to smash or soften up enemy resistances before ground forces punched through. There were crucial differences: the heavy fire came from the air, not from artillery, and it came very quickly and accurately. But as dramatic and impressive as these differences were, they were not *fundamentally* new. They resembled the sort of warfare, though on a smaller scale, that Wass de Czege had envisioned in his *AirLand Battle* manual—which itself derived from principles of warfare that went back centuries.

Through the 1990s, when Marshall and the others were developing their ideas on transformation, they were only dimly aware of the work being done by Wass de Czege at Leavenworth and Mike Wyly at Quantico. Rumsfeld wasn't aware of it at all. If he had been—or, perhaps, if he had been a soldier in his youth instead of a Navy pilot, if he had consulted with Boyd and Wass de Czege as well as with Marshall and Wade back during his first tenure at the Pentagon—he might have seen the war in Afghanistan through a different lens. He might have drawn different lessons for the war in Iraq.

Different lessons might have sired different views not only on how many troops he needed, but more important, and very much related, what those troops would need to do after toppling Saddam Hussein.

• • •

Rumsfeld wasn't entirely to blame on this score. The military's top leaders, too, had failed to study the lessons of history.

In the spring and fall of 2002, the Army and the Air Force each held its seasonal war games. The Army's game, in late April, was called "Vigilant Warrior." The Air Force's, in mid-November, was called "Global Engagement." The games weren't field exercises but tabletop simulations—sophisticated versions of combat board games. On a Sunday night, dozens of officers, active-duty and retired, would assemble at the Army War College in Carlyle Barracks, Pennsylvania—or, in the case of "Global Engagement," at a U.S. Postal Service conference center in the Maryland suburbs of Washington. The next morning, the game would begin. There would be a Blue Team (playing the U.S. side) and a Red Team (playing the enemy). The game's managers—officers from Joint Forces Command or the Air Staff—would set the scenario, assess each side's moves, and announce the next event that moved the game along. The game would end on Friday, when senior officers would show up for a briefing.

Formally, these games were supposed to gauge the armed forces' requirements for combat ten or fifteen years in the future. In fact, these two games were rough rehearsals for the coming invasion of Iraq. The fictitious country being invaded was called "Nair"—an anagram of Iran—and its features clearly resembled a composite of Iran and Iraq.

Wass de Czege had retired from the Army in 1993. He had begun to run into resistance from the remnants of the Army's old guard, and he knew that if he stayed in the service much longer, he would come to be seen as a crank, if not a threat. He remembered that J. C. C. Fuller, the pathbreaking British officer-strategist of the interwar years, was seen as an irritant by his superiors. The British high command didn't pay attention to Fuller's ideas about maneuver and blitzkrieg, but the German generals did—and the Western world nearly went up in flames as a result. Wass de Czege didn't want to be a twenty-first-century Fuller, so, after retiring from the Army, he kept in touch with his old colleagues—consulting for the Army's Training and Doctrine Command, attending conferences, talking with the most promising colonels and majors that he saw rising through the ranks, and participating in war games.

He played a Blue Team officer in the Army's game that year and an Army adviser to a three-star general in the Air Force's game. The games ended the way everyone knew they would: Blue (the United States) won, Red (Nair) lost. But the games disturbed Wass de Czege because they skirted the main issue.

They didn't properly define the end of a war and so couldn't clearly settle which side had won.

Shortly afterward, still several months before the actual invasion of Iraq, Wass de Czege wrote and privately circulated a memo called " '02 Wargaming Insights," a memo that Rumsfeld, Franks, and those around them would have done well to read.

War games such as these, he observed, "tend to devote more attention to successful campaign-beginnings than to successful conclusions." They "usually conclude when victory seems inevitable to us (not necessarily to the enemy), at about the point [where] operational superiority has been achieved and tactical control of strategically significant forces and places appears to be a matter of time."

However, he noted, winning a war doesn't mean simply defeating the enemy on the battlefield. It means achieving the strategic goals for which the war was fought in the first place. This was basic Clausewitz—"War is politics by other means." By the same token, the war isn't *over* until those political ends are achieved.

In both of these war games, Wass de Czege pointed out, the Clausewitzian question—how to achieve those strategic goals—wasn't answered, wasn't even addressed, because the game ended too soon.

Important as it is to understand a war's early stages, he went on, "it is just as important to know how to follow through to the resolution of such conflicts." If the managers of these games had followed through and played for longer, after the enemy's army was defeated, they might have realized that they—and, by extension, U.S. military commanders generally—were underestimating "the difficulties of 'regime change' and the magnitude of the effort required to achieve strategic objectives."

• • •

The invasion of Iraq began on March 19, 2003. In the battlefield phase, it went, to a remarkable degree, as planned. The second part of the war—after Saddam fled and his regime crumbled—went disastrously, in part because it had not been planned at all.

Rumsfeld was so enamored of transformation—as a theory of war, as a tool for control, and as an explanation for what still seemed the triumph in Afghanistan—that he forgot, if he ever fully understood, that winning wars means more than hitting targets or winning battles. Rumsfeld didn't plan for Phase IV—securing and stabilizing the country after the capital has fallen—because he didn't think it would be necessary.

The theories that had riveted his attention—RMA, transformation, shock and awe—were recipes strictly for crushing armies and toppling regimes. War was an instrument of politics. Transformation might sharpen the instrument, but it offered no wisdom about the politics. Some of the theorists, especially Deptula and Wade, were explicit on this point. They cautioned that their ideas had little or no relevance when it came to such matters as what to do after the fighting was finished. But these caveats were easy to overlook.

Rumsfeld was not alone in his failure to think about the postbattle phase. As Wass de Czege noted in his memo on the war games, senior military leaders weren't thinking about it, either. There were no U.S. Army field manuals still in print on the subject of how to end a war. In the entire Army structure, there was just one active-duty unit devoted to civil-military operations: the Ninety-sixth Civil Affairs (Airborne) Battalion, at Fort Bragg, North Carolina—consisting of fewer than two thousand soldiers—and just two more battalions in the Reserves.

The U.S. Army's Third Infantry Division swept up through the Iraqi desert with impressive speed, fought off guerrilla marauders on the way, captured the Baghdad airport, and from there rolled into the capital. But the division's official "after-action report" noted that the Army "did not have a dedicated plan to transition quickly from combat operations to SASO," the military acronym for "stability and support operations." Its commanders put a large premium on capturing the Baghdad airport, but—remarkably— they had no plan for using its facilities to fly in personnel or materials that might have helped impose order.

During World War II, the Army had an enormous civil-affairs apparatus; the occupation of Germany was planned in elaborate detail well before the war was over. Over the subsequent decades, postwar planning dwindled to a lost art. There was no opportunity to practice it. Korea was a stalemate, Vietnam a rout. Wars in the Western hemisphere were minor and manageable. Desert Storm's shady aftermath—the survival of Saddam, his repression of local rebels—could conveniently be attributed to the UN Security Council's resolution that authorized the war and allowed for no missions beyond ousting the Iraqi Army from Kuwait.

The failure to plan for an aftermath was also a product of institutional incentives. During the Cold War, officers were promoted on the basis of their performance in combat or, more often, their success at managing big-ticket weapons programs. Joining the civil-affairs battalion or the military police was no way to get ahead. So the best officers stayed away, and the function dwindled.

Rumsfeld had no interest in even thinking about Phase IV because the whole point of transformation was to keep wars fast and short. Nor was much of the Army brass bothered that the secretary of defense wasn't issuing orders for postwar operations. When Baghdad fell in late March, Tommy Franks told his generals that most of them would be going home by summer and that the American occupation would be down to thirty thousand troops by early autumn.

•   •   •

On May Day, 2003, President Bush, flying in the copilot's seat of a Navy S-3B Viking turbojet, swooped onto the deck of the aircraft carrier USS *Abraham Lincoln*, jumped out of the plane wearing a tight padded flight suit, and before a cheering crowd of sailors standing beneath a huge banner reading MISSION ACCOMPLISHED, declared, "Major combat operations in Iraq have ended. In the battle of Iraq, the United States and our allies have prevailed."

At that moment, he—and most of those around him—believed it. The dreams about a new kind of war and a new level of American supremacy seemed to have come true. The possibilities seemed limitless. The previous January, in his State of the Union address, Bush had referred to an "axis of evil" consisting of Iraq, Iran, and North Korea. Baghdad was down. It was time to confront the next tyrant—Kim Jong Il and his Hermit Kingdom of Pyongyang.

2

The Fog of Moral Clarity

George W. Bush entered the White House with two convictions about the conduct of foreign policy: America would no longer pursue international treaties—or honor existing ones—for the sake of doing so; and anything that Bill Clinton had done as president was, unless proved otherwise, wrong.

These two notions together guaranteed a crisis with North Korea, the most closed society in the world, ruled by a self-styled Communist dictator who had the technology and materials to do what Saddam Hussein could only dream of doing in Iraq—he could build nuclear weapons. Clinton dealt with the threat by making a deal with the dictator; Bush was more inclined to get rid of the dictator.

Clinton too had faced a crisis with North Korea, one that very nearly led to war, but he resolved it through a shrewd mix of force and diplomacy. Officials and analysts who studied that crisis came away with an idea of how to deal with North Korea's regime. Its reigning dictator, Kim Jong Il—like his father, Kim Il Sung, before him—was an eccentric monster, but he wasn't irrational. His negotiating style revealed clear patterns; if you recognized and exploited these patterns—if you learned the lessons of recent history—you could replicate, and build on, Clinton's success.

But Bush wasn't interested in lessons of the past; this was a new era. He didn't care about the patterns of others, certainly not those of some fleabag dictator. And he didn't regard any feat of Bill Clinton's as worthy of emulation.

The crisis that would occupy both Clinton and Bush was triggered in the late 1980s, during the presidency of Bush's father, George H. W. Bush, when the CIA discovered that the North Koreans were building a reprocessing facility near their nuclear reactor at Yongbyon, sixty miles north of the capital, Pyongyang. The news was very unsettling. When finished, this facility would be able to take the nuclear fuel rods from the reactor and convert them into plutonium—the main ingredient of an atomic bomb.

The first President Bush launched a policy of "comprehensive engagement" with North Korea—an all-fronts diplomatic campaign to keep Kim Il Sung from completing the facility or, short of that, from reprocessing the fuel rods. The campaign had little effect until September 27, 1991, when Bush announced that he was unilaterally dismantling all U.S. tactical nuclear weapons worldwide. He made this announcement in the context of rapidly warming relations between the United States and the Soviet Union amid the winding-down of the Cold War. But the move would also eliminate the hundreds of tactical nukes—most of them on short-range missiles—that America had deployed in South Korea decades ago to deter a North Korean invasion.

This tangible gesture unleashed a torrent of diplomatic activity. At the end of the year, after American officials confirmed that they had removed all nuclear weapons from the region, the leaders of North and South Korea—who had never signed a peace treaty to end the war of 1950–1953—negotiated a mutual nonaggression pact. And North Korea, which had signed the Nuclear Non-Proliferation Treaty back in 1985, signed the NPT's "safeguards" agreement, allowing the International Atomic Energy Agency to station inspectors and cameras inside its reactors and to place the nuclear fuel rods under lock and key.

By the time Clinton was elected president, relations were breaking down. North Korea refused to let the IAEA's inspectors inside a building that stored nuclear waste. The South Korean government arrested a ring of North Korean spies. The annual U.S.–South Korean military exercises, known as "Team Spirit," which Bush had suspended at the start of 1992, were scheduled to resume.

In March 1993, just over a month after Clinton took office, a Pyongyang spokesman denounced Team Spirit as a "nuclear war game preliminary to the invasion of North Korea." Kim Il Sung put the country on alert, ordering a dusk-to-dawn blackout and holding a massive rally—over one hundred thousand attended—in the capital.

On March 11, Kim announced that he intended to withdraw from the Non-Proliferation Treaty, kick the international inspectors out of the reactor, break the locks on the fuel rods, and reprocess them into plutonium. But he stopped short of actually taking those steps.

In response, Clinton pushed the United Nations Security Council to consider sanctions against North Korea. Kim's spokesmen proclaimed that sanctions would be considered an act of war. Clinton's generals drew up plans to send 50,000 troops to South Korea—bolstering the 37,000 that had been there for decades—as well as over 400 combat jets, 50 warships, and additional battalions of Apache helicopters, Bradley fighting vehicles, multiple-launch rockets, and Patriot air-defense missiles. Beyond mere plans, Clinton ordered in an advance team of 250 military personnel to set up logistical headquarters that could manage the massive influx of firepower.

These moves were designed to send a signal to the North Koreans that the president was willing to go to war to keep the fuel rods under international control. In June, Robert Gallucci, the State Department's ambassador-at-large and assistant secretary for politico-military affairs, was dispatched to tell Kang Sok Ju, North Korea's vice-minister of foreign affairs, that Clinton would regard refueling the reactor as a "red line," which, if crossed, could trigger a U.S. military response.

In early 1994, CIA analysts warned of a heightened danger of war on the Korean peninsula. On May 19, Clinton and his top advisers met in the Cabinet Room with Secretary of Defense William

Perry; the chairman of the Joint Chiefs of Staff, General John Sha-likashvili; and the commander of U.S. forces in Korea, General Gary Luck.

Perry briefed the results of a detailed military review. The United States could strike the Yongbyon reactor and set back North Korea's nuclear program by several years—but the North Koreans, whom he likened to "adolescents with guns," would almost certainly strike back against its foes in the region. The subsequent war would kill or injure half a million American and South Korean troops and as many as a million South Korean civilians. It would also cost over $60 billion and depress the South Korean economy by as much as $1 trillion.

Clinton continued to prepare for a vast mobilization of troops and armaments, as a deterrent to North Korean aggression. But he also saw that there were no good military options and that the very act of mobilizing might be viewed as a threat by the North Koreans—that, in other words, the act of preparing for war might increase the likelihood of war erupting.

He also figured that the North Koreans might be starting to realize that they had boxed themselves in—and might be looking for a face-saving way out.

A possible way out materialized on June 1, when Clinton received a phone call from former president Jimmy Carter, offering his services as a go-between to help resolve the crisis.

The call was not coincidental. Shortly after Clinton's meeting with Perry and the generals, Jim Laney, the U.S. ambassador to South Korea—and a former president of Emory University in Atlanta, where Carter had set up his post-presidential research center—called Carter, outlined the gravity of the crisis, and urged him to step in.

• • •

Carter was, in a sense, an ideal choice for such a gambit. Early in his own presidency, he announced that he would withdraw all U.S. troops from South Korea. He retracted the policy after it met fierce opposition, even from liberal Democrats. But it endeared him to Kim Il Sung, who subsequently sent Carter annual invitations to come visit.

The White House would portray Carter's trip as an unofficial, strictly private visit. But Clinton's cabinet was divided over whether to let Carter go under any circumstances. Those who had worked in Carter's administration—most notably Secretary of State Warren Christopher and National Security Adviser Tony Lake—vehemently opposed the idea. Carter, they warned, was a loose cannon; he would go beyond his orders. Vice President Al Gore favored the trip, for the same reason Clinton eventually approved it—that it might give Kim Il Sung an escape hatch, a way to walk back from the brink without appearing to buckle under pressure from the U.S. government.

Both sides in this debate turned out to be right. Carter did go beyond his instructions, negotiating the outlines of a treaty and announcing the terms live on CNN, notifying Robert Gallucci—who, at the time of the phone call, was in a White House cabinet meeting—just minutes before going on the air. Yet, at the same time, Kim did agree to back down. He agreed to keep the inspectors and fuel rods in place, if the United States gave him something in exchange.

Carter hadn't been the most appealing choice for an emissary, but he was the most likely to spur a deal that would halt North Korea's nuclear program and halt the juggernaut toward a catastrophic war. To Clinton's mind, that's what mattered.

Formal negotiations began in Geneva soon after Carter completed his trip. Three weeks later, on July 8, Kim Il Sung died at the age of eighty-two and was replaced by his son, Kim Jong Il. Clinton held out a token in the form of a gracious letter of condolence. Word got back that the note was much appreciated by the "Dear Leader" (Kim Jong Il's self-appointed nickname, to distinguish him from his father's designation, "Great Leader"). Even so, the two sides went through fifty maddening negotiating sessions before they signed a formal accord, on October 21, based on the outlines of the Carter-Kim meeting.

The accord was called the "Agreed Framework," to stress that it was an interim accord, not a full-blown treaty (and to evade the Senate ratification that a formal treaty would require). Still, its terms were elaborate and specific. North Korea would renew its commitment to the Non-Proliferation Treaty, lock up the fuel rods, and keep the inspectors on-site. In exchange, the United States, with financial backing from South Korea and Japan, would supply North Korea with two light-water nuclear reactors for electricity (these kinds of reactors were explicitly allowed under the NPT), a huge supply of heavy fuel oil, and a pledge not to invade its territory. The accord also specified that upon delivery of the first light-water reactor (the target date for this was 2003), intrusive inspection of suspected North Korean nuclear sites would begin. After the second reactor arrived, North Korea would dismantle its reprocessing facility and ship the fuel rods out of the country.

North Korea would essentially give up the ability to build nuclear weapons.

Other, less publicized sections of the accord pledged both sides to "move toward full normalization of political and economic relations." Within three months of its signing, the two countries were to lower trade barriers and install emissaries in each other's capitals. The United States was also to "provide formal assurances" that it would never use, or threaten to use, nuclear weapons against North Korea.

Initially, the North Koreans kept their side of the bargain. The Americans did not. Congress balked at the financial commitment. So did the South Koreans. The light-water reactors were never funded. Steps toward normalization were never taken. In 1996, a North Korean spy submarine washed up on South Korean shores. In reaction, the Seoul government—which had been leery of the Agreed Framework all along—suspended not only its financing of the reactors but also its share of heavy oil. Pyongyang retaliated with typically inflammatory rhetoric.

By the middle of 2000, relations began to warm again. Kim Jong Il invited Clinton to Pyongyang, promising to sign a treaty banning the production and export of long-range missiles. Clinton's secretary of state, Madeleine Albright, made the advance trip in October.

Kim Jong Il was far more erratic than his father. Tales were legion not only of his savage cruelty but also of his egomaniacal extravagances and bizarre ambitions. In one of his weirder acts, he kidnapped a prominent South Korean film director named Shin Song-ok and held him for over a decade, forcing him to shoot movies, including a Communist revision of *Godzilla*, in hopes of spawning a North Korean film industry.

Yet some of Albright's aides, who watched her negotiate with Kim over a twelve-hour period, were struck that he could behave quite rationally when he wanted, discussing and resolving issues in detail.

After the talks, Robert Einhorn, Albright's chief negotiator, stayed behind with his staff to hammer out the details of an accord. They worked at a frantic pace with their North Korean counterparts. But time ran out. With only weeks to go before the end of his second term, Clinton chose to devote his remaining time—futilely, as it turned out—to nailing down a treaty in the Middle East instead. The unsettled outcome of the 2000 presidential election, and the prolonged Florida recount, suspended all other diplomatic activity. Technical disputes over a missile deal remained unresolved. But as Clinton left the White House, the stage was set for diplomatic progress.

Meanwhile, the fuel rods remained locked up. The North Koreans didn't build a single atom bomb. And war in northeast Asia didn't seem remotely on the horizon.

• • •

A few days before George W. Bush took office in January 2001, a half-dozen members of Clinton's national security team crossed the Potomac River to the northern Virginia home of retired general Colin Powell. Bush had named Powell—an immensely popular black man who had written a best-selling autobiography and had seriously considered running for president himself—as his secretary of state, a choice widely viewed, and praised, as a signal that the new administration would pursue a moderate, internationalist foreign policy.

The Clinton team briefed Powell for two hours on the status of the North Korean missile talks. Halfway into the briefing, Condoleezza Rice, Bush's designated national security adviser, showed up, having just flown in from meeting with the president-elect in Texas. The Clinton officials were pleased with Powell's reaction to their briefing; he seemed enthusiastic, leaning forward in his chair, asking several questions. Rice made them wonder, though; she was leaning backward, a skeptical expression on her face.

The contrast foretold the internecine feuds that would rack Bush's presidency.

In early March, barely a month into Bush's term, Kim Dae Jung, the new president of South Korea, made a state visit to Washington. On the eve of the visit, Powell held a press conference and told reporters, "We do plan to engage with North Korea to pick up where President Clinton and his administration left off. Some promising elements were left on the table, and we'll be examining those elements."

The headline in the next day's *Washington Post* blared, "Bush to Pick Up Clinton Talks on North Korean Missiles." Early that morning, Powell received a phone call from Rice, saying the president was angry; he had no intention to engage with North Korea, much less to pick up where Clinton left off, and Powell had to backpedal in a hurry. A week later, Powell said, during an interview with CNN, that he'd leaned "too forward in my skis." It was the first of many instances when Powell would find himself out of step with the rest of the Bush team—the lone pragmatist in a sea of ideologues.

If Bush's stance embarrassed Powell, it humiliated Kim Dae Jong. KDJ, as some Korea-watchers called him, was a new kind of South Korean leader, a democratic activist who had spent years in prison for his political beliefs and who had run for president promising a "sunshine policy" of opening up relations with the North. During the Clinton years, South Korea's ruling party had been implacably hostile to North Korea. Efforts to hold serious disarmament talks had been obstructed at least as much by Seoul's sabotage as by Pyongyang's stubbornness. Now South Korea had a leader who could be a partner in negotiating strategy—but the United States had a leader who wasn't interested.

In Bush's view, to negotiate with an evil regime was to recognize that regime, legitimize it, and—if the negotiation led to a treaty or trade—prolong it.

It was the same view that the neocons had held about détente with the Soviet Union. And loathsome as Moscow under Leonid Brezhnev was, Pyongyang under Kim Jong Il was, in terms of human rights, much worse. To Bush, the North Korean dictator personified evil. He would later tell one reporter on the record, leaning forward, waving his finger in the air, "I loathe Kim Jong Il!" At a private meeting with Senate Republican leaders, Bush called him a "pygmy" and compared him to "a spoiled child at a dinner table."

As for Kim Dae Jong, Bush openly regarded him as "a naïve old guy." KDJ had also committed a cardinal sin in Bush's book: on his way to Washington, he stopped off in Moscow and issued a joint statement with Russian president Vladimir Putin endorsing the preservation of the Anti-Ballistic Missile Treaty. Everyone knew that Bush placed a high priority on scuttling the ABM Treaty. He took KDJ's Moscow statement as a personal affront.

When Kim Dae Jong arrived in Washington, Bush publicly criticized him and his sunshine policy. Bush and his advisers, especially Donald Rumsfeld and Vice President Dick Cheney, decided not only to isolate North Korea, in the hopes—in their minds, the near-certainty—that the regime would crumble, but also to ignore South Korea, in hopes that its next election would restore a conservative to office.

Bush turned out to be the naïf. Kim Jong Il survived U.S. pressure. And Kim Dae Jung was soon replaced by Roh Moo Hyun, a populist who ran on a campaign that was not only pro-sunshine but anti-American.

After the attacks of September 11, North Korea publicly issued a statement of sorrow over the American deaths and of opposition to all forms of terrorism. Kim Jong Il also sent a private message to Bush, through Swedish diplomats in Pyongyang, expressing condolences.

But Bush did not respond to the message. In his State of the Union address the following January, Bush characterized North Korea, Iran, and Iraq as the members of an "axis of evil." And the only thing to do with evil was to defeat it. By merely speaking those words, with the suggestion they carried, Bush was declaring that he had both the power and the moral right to follow through with action if needed.

A month later, he made his first trip to Seoul. Heading up the advance team were James Kelly, the assistant secretary of state for Asian affairs, and Charles "Jack" Pritchard, the director of the National Security Council's Asia desk during the Clinton years and now Bush's North Korean envoy. Everywhere they went in Seoul, Kelly and Pritchard were asked if there was going to be a war. President Roh told them that he woke up in a sweat every morning, wondering if Bush had done something unilaterally to endanger the Korean peninsula.

• • •

By this time, the Agreed Framework was unraveling. It was clear that the light-water reactors were never going to be built. Normalization of relations was a nonstarter. Finally, the CIA got wind that as far back as the late '90s, the North Koreans may have been acquiring centrifuges for enriching uranium, most likely from Pakistan.

Enriching uranium was an alternative way to build nuclear bombs—less potent and much more time-consuming than reprocessing fuel rods into plutonium. It was debatable whether enrichment *violated* the Agreed Framework, which dealt with the manufacturing of plutonium. Nor was it clear that the North Koreans had set up an enrichment program; the evidence on that point was ambiguous. But it was a sneaky end run and may have been a violation of the Non-Proliferation Treaty (which allows uranium enrichment but only if the government notifies the IAEA and opens the process to inspection).

On October 4, 2002, Jim Kelly flew to Pyongyang to confront North Korean officials with the evidence of the centrifuges. They admitted it was true. For nearly two weeks, the Bush administration kept this meeting secret. The U.S. Senate was debating a resolution to give President Bush the authority to go to war in Iraq. The public rationale for the war was that Saddam Hussein possessed weapons of mass destruction. If it were known that North Korea might also be starting to make WMDs—and nuclear weapons, at that—it would have muddied the debate over Iraq. Some would have asked why Bush saw a need for war against Iraq but not against North Korea. The Senate passed the resolution on October 11. Not until October 17 did the administration publicly reveal what it had known for weeks about North Korea's centrifuges.

On October 20, Bush announced that he was formally canceling the Agreed Framework. He halted oil supplies to North Korea and urged other countries to cut off all economic relations with Pyongyang.

The North Koreans—perhaps realizing that once again they had gone too far and boxed themselves into a corner—tried to replay the crisis of 1993–94. In late December, they expelled the international inspectors, restarted the nuclear reactor at Yongbyon, and unlocked the container holding the eight thousand nuclear fuel rods. On January 10, 2003, they withdrew from the Non-Proliferation Treaty. However, they also released a statement, offering to reverse their actions and retract their withdrawal if the United States resumed its obligations under the Agreed Framework and signed a nonaggression pact.

Another sign that Pyongyang was looking for a diplomatic way out came on the same day, when delegates from North Korea's United Nations mission paid a visit to Bill Richardson, the governor of New Mexico and a former UN ambassador during the Clinton administration. Richardson had negotiated with North Koreans before. As a congressman, he once traveled to Pyongyang to retrieve the body of a constituent whose U.S. Army helicopter had been shot down after drifting across the Demilitarized Zone. He later arranged the return of an American hiker who was arrested as a spy after inadvertently crossing the North Korean border.

Since President Clinton had used Jimmy Carter as an "unoffi- cial" intermediary to jump-start nuclear talks in 1994, North Kore- an officials apparently inferred that this was the Americans' way of "saving face" in dealing with out-of-favor regimes—to have middle- men do behind the scenes what presidents could not do publicly.

Richardson was willing to serve as a middleman. During the two days of talks in Santa Fe, he stayed closely in touch with the State Department. But nothing came of the gambit. The North Ko- rean foreign ministry had long employed a group of experts on American affairs; they played an important role in devising policy toward the United States. But their expertise, it seemed, had limits. They didn't realize that Bush would have nothing to do with Rich- ardson, who was not only a Democrat but a Clinton Democrat.

On January 13, two days after the Santa Fe meetings, Jim Kelly tried to keep a line open. At a press conference in Seoul, he sig- naled that he understood what the North Koreans were doing and that a negotiated settlement might still be possible. "Once we get beyond nuclear weapons," he told reporters, "there may be oppor- tunities—with the United States, with private investors, with other countries—to help North Korea in the energy area."

But Kelly was speaking out of turn. The White House made no subsequent overtures. Kelly, like his boss Powell, may have be- lieved that the crisis could be resolved by diplomatic means. But the revelation about North Korea's secret acquisition of centrifuges strengthened the hands of the administration's skeptics—especially Cheney and Rumsfeld—who felt that North Korea could not be trusted in negotiations and, more to the point, that negotiations were the wrong way to deal with such regimes in the first place.

Bush was foremost among the skeptics. He had no desire to negotiate with North Korea over its nuclear weapons or its energy needs. To Bush, this refusal was a matter of principle. Jack Pritch- ard later recalled reading National Security Council memos out- lining this no-negotiations policy explicitly.

The policy's rationale: to preserve "moral clarity."

• • •

When their overtures to Richardson led nowhere, the North Koreans escalated tensions again. Over the next two weeks, U.S. spy satellites detected trucks pulling up to the Yongbyon reactor, where
the fuel rods were stored, then driving away toward the reprocessing facility.

When Kim Il Sung had *threatened* to take this step in 1993,
Clinton warned that doing so would cross a "red line." Nine years
later, when Kim Jong Il actually *took* the step, George W. Bush did
nothing.

Specialists inside the U.S. government were flabbergasted.
Once those fuel rods left the storage site, once the reprocessing
began, once plutonium was manufactured, the strategic situation
changed—and the prospects for a verifiable disarmament accord di-
minished. Even if the North Koreans subsequently returned to the
bargaining table, even if they agreed to drive the fuel rods back, no
one could be certain that they'd disarmed totally. No one could know
whether they still had some undeclared plutonium hidden. (Even
before this crisis, the CIA estimated that the North Koreans might
have built one or two bombs from the plutonium they had reprocessed a dozen or so years earlier, when Bush's father was president.)

To Bush, the important thing was to keep the moral high
ground and to keep the pressure on Kim Jong Il. No one discussed
the possibility that it might also be a moral stance to prevent North
Korea from going nuclear—or that rhetorical pressure on Kim Jong
Il might have no effect.

In January 2003, Bush, Cheney, and Rumsfeld may have been
too preoccupied with the impending invasion of Iraq to pay much
attention to North Korea. Then again, they were preparing for
war against Iraq on the grounds that Saddam Hussein *might* have
a covert program to *develop* nuclear bombs in the *future*. Yet
here was Kim Jong Il, openly hauling out the materials to *build*
the stuff of A-bombs *now*.

Bush and his advisers did take some steps to counter the move. In early March, they sent a fleet of combat planes—twelve B-52s, twelve B-1s, twenty F-15s, and six F-117A Stealth aircraft—to bases in South Korea and Guam, well within striking range of North Korea. The public explanation for the move was to assure friends and foes that the imminent invasion of Iraq would not prevent the United States from protecting its interests in the Pacific. However, the move was also clearly a bit of "coercive diplomacy" against Kim Jong Il—a threat of the storm that could come his way if he didn't back down.

Kim Jong Il may have taken it that way. On March 10, his spokesmen accused the United States of planning a "nuclear attack" against North Korea. For the next several weeks, the "Dear Leader" was nowhere to be seen. U.S. intelligence agencies figured that he had taken shelter. But more to the point, he didn't back down. The mobilization of air power failed both as coercion and as diplomacy.

Saddam Hussein's regime fell on April 9, after a stunningly fast war that sparked far less military resistance than many expected. The notion of toppling dictators elsewhere—perhaps the other two spokes on the axis of evil—suddenly seemed tantalizing.

Rumsfeld, at the peak of his swagger and influence, wrote a secret memo that opposed negotiating a deal that, in his view, would only strengthen North Korea's economy and prolong Kim Jong Il's rule. Instead, he proposed teaming up with China to press for "regime change" in North Korea.

Overthrowing Kim Jong Il had been a long-prominent item on the neoconservatives' agenda, second only to overthrowing Saddam Hussein. When Bush's father launched his "comprehensive engagement" policy back in 1989, one of its most fervent opponents was Paul Wolfowitz, who was then undersecretary of defense. In his Clinton-era exile, Wolfowitz bitterly decried the Agreed Framework. William Kristol, chairman of the American Enterprise Institute—a neocon think tank that, during the Clinton years, had pushed strenuously for regime change in Iraq—testified before the Senate Foreign Relations Committee in February 2002, soon after the 9/11 attacks, that "American policy must be to change the North Korean regime, not simply to contain it or coexist with it."

There was no basis for Kristol's remark, no reason to think North Korea could no longer be contained. After 9/11, containment itself—as a policy toward any vaguely hostile power—was regarded as too passive, too risky. Diplomacy—to make the power less hostile—was seen as immoral. So regime change was the only alternative.

•   •   •

Kim Il Sung had risen to power through guerrilla warfare against Japan, and he governed in the same manner. As a national proverb put it, Korea was "a shrimp among whales," and both Kims—the only two leaders in North Korea's history—mastered the art of playing the large countries around them off one another. Their approach to diplomacy was to foster an atmosphere of "drama and catastrophe," a prolonged cycle of crisis, intimidation, and brinksmanship.

In the game of highway chicken, North Korea was the shrewd lunatic who very visibly throws his steering wheel out the window, forcing the other, more sober driver to veer off the road before the two collide.

At first glance, Bush might be excused for refusing to play this game. At second glance, though, what choice did he have? The whole world was traveling on that road. And it *was* possible to play Kim Jong Il's game—it *had been* played, by the Clinton administration, with fruitful results.

Bush and his aides considered the options. The Joint Chiefs, whose staff routinely prepares war plans for all conceivable contingencies, had just finished revising the war plan for Korea. Called Operations Plan 5030, it gave American commanders the authority to take provocative action against North Korea during a crisis, before a war started. For instance, they could conduct maneuvers or hold surprise military exercises, with the aim of flushing North Korean troops out of their barracks and onto heightened alert. Or

they could order spy planes to fly right up to the border, forcing the
North Koreans to scramble their jet fighters. The point of these
actions would be to strain the North Korean military's scarce resources and to sow enough confusion among its officers that they
might mount a coup against Kim Jong Il.

In July, the details of OPLAN 5030 were leaked to *U.S. News &
World Report*, perhaps as a deliberate ploy to throw the North Koreans into deeper panic. They probably already knew of the Pentagon's existing war plan for Korea, OPLAN 5027-98, which
envisioned launching preemptive air strikes against North Korean
artillery rockets and military bases, as well as mounting incursions
across the border, if U.S. intelligence agencies picked up any signs
of war preparations by Pyongyang. The war plan instructed U.S.
commanders to identify relevant targets and to assign specific
weapons for destroying them, so that they would be ready if a crisis
erupted suddenly. A revision of just the previous year, OPLAN
5027-02, contained plans for striking North Korea's weapons of
mass destruction. And a further revision, OPLAN 5027-04, still in
the works, adopted lessons from the Afghanistan and Iraq wars,
involving the use of Predator drones to find and attack key targets.

Even so, despite these elaborate war plans—to say nothing of
the dozens of combat planes recently, and theatrically, mobilized
to within striking distance of North Korea—Bush realized that war
was not a real option.

The problem was in part one of geography. Seoul, the capital of
South Korea, a city of seventeen million people, sat a mere fifty
miles south of the North-South border. The North Korean military
had, well within shooting range, 500 to 600 Scud missiles, 500 artillery guns, and 200 multiple-launch rockets—some of them loaded
with chemical warheads or shells.

Nothing had changed since the crisis of 1993–94, when the
generals told Bill Clinton that Pyongyang would almost certainly
retaliate against air strikes and that the ensuing war could kill or
injure a half million American and South Korean military personnel
and one million South Korean civilians. George W. Bush's generals
recited the same grim calculations.

In late April, Bush realized he had no choice but to sit down with the North Koreans. A new multilateral forum was created—the "six-party talks"—involving all the major nations with a stake in the outcome: the United States, the two Koreas, Japan, Russia, and China, which agreed to host the forum in Beijing.

Bush sent Kelly and Pritchard to Beijing for preparations. While they were there, Li Gun, North Korea's experienced deputy foreign minister, announced that his country now had nuclear weapons—he referred to them as a "deterrent"—but that Kim Jong Il would give them up, and return to the Non-Proliferation Treaty, if the United States dropped its "hostile attitude."

Back in Washington, Kelly said that the North Koreans, through the Chinese, had offered a "bold, new proposal." But Bush dismissed their proposal as spin, telling one reporter, "They're back to the old blackmail game." Until the North Koreans disarmed, he said several times, even to sit down with them would amount to "appeasement," giving in to "blackmail," "rewarding bad behavior."

Still, it was clear that efforts to destabilize or coerce Kim Jong Il's regime were not succeeding. In May, Bush ordered the fifty planes in Guam and South Korea to fly back to their home bases. And yet, though Bush recognized that war was not an option, he wasn't quite ready to pursue an alternative.

•   •   •

On July 13, North Korean officials announced that they had reprocessed all eight thousand fuel rods—which, American scientists estimated, would produce enough plutonium for at least five atom bombs. There was no way of knowing whether the North Koreans' claim was true, though U.S. atmospheric sensors did detect traces of Krypton-85, a chemical by-product of reprocessing, wafting near the Yongbyon reactor.

The first round of the six-party talks began on August 27. Kelly was allowed, for the first time, to meet one-on-one with his North Korean counterpart—but only for twenty minutes and only if delegates from the other four powers were in the same room. (The two could, however, chat alone in a corner.) He was forbidden to make any offers or to suggest even the possibility of direct negotiations, and he was instructed to start the private chats by saying, "This is not a negotiating session. This is not an official meeting."

For the previous year and a half, Colin Powell had favored a diplomatic solution to the Korean crisis, while Donald Rumsfeld and Dick Cheney opposed it. The August meeting in Beijing was Bush's idea of a middle path, but it constituted no path at all. He let Kelly talk, but didn't let him say anything of substance.

Even so, the bureaucratic warring persisted. John Bolton was the undersecretary of state for arms control and nuclear proliferation. Cheney had placed him in the job to act as his mole inside Foggy Bottom. Just before the six-party talks got under way, Bolton gave a speech in which he called North Korea "a hellish nightmare" and Kim Jong Il "a tyrannical dictator." True enough, but it was odd invective for a senior official to issue on the eve of an international summit.

As the talks got under way, Jack Pritchard—one of the few administration officials who had ever talked with North Korean diplomats—resigned in protest. His job title was envoy for North Korean negotiations, yet he was prohibited from conducting negotiations. He asked himself, "What am I doing in government?" Pritchard had heard, from reliable quarters, that White House and Pentagon higher-ups referred to him as "the Clinton guy" and didn't want him involved in the six-party talks, lest he take them too seriously. Powell asked him not to quit, or at least not do so publicly. Pritchard respectfully declined on both counts. He helped set up the six-party talks, left when they started, and went to work at the Brookings Institution. He explained his reasons for quitting to anyone who asked.

Not until mid-June 2004, ten months after the six-party talks began, did President Bush put a proposal—a set of incentives for North Korean disarmament—on the table. The offer was this: Pyongyang had three months to declare that it would dismantle its nuclear weapons program; once that declaration was made, the

United States would provisionally pledge not to invade North Korea's territory or topple its regime, and the other powers would send Pyongyang an enormous amount of fuel oil each month.

Remarkably, the proposal was a resuscitation of Clinton's Agreed Framework—minus the light-water reactors and the restoration of diplomatic relations. The North Koreans had been asking Bush to revive Clinton's accord for a year and a half, ever since they overplayed their hand and unlocked the fuel rods. But now Bush's bid was a classic case of too little, too late. Kim Jong Il had considerably strengthened his hand. He had plutonium now; he claimed to have nuclear weapons. More to the point, that's *all* he had. For him to trade in his only means of any leverage, the only bargaining chips that were compelling the United States to talk with him—to his mind, the only chips that were deterring the United States from attacking him—Bush would have to offer a lot more.

Nearly another year went by before further steps were taken, and they were initiated by North Korea. On May 13, 2005, Bush allowed two high-ranking U.S. officials—Jim Foster, the State Department's director of Korean affairs, and Joseph DiTrani, who had replaced Pritchard as the special envoy to North Korea—to travel secretly to New York and meet with Park Gil-yon, Pyongyang's ambassador to the United Nations. Park had called for the meeting to ask two questions: Did the Bush administration respect North Korea's sovereignty? And did it have any intention of launching an attack? Foster and DiTrani assured Park on both points.

Soon after, the six-party talks resumed. On September 19, all the parties signed a "Joint Statement," whereby North Korea vowed to give up its nuclear weapons program and rejoin the Non-Proliferation Treaty, while the other five powers promised to provide massive energy assistance and respect Pyongyang's sovereignty.

The statement was widely hailed as a breakthrough. Condoleezza Rice had replaced Colin Powell as secretary of state at the start of Bush's second term that January. Rice had been national security adviser in the first term and Bush's mentor on foreign policy since the late '90s when he started running for president. Unlike Powell, Rice had Bush's ear and talked with him every day. Some observers saw the Joint Statement as the sign of a return to state-craft and diplomacy.

In fact, it was nothing of the sort. Pyongyang was still insisting on a light-water nuclear reactor; Washington had no interest in supplying one—or in offering an alternative inducement.

The Joint Statement was a finessing of this deadlock, not a prelude to resolution. According to the carefully worded document, North Korea would abandon its nuclear program and "*at an early date*" rejoin the Non-Proliferation Treaty. The other five powers "agreed to *discuss* at *an appropriate time* the subject of the provision of a light-water reactor." There were no deadlines, no commitments to action.

Christopher Hill, an experienced diplomat who had replaced Jim Kelly as assistant secretary of state for East Asian affairs, wanted to go to Pyongyang to hammer out the differences. Cheney, whose influence was undiminished, argued against the trip. For an official of Hill's level to step foot in North Korea would imply American recognition of North Korea's legitimacy in the community of nations. Kim Jong Il would manipulate the trip to his advantage. It would be like Madeleine Albright's trip to Pyongyang in 2000. It was, in short, too reminiscent of Clinton. Bush sided with Cheney. The trip was off.

In June 2006, North Korea announced it would soon test a long-range missile—its first such test since 1998. The regional powers protested, including China, Pyongyang's closest ally. Bush was particularly miffed. "North Koreans have made agreements with us in the past," he said, "and we expect them to keep their agreements—for example, agreements on test launches."

Bush's protest was not only ironic but wrong. The North Koreans *had* declared a moratorium on missile tests, back when they were holding talks with the Clinton administration on an outright missile ban. But it was a *unilateral* moratorium, not an agreement "with us," as Bush put it, and they said it would remain in effect only as long as the missile talks continued. Bush had shut down those talks during his second month as president, when he made it clear to Colin Powell that he would not be picking up where

Clinton had left off. North Korea waited four years, till March 2005, to announce that the moratorium was over. Then they waited another year and a quarter to follow up with action. No one should have been surprised. If Bush had wanted them to keep the moratorium going, he should have kept the talks going.

The test, conducted with fanfare on the Fourth of July, was a dud; the missile sputtered and crashed thirty-five seconds after liftoff.

Three months later, on October 9, the North Koreans pulled off a more sensational test—the underground explosion of an atomic bomb, the first time they had ever attempted that. It was a small bomb. They'd alerted Russia, in advance, that they would be setting off a nuclear device with the explosive power of four kilotons (the equivalent of 4,000 tons of dynamite); it turned out to be well under one kiloton. Nonetheless, by the standard definition, North Korea was now a nuclear-armed state.

The United Nations Security Council voted, 13–0, to condemn the test. But little action followed. This too should have been no surprise. China held the key to leverage over North Korea; most of the country's trade passed across the Chinese border. But China's leaders had a strong interest in propping up Kim Jong Il's regime. First, his collapse would send hundreds of thousands—maybe millions—of North Korean refugees streaming across the border, a humanitarian disaster that China had no ability or desire to handle. Second, Kim Jong Il's survival ensured that American military forces in Asia would devote most of their effort to the defense of South Korea and Japan—and not so much to the defense of Taiwan.

Chinese officials were far from keen to see their erratic neighbor going nuclear. But, at least for the moment, they put more value on their own security interests than on the cause of nuclear non-proliferation.

And in 2006, the United States had very little leverage over China. America was a debtor nation, and Chinese bankers held the vast bulk of its debt, in effect subsidized its vast deficit spending. America couldn't persuade Chinese officials to alter their monetary policy. It certainly couldn't persuade them to alter their basic priorities for national security.

• • •

The Bush administration's whole approach to North Korea hinged on a premise that turned out to be untrue—that the United States had the power to set the terms of a new world order and, therefore, didn't need to compromise with competing concepts or interests.

The failure of American policy toward North Korea stemmed from a failure to grasp the implications of this new balance of power in Asia. It also stemmed from a failure to understand—a willful refusal even to try to understand—Kim Jong Il's motives in this standoff, the patterns of behavior he displayed, and the strategic options for dealing with them. Kim's eccentricities had little to do with it. Had he been the sanest leader on the planet, he would have had a rational motive to develop a nuclear arsenal. His diplomats had studied the two Gulf Wars carefully, and concluded that Saddam Hussein's big mistake lay in not having nuclear weapons to deter U.S. intervention. They made precisely this point in an official statement released back in April 2003, just after American tanks rolled into Baghdad: "The Iraq war teaches us a lesson that, in order to prevent a war, and defend a country's security and a nation's sovereignty, it is necessary to have a powerful physical deterrent."

When Jack Pritchard started dealing with North Korea, he scoffed at the official fears of an American attack, viewing them as propaganda. But over the years, he came to regard them as (however unfounded) genuine; the North Koreans really seemed to believe them. And he saw that Bush's rhetoric only inflamed their fears, sharpened their suspicions, and hardened their determination to build a counterweight. A plutonium counterweight had the appeal of being not only particularly potent but also within their technical grasp.

Bush's father spurred enormous diplomatic progress near the end of his presidency by *doing* something that appealed to North

Korea's tangible interests—namely, by withdrawing all of America's tactical nuclear weapons from the peninsula. The conceptual breakthrough during Clinton's crisis with Pyongyang came at a White House meeting in October 1993, when Robert Gallucci suddenly realized why the North Koreans had been rejecting the administration's disarmament proposals—because all of its proposals required the North Koreans to disarm long before they required the United States to reward them for doing so. The talks took off after the Clinton team made proposals that called on the two sides to take steps simultaneously.

Those who took part in those talks, which led to the Agreed Framework, observed and made note of distinct patterns in the North Koreans' negotiating style. For instance, disputes were almost always resolved in small, informal settings, even in after-hours chats, not in the large, formal sessions. The North Koreans would begin talks with a hard-line stance; at some point, they would become very flexible; then, in the endgame, they would follow a hard line again, often reversing earlier compromises, in order to squeeze the last possible concession out of the American negotiators.

At least for the first six years of his presidency, Bush and his closest aides had no interest in studying the past or in talking with anyone who had lived it. They insisted that North Korea dismantle its nuclear program as a *prerequisite* to substantive talks. They were through with mindless concessions and maddening gamesmanship. They would not authorize substantive talks in informal sessions. They blew off the North Koreans at the first sign of hardening. They assumed that a tinhorn tyrant like Kim Jong Il would fold when confronted with the mere demonstration of American might.

And so the North Koreans went nuclear, and the most powerful nation on Earth did nothing to stop them.

• • •

Bush may have rationalized that it didn't matter because, if Kim Jong Il dared to put nuclear warheads on missiles and launch them in anger, America's latest wonder weapon, the ultimate emblem of its technological supremacy, would intercept and destroy the missiles during their trajectory through outer space. On August 17, 2004, during a campaign speech at a Boeing defense plant in Ridley, Pennsylvania, Bush proclaimed, clearly with North Korean nukes in mind, "We say to those tyrants who believe they can blackmail America and the free world: 'You fire, we're going to shoot it down.'"

He would soon be disabused of this dream, too.

3

Chasing Silver Bullets

Back in September 1999, in his speech at The Citadel, the first major foreign policy address of his presidential campaign, George W. Bush talked not only about military transformation but also about the need for a weapon that could shoot down enemy missiles in the event of a nuclear attack.

"At the earliest possible date," he said, "my administration will deploy anti-ballistic-missile systems . . . to guard against attack and blackmail." Since 1972, when the United States and the Soviet Union signed the Anti-Ballistic Missile Treaty, we had essentially halted a once-ambitious ABM program. But now, Bush dismissed the treaty as "an artifact of Cold War confrontation" and pledged that as president, he would sweep it into history's dustbin. "I will have a solemn obligation to protect the American people and our allies," he said, "not to protect arms-control agreements signed almost thirty years ago."

That passage of the speech came straight out of Republican Party gospel. Specifically, it came from "The Contract with America," the "detailed agenda for national renewal" that Congressman Newt Gingrich had coordinated during the 1994 congressional elections, which brought a Republican majority in the House after forty years of Democratic control and elevated Gingrich to the post of House Speaker. Among its pledges was passage of a bill "to deploy at the earliest possible moment an antiballistic missile system that is capable of providing a highly effective defense of the United States against ballistic missile attacks," including attacks "from 'third world' countries."

The Contract—which also called for tax cuts, welfare cuts, tort reform, stiffer prison sentences, and other planks of the conservative Republican agenda—was an appeal to revive the spirit of Ronald Reagan's presidency. Reagan had been the first president in twenty years to take ABMs seriously, delivering a nationwide television speech on March 23, 1983, that called on American scientists "to give us the means of rendering these nuclear weapons impotent and obsolete." Reagan tripled the Pentagon's research-and-development program for missile defense, to $3 billion annually, and approved an ambitious scheme that included laser weapons in outer space, thus giving rise to the program's nickname, "Star Wars." But even Reagan's plan fell short of the $10 billion a year that Bush would spend on missile defense. And not even Reagan went so far as to abandon the ABM Treaty.

Like Reagan, like most presidents briefed for the first time on the horrific details of the nuclear war plan, Bush wondered why anyone would oppose defenses. What was wrong with trying to protect the American people from the ravages of nuclear war? As Bush would later put it in an August 2004 campaign speech in Pennsylvania, "I think those who oppose this . . . system really don't understand the threats of the twenty-first century. They're living in the past. We're living in the future. We're going to do what's necessary to protect the country."

Reagan, Gingrich, Bush, and others thought that opposition stemmed from an arms-control doctrine dating back to the 1960s, called MAD, for Mutual Assured Destruction, in which the superpowers deterred nuclear war through the threat of retaliation: if either side launched a nuclear first strike, the other would respond with an annihilating blow. By this logic, missile defenses were "destabilizing," because they could blunt a retaliatory second strike and thus be used as protective cover for a first strike.

ABM proponents thought MAD was just that—*mad*—an abrogation of the right of national defense for the sake of a theory. After the Cold War was over, the theory seemed particularly bankrupt. Missile-defense advocates were no longer talking about a vast ABM system against the Soviet Union, but a much smaller system designed to thwart attacks by rogue regimes that might acquire a handful of nuclear weapons.

But their premise was mistaken. The original and most outspoken critics of ABM systems were not arms-control theorists or antinuclear activists, but rather physicists and engineers, most of whom had helped build nuclear weapons—some of whom had helped design ABM systems. And they opposed the ABM not so much because it was "destabilizing," but because they had concluded it simply would not—and probably could not—work.

• • •

The debate over missile defenses dated not to Reagan's Star Wars or even to the 1972 ABM Treaty but much further back, to the mid-to-late 1950s, when weapons scientists inside the government, carrying high-level security clearances, first discovered the technical obstacles. Roughly every ten years since, the debate has repeated itself, with the same arguments, often among the same people. And each repetition has followed the same pattern, with the president and his aides at first enthusiastic about some technological advance that makes shooting down missiles seem suddenly feasible—then realizing that the same old technical obstacles remain.

If Bush and his aides had known this history—if they had known that the main critique of missile defenses was not political or philosophical but rather technical—they might have stepped more gingerly before tripling the missile-defense budget yet again, withdrawing from the ABM Treaty, and rushing a brand-new missile-defense system into production and deployment without having any idea whether it could really defend against an attack. But they didn't know the history; they thought that history was irrelevant anyway; and so they plunged ahead.

The history began before either America or Russia had ballistic missiles with the range to strike each other's territory. In 1945, as the Second World War was coming to an end, the U.S. Army contracted Bell Telephone Laboratories and Western Union to develop an antimissile defense system called Project Nike. The Navy commissioned Johns Hopkins University to work on a similar project called Bumblebee. When the Air Force became an independent service in 1947, it hired Boeing to develop a competing system called BOMARC. Over the next decade, all three services did research and development on a variety of ABM projects under the code names Thumper, Hermes, Terrier, Tartan, and Wizard, among others.

Most of these projects followed similar principles, involving a network of radars and antimissile missile batteries deployed all across the nation. The radars would track the nose cones of enemy missiles as they plunged toward the United States. The antimissile missiles would be launched toward the nose cones and blow up once they got near, destroying the nose cones with the blast (in most of these schemes, a nuclear blast).

In August 1957, President Dwight Eisenhower's secretary of defense, Neil McElroy, convened a panel to select the most promising of these systems and to impose a division of authority. The panel ruled that the Air Force would build early-warning radars to detect an enemy missile attack; the Army would build the weapon system that tracks and shoots down the enemy missiles. In short, the Army was to proceed with its Nike-Zeus interceptors, while the Air Force and the Navy were to drop their ABM programs.

Throughout the 1950s, Eisenhower had kept a firm cap on the defense budget, and the three services—Army, Navy, and Air Force—fought bitterly over their share. When the Army won the battle over which service would build the antimissile missile, Lieutenant General James Gavin, chief of the Army's R&D directorate, crowed that the Nike-Zeus would soon replace strategic bombers—the Air Force's B-47s and B-52s—as the nation's chief nuclear deterrent.

The Air Force fought back. While its scientists were doing their own ABM research, they discovered that the whole concept had severe problems. First, their calculations indicated that an enemy could build offensive missiles far more cheaply than the U.S. could continue to build defensive missiles; in other words, in an offense-defense arms race, the offense would win. Second, they realized that an enemy could easily pack a missile's nose cone with more than one warhead, which the ABM's radar could not track, or with several decoys, which the radar would be unable to distinguish from the actual warhead.

Now that they were out of the ABM game, the Air Force chiefs made McElroy aware of these problems.

The chiefs were clearly motivated by internecine rivalries with the Army, but McElroy realized that they also might be right. So he set up a committee of scientists, all with experience at designing missiles, to investigate the claims. On April 2, 1958, the Reentry Body Identification Group, as the panel was called, submitted its report, confirming the Air Force critique and outlining several additional ways that the offense could overwhelm or confuse the defense.

McElroy had recently set up the Advanced Research Projects Agency to supervise programs involving technical expertise. Scientists in ARPA's missile-defense unit reviewed the group's report and agreed with its findings. Nike-Zeus seemed doomed. In 1959, the issue was reviewed again by a special panel of the President's Science Advisory Council or PSAC. It was an impressive panel, to say the least, including Hans Bethe, who had directed the Theoretical Physics Division at Los Alamos during the development of the atomic bomb and, five years later, helped design the hydrogen bomb; Wolfgang Panofsky, director of the High-Energy Physics Lab at Stanford University; Harold Brown, director of the Lawrence Livermore weapons lab; and Jerome Wiesner, an MIT physicist who, two years earlier, had served on the Gaither Commission, which forecast (inaccurately, as it turned out) a threat of Soviet missile superiority by the turn of the decade.

The panel reached the same conclusion as all the previous panels, and recommended that Nike-Zeus not be built without substantial changes in its design.

Now the Army fought back. Its public-relations office placed ads in mass-circulation magazines, touting the Nike-Zeus. The program managers distributed contracts and subcontracts to thirty-seven states, in an effort to maximize corporate lobbying and congressional support. After John F. Kennedy won the 1960 presidential election, he was flooded with mail and phone calls urging him to keep Nike-Zeus going.

Kennedy was initially inclined to support the program. He had, after all, campaigned on a platform of increasing the defense budget and closing the "missile gap" with the Soviet Union. (Not until the spring of 1961, when photos from the first reconnaissance satellite came in, did he discover that there was no missile gap—or, rather, that there was, but the United States was far ahead, not behind.) However, Kennedy had named Jerry Wiesner, who had served on the PSAC panel, as his science adviser. Wiesner educated Kennedy about the technical problems that he, Hans Bethe, and the other scientists had uncovered. Kennedy was also briefed by Jack Ruina, a member of the 1958 Pentagon panel and now the director of ARPA.

Meanwhile, the Army was moving forward on an improved ABM, called Nike-X, which incorporated a new "phased-array" radar that could scan a much wider area of the sky. The Nike-X also contained a dual missile system consisting of a long-range ABM called Spartan, which would intercept missiles when they were still in outer space, and a short-range one called Sprint, which would shoot down missiles once they entered the atmosphere.

The Army wanted to deploy Nike-Zeus, then upgrade the system when Nike-X was ready. But Kennedy's secretary of defense, Robert McNamara, had a different idea.

• • •

McNamara was a new kind of defense secretary. During World War II, he had worked in the Statistical Control Office of the Army Air Corps as part of a group from the Harvard Business School that used new techniques of operations research and systems analysis to make the U.S. bombing campaign more efficient. After the war, he

and nine others from the Stat Control Office were hired by Ford
Motor Company to rationalize its management system. At age
forty-four, McNamara had just become the youngest president in
Ford history when Kennedy tapped him to run the Pentagon. To
help him rationalize weapons procurement and military strategy,
McNamara created an Office of Systems Analysis inside the Penta-
gon and filled it with young defense analysts, mainly from the
RAND Corporation, who, like his Harvard group during World
War II, came to be called the "whiz kids."

Initially, McNamara favored the Army's plan to deploy Nike-
Zeus. But when Nike-X came up on the drawing boards, he concluded that Nike-Zeus was already outmoded; he canceled the
program and stepped up funding for research and development,
but not yet production, of Nike-X.

McNamara still supported the idea of an ABM system, but
that changed in January 1964, when Harold Brown, another member of the 1959 PSAC panel, showed him a study that had been
conducted by an Air Force general named Glenn Kent.

Brown was now director of the Pentagon's research and engineering department. Kent was an unusual general—a mathematician who had directed the Air Force planning office in the late
1950s. He had taken leave in 1961 to study defense policy at Harvard for a year, then returned to the Pentagon as Brown's military assistant.

When Kent came on board, the Joint Chiefs of Staff had just
finished a computer war game designed to measure the impact of
ABMs on the results of a "nuclear exchange" between the United
States and the Soviet Union. The conclusion was that ABMs would
dramatically reduce the damage wreaked by a Soviet attack. (The
Chiefs by this time were unanimously in favor of an ABM; the Army
and Air Force had settled their rivalry by backing each other's budgets in common cause against McNamara, who was daringly cutting
programs right and left.) Kent noticed something strange in the war
game's methodology. It assumed that the Soviet Union would attack
with a particular number of warheads, then calculated how many
ABMs would be needed to shoot down a high percentage of those

warheads. Kent pointed out to Brown that this method didn't take into account the interactions of a real-world arms race. The construction of an American *defensive* system would almost certainly prompt the Soviets to expand their *offensive* arsenal. A more realistic analysis, Kent said, would calculate how many ABMs would be needed to thwart an enemy attack—and at what price—given a wide range of possible Soviet arsenals and tactics.

Brown ordered him to do that analysis and to broaden it, looking not only at ABMs but also at other methods of limiting the damage from a Soviet attack, including fallout shelters and preemptive offensive attacks.

Over the next several months, Kent worked on the calculations, drawing twenty-nine graphs covering a variety of assumptions and scenarios. The calculations revealed that "damage-limiting" strategies generally were fairly hopeless. Under certain conditions, a combination of ABMs, fallout shelters, and preemption could reduce the damage of a Soviet attack by as much as 60 percent—in terms of Americans killed and American industry destroyed. However, if the Soviets responded to the defensive measures by building or launching more missiles, they would nullify the effect and do so far more cheaply. In short, ABMs would cost too much and would not reduce the massive death and destruction caused by a Soviet attack.

McNamara read Kent's study and fully grasped its implications. He backed off ABMs altogether. He tried to buy off the Army brass, rejecting their requests for production funds but giving them loads of money—by 1967, nearly a half-billion dollars—for continued research and development.

But President Lyndon B. Johnson was under enormous pressure—from the Joint Chiefs of Staff and from powerful members of Congress—to build *some* kind of ABM system, and he ordered McNamara to comply. On September 18, McNamara gave an odd speech in San Francisco. In the first part, he laid out the many reasons why an ABM would be futile. In the second part, he announced that he was approving a new ABM system designed to defend against a limited attack that might be launched by China.

Two months earlier, after McNamara asked one of his aides, Morton Halperin, to write this speech, Halperin's boss, Paul Warnke, the assistant secretary of defense for international security affairs, dropped by McNamara's office. Warnke raised his eyebrows and asked, "China bomb, Bob?"

McNamara looked down, shuffled some papers on his desk, and muttered, "What else am I going to blame it on?"

• • •

It has been a recurring pattern throughout the history of arms procurement: when one rationale for buying a weapon proves untenable, its most impassioned advocates shift to a different rationale. The advocates *know* that the weapon is vital to the national defense; they figure that opposition stems from some ulterior motive (political hostility or pacifism or a rivalry with the branch of the armed services that's funding the weapon). For many, it would be too drastic a cognitive shift to reassess the wisdom of a project; better to devise a new argument that justifies it.

When James Schlesinger was secretary of defense under Richard Nixon, he thought the Navy was too large. He asked the chief of naval operations to calculate how many aircraft carriers he would need if the president decided to drop the mission of defending the Indian Ocean. At the time, the Navy had thirteen carriers, two of them tasked to the Indian Ocean. The chief ordered a study; the answer came back: the Navy would still need thirteen carriers. It was thirteen carriers that the Navy wanted; no matter how the president might change the mission, the answer would be the same— only the rationale for them would change.

This pattern of shifting rationales has been particularly acute in the history of the ABM, because the desire for a nuclear defense is understandably strong—and because the case for specific ABM systems has fallen apart so repeatedly.

In October 1965, two years before McNamara's reluctant shift to an anti-China ABM rationale, the President's Science Advisory Council assembled yet another panel to assess Nike-X, in much the same way that Eisenhower's PSAC had assessed Nike-Zeus. Their conclusion was the same: Nike-X "can probably be exhausted by the use of light, relatively unsophisticated . . . decoys" and would therefore be ineffective against an attack by not only the Russians but also the Chinese.

Still, China had a much smaller arsenal than Russia; at the time it had no intercontinental ballistic missiles. If McNamara couldn't stop the ABM, he could at least create a rationale that would sharply limit how many antimissile missiles the Army could justify buying.

But the Joint Chiefs saw the concession as an opening for reviving a much larger ABM system, and, seeing that McNamara was weakened—President Johnson had forced him to give way on a vaunted principle—they pushed more vigorously still. This time, it was the scientists' turn to fight back. In December 1967, Hans Bethe and Richard Garwin spoke about the technical problems of the ABM on a panel at the annual conference of the American Association for the Advancement of Science. Bethe had just won the Nobel Prize for physics. Garwin had worked on the 1965 PSAC panel.

After the discussion, Gerard Piel, the organizer of the conference and also the publisher of *Scientific American*, approached Bethe and Garwin and asked them to turn their remarks into an article for his magazine. They were reluctant. Both of them had high-level security clearances. And like most weapons scientists, they were hesitant, as a matter of principle, to speak out publicly on such matters. Piel begged them. Besides being a pioneer in science journalism—he had written about science for *Life* magazine in the 1940s before buying, and subsequently enlivening, *Scientific American*—Piel was passionate about nuclear disarmament and thought the public needed to hear what Bethe and Garwin were saying about this new weapon system. After much cajoling (he "almost broke our arms by twisting," Garwin would later remember), Piel convinced them.

After undergoing an official security review, to ensure that it contained nothing classified, the article appeared in the May 1968 issue. Like the panel discussion the previous December, it was a reprise of the criticisms lodged over the previous decade by various top secret scientific panels in the White House and the Pentagon. But now Bethe and Garwin were making the points, albeit in sanitized form, to the public.

Around this time, the war in Vietnam was turning disastrous, spurring protests in the streets and skepticism on Capitol Hill—not just about the war but about Pentagon policies generally. The ABM was the most high-profile weapon system in the budget. Opposition was also stirring in areas of the country where the Army planned to deploy the large interceptors and radar dishes. The Bethe-Garwin piece came along at just the right moment, and it caused a huge splash. Senators began to consult scientists who had worked on the panels of the late 1950s and '60s. Congressional hearings were held on the subject, and many of these scientists were called to testify. In some committees, it marked the first time that nonadministration witnesses had ever testified on military matters.

When Richard Nixon became president in January 1969, the debate shifted. A few weeks into the administration, Nixon's national security adviser, Henry Kissinger, went over to the Pentagon and laid down the orders: there will be an ABM system; it will be cheaper than Johnson's ABM; and it will shoot down Soviet missiles, not just Chinese missiles.

The Pentagon's R&D director, John Foster, concluded that under these guidelines, defending cities was out of the question; even if the mission were feasible, it would be too expensive by Kissinger's criteria. Foster came up with a new mission for the ABM: defending not America's cities but rather its ICBMs.

This was a dramatic shift in rationale, and in a sense, it was a bit more plausible. For much of the 1960s, the Soviet Union had only a small number of nuclear missiles, and America's Minuteman ICBMs were buried in blast-resistant concrete silos; the idea of a Soviet nuclear threat was very abstract. But by the end of the decade, the Soviets were building a new generation of ICBMs with warheads powerful enough, at least theoretically, to destroy the Minuteman silos. America's ICBMs suddenly seemed vulnerable. Maybe ABMs could defend them from an attack.

On March 14, Nixon made the announcement. The Sentinel ABM, the Nike-X derivative to defend against a Chinese attack, was canceled and would be replaced by a new ABM, called Safeguard, to protect the Minutemen from a Soviet first strike. The new rationale blunted the critics' case somewhat. Defending ICBM sites was easier than defending cities. Under the old concept, if one enemy warhead made it through the defenses, a city would be destroyed. Under the new concept, if one warhead made it through, one ICBM would be demolished; since a single ICBM wasn't so valuable, the defense didn't have to be foolproof.

Still, despite the new name and mission, Safeguard was technologically the same old ABM system, and it didn't take long for the scientists to point out that it had the same vulnerabilities. In January 1970, Nixon's science adviser, Lee DuBridge, sent the president a report from the PSAC's Strategic Military Panel, concluding that Safeguard "will be obsolete within three to four years after it is first deployed." Nixon was furious, but he felt he could reject the findings in good conscience, since the panel's director, Stanford physicist Sidney Drell, had been a member of the 1965 PSAC panel, the Democrats' panel.

Kissinger wrote in the margins of DuBridge's memo: "We must get PSAC out of strategy." Don't heed the message; kill the messenger.

• • •

But a bigger shock came in the spring. On April 9, 1970, Kissinger's assistant on strategic issues, Laurence Lynn, met in DuBridge's White House office with two senior executives from Bell Telephone Laboratories, Safeguard's prime contractor. The executives had called the meeting to announce that they wanted out of the ABM business. They recited all the ways that Safeguard could be overwhelmed by the offense, and concluded—as Lynn put it afterwards in a secret/eyes-only memo to Kissinger—that Bell no longer wanted "to be associated with a program which cannot technically perform the missions the government claims it will perform."

Nixon and Kissinger were shocked. Nixon wrote in the margins of the memo, "My guess is that the real reasons are their scientists"—who might have been influenced by all the Nobel laureates opposing the system— "and P.R. fears." Whatever the motive, they knew this was a disaster. Once Congress found out that the prime contractor was giving up lucrative business on the grounds that Safeguard wouldn't work, the program was doomed.

One week after Lynn's meeting with the Bell executives, the first Soviet-American nuclear arms control talks got under way in Vienna. The administration kept Safeguard alive and persuaded Bell to stick it out by calling it a "bargaining chip" at the arms talks, a lever to force the Soviets to reduce their offensive weapons. Bell stayed in the program. Two years later, on May 26, 1972, Nixon and Soviet premier Leonid Brezhnev signed the Strategic Arms Limitation Treaty, known as SALT, and the Anti-Ballistic Missile Treaty. SALT didn't reduce offensive nuclear missiles, but it did prohibit both sides from building more. The ABM Treaty, however, put a very tight clamp on antimissile missiles. The treaty restricted each side to two ABM sites of no more than one hundred interceptors each: one site to defend ICBMs, the other to defend the nation's capital. It also banned ABM tests at sea or in outer space, and it set restrictions on various technical aspects of antiaircraft radars to ensure that they couldn't be upgraded to ABM radars.

In 1974, President Gerald Ford met with Brezhnev in Vladivostok and signed a protocol further restricting each side's ABMs to just one site. Soon after, the United States dismantled the one Safeguard battery that it had deployed, just a year earlier, next to the Minuteman missiles at Grand Forks Air Force Base, North Dakota. The Soviets had installed sixty-four ABM missiles near Moscow. The treaty allowed them to build another thirty-six, but they didn't bother; nor did they maintain the existing sixty-four, which rotted in the ground.

For the next nine years, nobody said much about ABMs. The Cold War continued. Tensions flared and abated, as before. The offensive nuclear arms race proceeded apace, as—through the new technology of MIRVs, or multiple independently targetable reentry vehicles—the United States and the U.S.S.R. expanded the number of warheads on top of each missile. Still, the balance of power kept either side from starting a major war.

Then, on March 23, 1983, two years into his presidency, Ronald Reagan gave a prime-time television address. The speech was supposed to be about impending increases in the military budget. But it ended with a surprise—the announcement of a renewed, far more ambitious project to build not merely a partial defense against a missile attack but rather a foolproof shield.

"I have become more and more deeply convinced," Reagan said, "that the human spirit must be capable of rising above dealing with other nations and human beings by threatening their existence. . . . Wouldn't it be better to save lives than to avenge them? . . . What if free people could live secure in the knowledge that their security did not rest upon the threat of instant U.S. retaliation to deter a Soviet attack; that we could intercept and destroy strategic ballistic missiles before they reached our own soil or that of our allies?"

He then recited the line that drew everyone's attention: "I call upon the scientific community in our country—those who gave us nuclear weapons—to turn their great talents now to the cause of mankind and world peace, to give us the means of rendering these nuclear weapons impotent and obsolete."

Reagan wrote that final sentence himself, over the objections of his advisers, who cautioned that it might overstate what was technically feasible. Reagan was a bristling hawk. Since the mid-1960s, when he became a national spokesman for the ascendant right wing of the Republican Party, he had given many speeches advocating victory, not merely containment, in America's struggle with the Soviets.

He had long thought America could achieve victory by launching an arms race that would drive Moscow into bankruptcy. Now that he was president, that's what he set out to do.

• • •

The Cold War was as tense as it had been in twenty years. The Soviets had recently invaded Afghanistan and crushed the Solidarity workers' union in Poland. This was the time when the creative officers in the U.S. Army, Marines, and Air Force were devising new strategies to counter the growing sophistication of Soviet weapons in Europe. The Soviets were also beginning to deploy a new generation of ICBMs, the SS-18s and SS-19s, armed with six to ten warheads apiece, each more powerful and accurate than those on their earlier missiles. Reagan's secretary of defense, Caspar Weinberger, warned of a looming "window of vulnerability," during which the Soviets could launch a disarming first strike against America's ICBMs. He ordered a 13 percent hike in the defense budget, the largest peacetime increase in U.S. history. Most of the extra money was spent on conventional weapons—tanks, airplanes, ships, and so forth. But he also boosted spending on every nuclear weapon that was in the arsenal and a few that weren't.

In early 1982, Weinberger signed a top-secret document called the "Defense Guidance," which called for nuclear weapons that could "prevail" in a "prolonged nuclear war." Every administration in the Cold War era, even John Kennedy's, had plans on using nuclear weapons not only to deter wars but also, if necessary, to fight them. But these plans were rarely discussed and not taken very seriously; they were seen as desperate options that, at best, might mitigate a nuclear catastrophe only slightly. Yet several of Reagan's top officials talked about "limited nuclear war" openly, even with gusto.

Despite it all, and though his advisers worked strenuously to keep his views on the subject under wraps, Reagan himself abhorred nuclear weapons. He regarded the whole concept of deterrence—of preventing a nuclear attack through the threat of retaliation—as immoral. He was sincere about the rhetoric of his Star Wars speech—not just its key passages, but the idea of delivering it and the idea of making the development of a missile shield a top priority. These were Reagan's ideas and, in the corridors of power, very nearly Reagan's alone.

The Republican Party platform at the 1980 Convention had proclaimed, "We reject the mutual-assured-destruction (MAD) strategy of the Carter administration" and called for "vigorous research-and-development" into "modern ABM technologies." But even most Republicans dismissed this as standard boilerplate. In the first two years of Reagan's presidency, amid the huge surge in spending on nuclear armaments, nobody in the Pentagon or the White House was taking a serious look at missile defense. At one point, Weinberger asked his R&D chief, Richard DeLauer, and the Joint Chiefs of Staff if a missile-defense system was worth pursuing. They replied that it wasn't.

Reagan's science adviser, George "Jay" Keyworth, knowing of Reagan's interest in the subject, appointed a panel to examine the feasibility of new ABM technologies. Keyworth was an acolyte of Edward Teller, who thirty years earlier had designed the hydrogen bomb and was now a leading Star Wars supporter. The panel was chaired by Edward Frieman, a physicist and the vice president of Science Applications, Inc., which had done studies in support of an ABM system in the late 1960s and early '70s. Even so, after a year-long review, the panel concluded that none of the technologies were ready for serious funding, much less for deployment.

Yet Reagan was keen on the idea and had been well before his speech. During the 1980 presidential campaign, while talking to a reporter about the Soviet threat, he said he would like to turn scientists loose on a project to build a "line of defense" that might "defend our population" from a Soviet nuclear attack.

On December 22, 1982, at a meeting with Weinberger, the Joint Chiefs, and his top White House staffers, Reagan asked, out of the blue, "What if we began to move away from our total reliance on offense to deter a nuclear attack, and moved toward a relatively greater reliance on defense?" He noted that every weapon ever invented was followed by a defense against it—the sword, then the shield. Can't our technology produce some shield that could blunt the sword of nuclear weapons? Reagan wanted the Chiefs to report back to him on the possibilities by February.

After the meeting, one of the Chiefs called William Clark, Reagan's national security adviser, and asked, "Is he serious?" Clark said that he was.

The group met again on February 11. The Chiefs, who never like to tell a president no, said the notion wasn't impossible. That was good enough for Reagan, who told them to get started. That night, he wrote in his diary what amounted to a first draft of the line that would dominate his speech six weeks later: "What if we were to tell the world that we wanted to protect our people, not . . . avenge them; that we are going to embark on a program of research to come up with a defensive weapon that could make nuclear weapons obsolete?"

Nobody outside Reagan's inner circle knew about this part of his speech until a few days before he gave it. When Keyworth was told about it, he was stunned. Just a couple of months earlier, he had briefed Reagan on the discouraging results of the Frieman panel. Keyworth's national-security assistant, Victor Reis, was apoplectic about the speech and, soon after, resigned over the issue. Weinberger, the Chiefs, and Secretary of State George Shultz were appalled as well, thinking that the president was at the very least premature.

Reagan was immovable. He not only gave the speech but told Weinberger to pour as much money into the program as he could manage. The program was called the Strategic Defense Initiative, and Weinberger not only created an independent SDI Office but gave it $3 billion for advanced research and development, a massive boost from what had been, since the signing of the ABM Treaty, a low-level R&D project with a budget one-tenth that size.

The SDI Office issued lavish contracts for every ABM scheme that had ever been on a drawing board. One such scheme involved firing directed-energy beams at mirrors, which would be orbiting in outer space and which would direct the beams to hit Soviet missiles in midtrajectory. Another envisioned hitting the missiles with beams or projectiles fired from satellites in space. Still others involved multilayered systems—based on the ground, in space, and at sea—shooting at Soviet missiles at various stages of their flight.

Reagan may have been alone, at least among high-level officials, in believing the dream might come true. The Frieman panel's findings marked only the first expression of scientific doubt. Most of the old ABM flaws were discovered anew, along with some new ones. The multilayered version of SDI relied on highly complex computer networks that would link the sensors detecting a missile attack to the weapons assigned to shoot the missiles down. A panel of computer scientists, all of whom favored SDI in principle, met for a seventeen-day conference in the summer of 1985 and emerged pessimistic. The system's software, they calculated, would have to contain ten million lines of error-free code, a requirement that struck them as infeasible, to say the least. When commercial software was put out on the market, errors were routinely discovered; engineers worked for weeks, even months, before the software was fully debugged. Yet there would be only one nuclear attack, at most; the SDI's software would have to work on the first try. Maybe it would, but to make it work, the engineers, at a minimum, would have to develop the software first and the hardware later, whereas the SDI managers were going about it the other way around. Finally, if the enemy set off a nuclear bomb as far as a thousand kilometers away from a piece of Star Wars hardware, the explosion would release a high-energy neutron flux, which would erase the semiconductors' memory. In other words, an enemy could easily shut the system down as the first stage of an attack.

And yet, once Reagan announced the program and told his Cabinet officers that he would tolerate no dissent, a lot of people found a lot of reasons to support it with enthusiasm. Defense contractors made serious money on projects that had lain dormant for years. The armed services started pushing systems that had the slightest connection to missile defense, knowing that anything labeled "SDI" was sure to win full funding and then some.

• • •

On a strategic level, some officials saw SDI—as Nixon had ultimately seen Safeguard—as a potential "bargaining chip" at arms negotiations, something that the United States could offer to give up in exchange for sharp reductions in the Soviet Union's offensive nuclear arsenal. Of course, SDI would have value in this regard only if the Russians believed it might work—and it seems they did.

A study sponsored by the U.S. Arms Control and Disarmament Agency revealed that 70 percent of Soviet worldwide propaganda messages were aimed at discrediting SDI. That was the first tip-off that the Russians viewed the program as a threat. Around this time, Andy Marshall and Charles Wolf were writing their report about the dire straits of the Soviet economy and urging the Pentagon to invest more money in weapons programs that would force the Russians to spend much more money in response—maybe, ultimately, more money than they could afford. A space-based ABM—whether or not it amounted to anything real—might be one of the programs that sharpened Moscow's pain.

Years later, after the Soviet Union imploded, secret Kremlin documents, declassified by Russia's new government, revealed that Marshall and Wolf were right. But the documents also revealed that Reagan was lucky. By the time various pressures began to be felt inside the Politburo, the Soviet Union's first true reformer, Mikhail Gorbachev, had risen to power.

At a Politburo meeting in March 1986, Gorbachev told his colleagues, "Maybe we should stop being afraid of the SDI!"—a clear confirmation that they *were* afraid. "Of course, we cannot be indifferent to this dangerous program. But they," he went on, referring to Reagan and his aides, "are betting precisely on the fact that the U.S.S.R. is afraid of SDI. . . . That is why they are putting pressure on us—to exhaust us."

Gorbachev asked his science adviser, Yevgeny Velikhov, if these fears were justified. Velikhov replied in much the same way as science advisers to American presidents had replied when asked about the effectiveness of ABMs: the project was fanciful, and Soviet engineers could easily develop countermeasures to saturate the defenses. However, perhaps succumbing to pressure from his own military-industrial complex, Velikhov advised that it might be a good idea to build more missiles, just in case.

In October, Gorbachev prepared for his first summit with Reagan, to be held in Reykjavik, Iceland. He planned to offer Reagan a groundbreaking disarmament plan, including a 50 percent reduction in both sides' offensive nuclear warheads. Speaking at a Politburo session on the eve of his departure, Gorbachev warned that if he didn't propose these cuts, "we will be pulled into an arms race that is beyond our capabilities. . . . The pressures on our economy will be unbelievable."

As the summit began, Reagan went far beyond Gorbachev's proposal. To the alarm of his aides, who were not let in on the decision, Reagan suggested that the two sides get rid of nuclear weapons altogether and jointly build an SDI system to guard against a nuclear revival or a threat from third parties. Gorbachev dismissed the notion. "I do not take your idea of sharing SDI seriously," the minutes reveal him telling Reagan. "You don't want to share even petroleum equipment, automatic machine tools, or equipment for dairies, while sharing SDI would be a second American revolution—and revolutions do not occur all that often."

Reagan replied, "If I thought that SDI could not be shared, I would have rejected it myself."

Gorbachev said he would accept the proposal for total disarmament if Reagan pledged not to test nuclear weapons in space—a crucial element of SDI. Reagan would not accept that condition.

The Reykjavik summit fizzled. But Gorbachev returned to Moscow persuaded that Reagan—who had earlier struck him as a "caveman"—honestly had no intention of launching a first strike against the Soviet Union, and he made this point to the Politburo. He could proceed with perestroika, which involved not only economic reforms but—as a necessary precondition—massive defense cuts and a serious outreach to the West. He needed assurances of security in order to move forward with his domestic upheaval, and Reagan had given him those reassurances.

During his last couple of years as president, Reagan proposed extravagant arms reductions. His hawkish aides went along with them, thinking that the Soviets would reject them and that the United States would thereby win a propaganda victory. Then, to the surprise of everyone, except perhaps Reagan, who advanced the proposals sincerely, Gorbachev accepted them. This sequence happened a few times, resulting, most prominently, in the elimination of all intermediate-range missiles in Europe.

In the end, Reagan and Gorbachev needed each other. Gorbachev needed to move swiftly if his reforms were to take hold. Reagan exerted the pressure that forced him to move swiftly and offered the rewards that made skeptics in the Politburo agree that the cutbacks were worth the trade. A more traditional American president might have been too cautious, too conventional, to push such radical proposals. At the same time, Reagan was incredibly lucky to have a radical like Gorbachev on the receiving end. If either of Gorbachev's two stuffy predecessors had lived longer—if Yuri Andropov's kidneys hadn't given out, or if Andropov's successor, Konstantin Chernenko, hadn't died after a mere thirteen months in office—Reagan's bluster and passion might have come to naught and only aggravated tensions; the Cold War might have raged on for years and ended less peacefully.

Fifteen years later, when George W. Bush invoked the reforms in Russia as a model of possible reforms in the Middle East, he didn't take into account the historical novelty—the near-uniqueness—in the confluence of Reagan and Gorbachev.

• • •

Reagan didn't cancel SDI—he never had to cash it in as a bargaining chip—but after his vice president, George H. W. Bush, succeeded him in January 1989, the program faded away. That autumn, the Berlin Wall fell. Two years later, the Soviet Union imploded. The Cold War was over, and the threat evaporated. Bush's national security adviser, retired general Brent Scowcroft, had never been a fan of SDI. While Reagan was still president, Scowcroft had led a panel at the Aspen Institute that opposed rapid deployment of missile defenses. Under pressure to produce a "peace dividend," Bush ordered major cuts in the military budget. The Joint Chiefs of Staff moved to protect their top priorities. Missile defense was not among them. SDI was slashed.

When Clinton became president in 1993, he cut the program still further. His first defense secretary, Les Aspin, shut down the SDI Office and replaced it with the Ballistic Missile Defense Office, which would report not to him directly but to an assistant secretary of defense. Aspin kept the program's budget fairly high, at $3.8 billion a year, but nearly all of it went to develop defenses against short-range missiles in the European theater, an activity that the ABM Treaty permitted.

• • •

Then came the 1994 midterm elections, the Republicans' take-back of the House of Representatives, and the triumph of Newt Gingrich and his "Contract with America," including the demand for deployment of a national missile defense system "at the earliest practical date."

But a defense against what? Russia was no longer a credible threat. So several strategic analysts focused—in some cases opportunistically, in other cases with genuine concern—on the potential threat from "rogue states," especially North Korea, Iran, and Iraq (which George W. Bush would later conjoin as an "axis of evil"). All three states were thought to harbor nuclear ambitions; North Korea was believed to have enough plutonium for a couple of A-bombs already, and it had tested a short-range missile. The rationale was shifting once more.

At the House Republicans' prompting, the Pentagon's Ballistic Missile Defense Office asked the CIA to produce a special National Intelligence Estimate, or NIE, on emerging missile threats, particularly from those three countries. The resulting report, released in 1995, concluded that no hostile nation would be able to pose a missile threat to the continental United States for at least fifteen years.

House and Senate Republicans were outraged. They accused the CIA analysts of "politicizing intelligence," of downplaying the threat in order to justify Clinton's inaction on missile defenses. Arlen Specter, chairman of the Senate Intelligence Committee,

ordered CIA director John Deutsch to review the estimate and
to report back.

Deutsch appointed a panel, chaired by Robert Gates, a former
CIA director in the Bush administration, to investigate. (A decade
later, Bush's son would call on Gates to take charge of the Pentagon
after forcing Donald Rumsfeld to resign.) Gates's report, finished
in December 1996, not only found "no evidence of politicization,"
but denounced the Republicans' allegation as "irresponsible."
Gates did criticize the CIA's analysts for excessive optimism on certain points, but he chided them much more for failing to present all
the evidence that supported their conclusion. "There was much
that could have been added to the main text of the Estimate that
would have strengthened the analysts' case," Gates's report stated.

In his report's final sentence, Gates wrote that on balance, the
case for the CIA's conclusion—that the United States was unlikely
to face an ICBM threat from a third-world country before the year
2010—was "even stronger than presented in the NIE." (The NIE
held up well; as of late 2007, none of those three countries was
close to building a nuclear-tipped missile that had the range to
strike the United States.)

And so, the Republicans did what legislators in their predica-
ment normally do—they convened another panel. And this time,
they put their own people in charge.

The Commission to Assess the Ballistic Missile Threat to the
United States, as the panel was called, would have a chairman and
eight other members, half named by Republicans (specifically by
Gingrich), half by Democrats (mainly by Carl Levin, who was
chairman of the Senate Armed Services Committee and a missile-
defense skeptic).

The commission's chairman was Donald Rumsfeld.

● ● ●

Gingrich had known Rumsfeld since 1965, when he was a senior at
Emory College and Rumsfeld, then a congressman from Illinois,
was making a series of speeches at college campuses on behalf of

Republican causes. They talked several times over the years. When Rumsfeld managed Bob Dole's campaign for president in 1996, Gingrich was one of his military advisers. (Paul Wolfowitz was another.)

Rumsfeld had lots of free time on his hands when Gingrich asked him to chair the ballistic missile commission. He had recently retired from a highly lucrative corporate career, was keen to get back into politics, and saw chairing some commissions as a way to raise his profile and get reeducated in the process. Gingrich knew that Rumsfeld favored a revival of the ABM and so viewed him as an ideal chairman of this panel.

Among the Democrats' picks was Richard Garwin, the physicist who coauthored the *Scientific American* critique of ABMs back in 1968 and who, over the decades, served on many defense-policy commissions for the White House, the Pentagon, and other government agencies.

Garwin was suspicious. He realized that the panel would be used—was, in fact, created—as a political tool, to help revive a large-scale ABM program. He looked up some articles by Stephen Cambone, the former Los Alamos researcher who had been picked as the panel's staff director, and saw that he was an ardent missile-defense advocate who favored scrapping the ABM Treaty and deploying a system as quickly as possible. Still, Garwin agreed to join. At best, he might exert some influence. In any event, membership on the panel would give him credibility if he decided, afterward, to criticize its report or any missile-defense system that might be built as a result.

The commission's first session took place on January 14, 1998, and Garwin found himself liking Rumsfeld's style. During the first week, Rumsfeld sensed—correctly—that the CIA wasn't giving him all the information he had requested. He called George Tenet, the CIA's director, to come to the panel's hearing room, and gave him hell. The commission's charter stated that it would have "full and timely" access to all the information it needed. Rumsfeld had once been a congressman and so still had a pass to the House floor. He threatened to use it and go tell Speaker Gingrich in person that

Tenet was breaking the law. Tenet gulped. Soon after, Rumsfeld and the commission moved from a room in the Old Executive Office Building to an office at CIA headquarters, in Langley, Virginia, so they could get quick access to whatever they needed.

The commissioners met forty-eight times over the next six months and called twenty-seven witnesses. Rumsfeld attended every session. He took care not to squelch anyone's view. When the report was drafted, passages were written and rewritten until everyone was satisfied. Rumsfeld insisted on consensus, knowing that a unanimous report would have the greatest impact.

To get unanimity, he insisted on two conditions from the outset. First, the report would not mention the words "missile defense." It would analyze the threat, but make no proposals for what to do about it. Second, the report would not be an alternative NIE; it would not pretend to judge whether foreign governments *would* build ICBMs but only whether they *could*.

Garwin and the other Democrats agreed to those conditions; in fact, they insisted on the first one. But they also realized that the conditions were a clever gambit. Focusing on a foreign power's potential capability, with no reference to its calculations or intentions, would unavoidably exaggerate the appearance of a threat. And whether or not the report discussed policy, the House Republicans would certainly use it to push for missile defenses; the fact that the report was unanimous would only make it a more potent tool.

During the sessions and the briefings, all the commissioners— Democrats included—were shocked by the disarray of the U.S. intelligence community. Analysts from one branch of the CIA would give them information that was contradicted by analysts from another branch. When the commissioners asked for clarification, it soon became clear that the two branches were not sharing information; in some cases, their analysts didn't have the same security clearances. Garwin was particularly dismayed by how sharply the agencies' technical expertise had deteriorated. During the Cold War, the CIA had lots of analysts who knew the technical minutiae of missiles and warheads. Now it seemed that there were almost none. The Soviet missile threat had vanished, and so had the missile experts.

On July 15, 1998, the Rumsfeld commission gave Congress a 307-page classified report and a shorter, unclassified executive summary. Gingrich scheduled a closed session of both houses, at which each commissioner gave a speech outlining the findings.

The report concluded that North Korea, Iran, and Iraq could acquire ballistic missiles armed with nuclear or biological weapons "within about five years of a decision" to do so, except for Iraq, which, because of the United Nations sanctions, would take ten years. (In retrospect, this was a jarring caveat, given Rumsfeld's subsequent role in invading Iraq on the grounds that Saddam Hussein had, or would soon have, weapons of mass destruction.)

In its 1995 National Intelligence Estimate, the CIA had assumed that a third-world regime would build missiles in much the same way the United States and Soviet Union had—through a vast industrial project, followed by several flight tests before deployment. But the Rumsfeld report speculated that such a country might acquire the technology, or the weapons themselves, surreptitiously from a foreign power. Intelligence indicated that North Korea and Iran were receiving foreign assistance already. Finally, if a country wanted nuclear or biological missiles not in order to launch an attack but merely to deter or blackmail the United States, their missiles wouldn't have to be very reliable or accurate; therefore, they would not have to conduct many tests. In other words, hostile regimes could develop an arsenal without much U.S. detection; they could take America by surprise.

At first, the report had little impact outside Congress. Then, on August 30, 1998, six weeks after its release, the North Koreans launched a Taepo Dong missile. They claimed that its purpose was to put a satellite into space, and it flew for only a thousand miles, far short of the range necessary to hit U.S. territory. The third stage had fizzled out; that was why it didn't go very far. Even if it had worked, there was no evidence that the North Koreans could fit a nuclear warhead in its nose cone. Still, it *was* a three-stage rocket, which meant they did know how to build a missile of potentially intercontinental range—an ICBM. And they had cobbled the three stages together from bits and pieces of existing rockets, just as the

Rumsfeld report had said they might do. They had not built a whole new missile from scratch, which is what the CIA's estimate assumed they would have to do.

Soon after the test, Rumsfeld gave a speech at the National Defense University in Washington. "God bless you, Kim Jong!" he said with glee.

• • •

The commission's work had enormous impact, not merely on decisions about missile defense but also on the broader course of history. After the 2000 presidential election, Rumsfeld's enhanced cachet in Republican circles, as well as his renewed expertise on a subject of enormous interest to the Republican president-elect, convinced George W. Bush to choose him as secretary of defense. Two key members of Rumsfeld's subsequent inner circle came from the commission. Stephen Cambone, the staff director, followed him into the Pentagon, first as his special assistant, then as his undersecretary of defense for intelligence. Paul Wolfowitz, one of the Republican-appointed commissioners, became his deputy secretary. Both would be deeply involved in the preparations and planning for the war in Iraq.

During the run-up to that war, Rumsfeld, Wolfowitz, and Cambone all applied lessons that they had learned from their time on the commission. When the CIA assured them that Saddam Hussein had no weapons of mass destruction or ties to Osama bin Laden, their instinctive reaction was doubt. The CIA had been wrong about North Korea; it was probably just as wrong about Iraq. The lack of clear, open evidence didn't mean anything; there hadn't been clear, open evidence of a North Korean missile either.

Rumsfeld created his own intelligence unit, in the upper echelons of the Pentagon, to sift through raw data, with the explicit aim of piecing together fragments of evidence to prove their case—just as on the ballistic-missile commission, they had focused their research on what North Korea, Iran, and Iraq might be able to do if they wanted, not on what they were actually doing. The main goal of the unit was to amass all the data that seemed to prove what they wanted to prove—and to ignore any data that didn't.

• • •

The commission had immense short-term impact as well. In 1999, after North Korea's rocket launch, the CIA released a revised NIE, adopting the Rumsfeld commission's standard—that capabilities were key, not intentions—and concluding that North Korea, Iran, and Iraq could threaten the United States with ballistic missiles before 2010 after all, a stark reversal of their earlier estimate.

On October 2 of that year, in an American missile-defense test over Kwajalein Island in the Pacific, a kinetic kill-vehicle—the new program's antimissile weapon, designed to destroy an incoming warhead not by blowing it up but by colliding with it at fifteen times the speed of sound—smashed into a mock warhead that had been launched from Vandenberg Air Force Base, California. A bullet hit a bullet.

Back in 1997, to stave off congressional pressure to put a missile-defense system into production right away, Clinton had offered two compromises. He doubled the program's R&D budget. And he devised a "three-plus-three" schedule. Three years would be spent designing and testing a system; if it proved feasible, the next three years would be spent putting it into the field.

Now it was 2000, the end of the three-year period of design and testing, as well as his final year as president. It was time to make the decision.

• • •

Meanwhile, Philip Coyle, the director of the Pentagon's Office of Operational Testing and Evaluation, was causing a stir. The OT&E office had been created back in 1983, by congressional mandate, after whistle-blowers revealed widespread rigging of weapons tests. The law required all major weapons to pass operational tests before they were deployed, and it required the OT&E director to supervise and sign off on the test reports.

In August 2000, as part of the Defense Department's "National Missile Defense Deployment Readiness Review," Coyle wrote a sixty-three page report, concluding that the system wasn't remotely ready. Not a single element of the system, he wrote, was yet "mature enough" to allow even "an adequate performance evaluation." The majority of tests had failed. Those that had succeeded did so because they followed "canned scenarios." Even the bullet-hits-a-bullet triumph the previous October was unrealistic. A beacon had been attached to the mock warhead—a sort of radar beeper—so that the kill-vehicle's guidance system could more easily find its target. No tests had yet been planned, much less conducted, that would involve distinguishing a warhead from decoys or shooting down more than one warhead at a time.

The program's managers knew that decoys were a serious challenge. (Every U.S. intelligence agency concluded that any country with the technology and know-how to build an ICBM would also know how to load it with decoys.) In 1997, the missile-defense office had planned to conduct a test involving a warhead and nine decoys. In '98, the plan was cut back to three decoys and in '99, to just one decoy, and Coyle wrote that this decoy did "not mimic in any way" the warhead. The antimissile radar would easily be able to distinguish the real warhead from the fake. In other words, the test did not legitimately simulate a real attack.

In his report's conclusion, Coyle listed fifty-two steps that needed to be taken before a rational decision on production could be made, and he expressed doubts that a system would be ready for many years, if at all.

Coyle was no green-eyeshade auditor. He was a physicist who had worked for three decades at the Lawrence Livermore weapons lab on directed-energy beams and other high-tech projects. Before coming to the Pentagon, he had been the lab's deputy director.

The Pentagon refused to release Coyle's report to Congress, but the White House got a copy. On September 6, Clinton announced that the system was not ready for operation. The final decision, he said, would be left to his successor.

• • •

When George W. Bush became president, this picture changed dramatically. On May 1, 2001, he gave a speech at the National Defense University, affirming his campaign pledge to build missile defenses. He announced that he had ordered Secretary Rumsfeld to explore the technological options, adding, "We must move beyond the constraints of the thirty-year-old ABM Treaty."

In June, Rumsfeld submitted his budget for the next fiscal year. It included a request of $8.3 billion for missile defense—a 57 percent increase over the previous year's funding. On September 7, members of the Senate Armed Services Committee considered an amendment to transfer $600 million of that sum to antiterrorism accounts. Rumsfeld said if they approved it, the president would veto the bill.

On September 11, Condoleezza Rice, Bush's national security adviser, was scheduled to give a speech on, as she put it, "the threats and problems of today and the day after, not the world of yesterday." The main topic was to be missile defense; her prepared text, which was later leaked to the press, said nothing about terrorism. She never delivered the speech because that morning, terrorists flew two passenger jetliners into the World Trade Center and another one into the Pentagon.

The attack suggested that ballistic missiles might not be the most likely threat facing America; that even if missile defenses could be made to work, a foe could simply strike with other, far cheaper and easier weapons. But it only galvanized Bush and Rumsfeld to push full speed ahead.

Up until 9/11, Bush had gone along with Secretary of State Colin Powell, who, though realizing the ABM Treaty's days were numbered, argued that the European allies should be consulted and that relations with Russia should be put on solid footing before the administration took such a drastic step. Cheney and Rumsfeld wanted to pull out of the treaty at the start of the term, to punctuate their declaration that a new era had arrived. But they didn't mind letting Powell win this round. There wasn't anything the Pentagon could do to violate the treaty—there were no antimissile missiles ready to test or deploy—for a year or so anyway.

By the end of 2001, violations were ready to proceed. The 9/11 attacks strengthened the Cheney-Rumsfeld position. Meanwhile, from Powell's viewpoint, several months of diplomacy with the Russians—including a friendly face-to-face meeting in June between Bush and Russian president Vladimir Putin—had created the framework for a new round of reductions in offensive nuclear missiles. A program that revived limited missile defenses no longer set off the Kremlin's alarms—at this point, anyway.

On December 13, Bush gave formal notice to Russia that the United States was withdrawing from the ABM Treaty (which, like most international accords, contained a clause permitting withdrawal six months after such notice).

Three weeks later, Rumsfeld laid out the scheme for a system—a multilayered network of satellites, sensors, and antimissile missiles, on the ground, at sea, in the air, and in space—that would try to intercept an attack in three phases: just after the enemy launched the missile up through the atmosphere ("boost-phase intercept"); as the top stage of the missile arced through outer space ("midcourse intercept"); and as the warhead plunged toward its target back on Earth ("terminal-phase intercept").

And this time, Bush and Rumsfeld poured in money not only to research and develop such a system but to build it and make it operational.

It was basically the same system that had been on the drawing boards for several years except, if anything, more complicated—the same system that Philip Coyle and others had criticized as impractical. Coyle was gone now. He had left the Pentagon when power changed hands from Clinton to Bush, and Rumsfeld was determined that whoever succeeded him would not wage the same rearguard battle.

Rumsfeld decided to exempt missile defense from the law that required major weapons to pass performance tests before being deployed in the field. He also classified details about tests at a higher level, accessible only to those with a compartmentalized security clearance. The director of the Office on Operational Testing and Evaluation would not have that clearance.

● ● ●

Coyle's replacement was a veteran missile engineer and weapons analyst named Thomas Christie. Through the 1980s and '90s, Christie had been a member of an informal group of maverick officers and civilian analysts known as "the military reform movement." (Colonel John Boyd, the retired Air Force fighter pilot who pioneered the theory of "maneuver warfare," was one of the movement's leading lights.) The reformers made a crusade of going after weapons that didn't work. Some of these officials had played a key role in drafting the law that required weapons to undergo testing and that created the independent office to evaluate those tests.

Christie wasn't quite as rebellious as many of his colleagues, some of whom thought that he had sold out when he agreed to go work in Rumsfeld's Pentagon. He was deeply committed to the principle of testing before buying; he thought it would be disastrous to spend billions of dollars deploying missile defenses without solid testing. But he knew that Rumsfeld was committed to the program, and he feared that raising a fuss might endanger his entire office.

He and one of his technical assistants, Larry Miller, figured out a way to get around Rumsfeld's attempt to shut them out. The Senate Armed Services Committee was scheduled to hold a hearing about missile defense on March 13, 2002. A committee staff member, Mitch Crosswaite, once worked with Miller in the Pentagon and shared his skepticism of a missile-defense system's feasibility. At Miller's prompting, Crosswaite put Christie on the witness list and planted a question with Senator Jack Reed, the top Democrat on the panel's subcommittee dealing with strategic issues. Reed, also a skeptic, happily went along.

After the administration witnesses described Rumsfeld's plan for a missile-defense system, Reed played his part, asking Christie if he had seen the plan. Christie said he had not. Reed was shocked, shocked, and easily persuaded the committee to insert language into the defense bill requiring Christie's office to write an annual report assessing the Pentagon's missile-defense tests and to submit the report to Congress.

In February 2003, Christie submitted his first report, and it was even more critical than Coyle's. In addition to the usual qualms and caveats that scientists had been expressing about ABMs for nearly a half century, Christie noted that the current system lacked an effective rocket booster; that there was no radar of sufficient bandwidth to track enemy missiles in space; and that the tests had a low success rate, even though no realistic decoys were involved and the mock warheads flew more slowly than real warheads would in an attack. In sum, he wrote in what he would later say was deliberate understatement, the system had "yet to demonstrate significant operational capability."

Just two months earlier, President Bush had announced that the first elements of an operational missile-defense system would be deployed by the fall of 2004. The program's managers had assured him so. These initial elements would include 10 antimissile interceptors buried in silos at Fort Greeley, Alaska; another 10 at Vandenberg Air Force Base, California; 20 interceptors on 9 Aegis cruisers; 192 upgraded Patriot air-defense missiles, deployed with U.S. troops abroad, to shoot down short-range ballistic missiles; and the radars to go with them.

Bush announced the timetable on December 17, 2002, boasting, "The United States has moved beyond the doctrine of Cold War deterrence reflected in the 1972 ABM Treaty."

Yet here was the Pentagon's chief tester, telling Congress that the United States had done no such thing.

• • •

To some of Rumsfeld's policy aides, it didn't matter whether a missile-defense system worked or not. The important thing was to get *something* out in the field to deter the North Koreans, who would have to worry that it *might* work.

The day before Bush's speech, the White House released National Security Presidential Directive NSPD-23, titled "National Policy on Ballistic Missile Defense." Its rationale for missile defenses wasn't so much that North Korea and other hostile regimes might actually launch an attack on the United States; it was that they might brandish their missiles to "blackmail us from coming to the assistance of our friends who would then become victims of their aggression." A commonly cited analogy was that if Saddam Hussein had had nuclear weapons before he invaded Kuwait in 1990, the United States might not have been able to rally the international coalition that pushed his troops back behind Iraq's borders; too many coalition governments, perhaps even the U.S. government, might have worried that Saddam would strike back at them. "To deter such threats," NSPD-23 stated, "we must devalue missiles as tools of extortion and aggression, undermining the confidence of our adversaries that threatening a missile attack would succeed in blackmailing us." A missile-defense system would be one way to force this devaluation. Missile defenses would also help "dissuade countries from pursuing ballistic missiles in the first instance, by undermining their military utility."

Christie's deputies occasionally argued about this logic with some of the deputies to Rumsfeld's policy aides. They didn't see how an ineffective missile-defense system would affect North Korea's, or anyone else's, behavior. "If I'm holding a gun on you," they would say, "and you know it's empty, is that a deterrent?" Or if the North Koreans did suspect the system worked, maybe they wouldn't give up; maybe they would build more nuclear weapons more rapidly. And maybe, if they attacked us, they would fire more missiles than they otherwise would, thinking we wouldn't be able to shoot them all down—in which case, if the defenses didn't work at all, an attack would wreak still more damage. Or maybe they would just go around the defenses, attacking us with cruise missiles, which fly through the atmosphere, underneath the radar of a ballistic-missile-defense system. Or they might fire ballistic missiles from boats just off American shores, which a missile-defense network wouldn't detect quickly enough. Or they could attack with suitcase bombs or hijacked planes.

The scheduled deployment date drew near, but little had improved. The Missile Defense Agency was canceling more tests than it was conducting, in part, its chief officers admitted, because the components weren't ready to be tested.

•   •   •

Rumsfeld thought a big shake-up was in order. In July 2004, he appointed General James Cartwright, the Joint Chiefs of Staff's director of acquisitions, to go out to Omaha and take charge of the U.S. Strategic Command, which had operational control over long-range nuclear weapons and space systems, including missile defenses.

The startling thing about this move was that Cartwright was an officer in the Marine Corps, the one branch of the U.S. armed forces that never had any involvement with nuclear weapons. It was a classic Rumsfeld move: throw the generals off balance. This time, the move backfired in a different way.

While directing weapons acquisition on the Joint Staff, Cartwright had struck up a good working relationship with Tom Christie. When he was appointed to run Strategic Command, Cartwright asked Christie to bring him up to speed on missile defense. He came to Christie's office and spent two hours asking questions. He spent another entire morning going over technical details with Larry Miller.

Cartwright was a straight shooter. His nickname was "Hoss," after the Hoss Cartwright character on the old TV Western *Bonanza*. At the end of the summer, just weeks before the date when the missile-defense system was supposed to achieve "initial operational capability," Cartwright briefed Rumsfeld on the program. The briefing relied heavily on the latest version of Christie's report to Congress. He told Rumsfeld bluntly that nothing was ready, that a lot more testing was necessary, and that at the moment he had no confidence in the program.

This wasn't one of "Clinton's generals" talking. This was Rumsfeld's own man. Rumsfeld passed the word on to Bush.

That fall, the presidential election dominated everything. Bush ran his reelection campaign mainly on the theme of national security. He had planned to tout the missile-defense program as one of his great accomplishments. This was why he had wanted at least part of a working system in place by the fall. In July, the first anti-missile interceptor was lowered into its silo at Fort Greeley, Alaska. But except for the one speech, at the Boeing plant in Ridley, Pennsylvania, Bush said nothing about missile defense. Nor did he say much about it after he was reelected to a second term. Rumsfeld no longer exuded much enthusiasm either.

Spending on missile defense continued soaring, to $10 billion a year and beyond, an amount much larger than the budget for any other single weapons program. It remained a great boon for contractors. And Bush still believed in the idea. To cut back would be to admit that the idea was wrong, that the money spent so far—over $100 billion since Ronald Reagan sparked its revival nearly twenty years earlier—had been a waste. Maybe it would work one day. Some enemies might think it works now. Meanwhile, there was still the hope that America's enemies might be vanquished, that the axis of evil would collapse, and that freedom would supplant tyranny across the planet.

As Bush began his second term, he adopted this hope as an article of faith and as the centerpiece of his foreign policy.

4

Breaking the World Anew

On January 20, 2005, in his second inaugural address, George W. Bush declared that the new central aim of American foreign policy would be to abolish tyranny and to spread freedom around the world. Global freedom had long been the nation's ideal. Now Bush was saying it was also "the urgent requirement of our nation's security and the calling of our time."

Speaking directly to victims of tyranny everywhere, Bush pledged that America "will not ignore your oppression or excuse your oppressors," that "when you stand for liberty, we will stand with you." And tyrants, he said, should know that good relations with America "will require the decent treatment of their own people."

The attacks of September 11—which were planned and executed almost entirely by Saudis, the subjects of a tyrannical but supposedly stable regime—had altered the equations of national security. Tyranny, it now seemed, breeds resentment and hatred, which in turn breeds terrorist violence, which threatens our survival. The end of tyranny will bring on the end of this resentment and hatred. Therefore, spreading freedom will make us more secure. Or, as Bush put it, "America's vital interests and our deepest beliefs are now one."

It was an appealing syllogism. Since the end of World War II, statesmen had been grappling with the tensions and trade-offs between American interests and ideals. To proclaim these dilemmas resolved not only amounted to bold rhetoric; it implied license for untethered American action. Anything done in the national interest could be said to serve the values of the greater good; American might and moral right were synonymous.

When Bush uttered these words, it seemed for a moment that there might be something to them. Just a few weeks earlier, Iraq had held the first free election in its history, and the televised broadcasts of smiling Iraqi people holding up their thumbs—purple with the ink stains that signified they'd cast a ballot—were irresistibly inspiring.

Shortly before then, in the former Soviet republic of Ukraine, hundreds of thousands of people gathered in Kiev's public square to protest a presidential election that had clearly been rigged in favor of the Moscow-backed candidate. In what came to be called the "Orange Revolution," in honor of the color of Ukraine's national flag, the rallies forced the vote to be annulled; a new election was held; and the rightful winner, the independent Viktor Yuschenko, this time took office.

A few weeks after Bush's address, massive rallies in Beirut, held under the banner of a "Cedar Revolution," forced the Syrian military to end its thirty-year occupation of Lebanon, and at least some of the protesters said that they were inspired by the examples of Iraq and Ukraine.

But in a matter of weeks, the celebrations turned sour.

● ● ●

After the attacks of 9/11, President Bush believed finally that his presidency had a mission. Before then, it wasn't so clear. Those around him thought that he sometimes acted as if he wasn't president. He seemed haunted by the circumstances of the 2000 election—his loss of the popular vote and the highly suspect nature of his victory in Florida. In his first eight months in office, Bush spent nearly half his time away from the White House, mainly on his ranch in Crawford, Texas. His more seasoned vice president, Dick

Cheney, seemed to be running things, especially when foreign leaders came to call. Bush's presidency seemed adrift.

The attacks changed all that. He was suddenly a wartime president, faced with an enemy that had not only attacked America but threatened Western civilization. His confidence stiffened after the 2002 midterm elections, which returned the Republicans to both houses of Congress and were widely seen as an affirmation of his legitimacy. His own reelection in November 2004, in which he won both the popular and electoral vote, solidified his standing. At his victory press conference, he exclaimed that he had earned "political capital" in the campaign and he intended to spend it, "now that I've got the will of the people at my back."

His mission, the reason he was put in the White House, was now clear: it was to fight terrorism and spread freedom, which, as he had said several times over the previous year, was "not America's gift to the world" but rather "God's gift to humanity."

The implications of this belief were enormous. It suggested that freedom was humanity's natural state. Democracy, in this view, was not a hothouse flower that needed careful tending; it was a lily of the field, requiring no toil to flourish.

Blow off the manhole cover imposed by a tyrant, and freedom would gush forth like a geyser.

Bush seemed to believe this; he said as much in private conversations as well as in public speeches. His most powerful advisers, Cheney and Rumsfeld, certainly did not believe it. Their thinking was more like that of hardheaded nineteenth-century nationalists; their aim was to maximize American power in the world. Yet spreading democracy and spreading American power were not inconsistent pursuits. The end points converged, even if the starting points were different. Cheney and Rumsfeld, old friends and collaborators, won so many bureaucratic battles—especially over issues like Iran, Iraq, and North Korea, where security and ideology were at stake—not only because they were seasoned infighters but also because their positions converged with Bush's instincts.

Not that Bush was by any stretch an international altruist. He saw himself, especially after 9/11, as a president of big ideas *and* bold action. His secretary of state, Colin Powell, a proudly pragmatic old-school Realist who frequently found himself outmaneuvered by the Cheney-Rumsfeld alliance, once told his chief of staff, Colonel Lawrence Wilkerson, that he could sometimes persuade the president of his views but that those who appealed to Bush's religious instincts *and* his "cowboy instincts"—which, Powell stressed, were not necessarily antithetical—would win him over every time. Cheney understood this especially well.

Bush's instincts on these matters were not formed by experience. Before he ran for president, he had had no schooling in international relations. In contrast with his father, a World War II veteran and seasoned diplomat, he had hardly ever traveled abroad. His thinking was shaped by his beliefs, and his beliefs were powerfully articulated and, at a crucial moment, profoundly shaped by his chief speechwriter, a self-described "socially conscious evangelist" named Michael Gerson.

• • •

Gerson was thirty-four—intense, earnest, and shy—when Bush hired him in 1999, as his presidential campaign kicked into gear. Gerson had graduated from Wheaton College in Illinois, the avowed Harvard of Christian colleges.

In 1985, just out of school, Gerson was hired as a speechwriter by Charles Colson, the Watergate felon turned evangelist. Colson had read an editorial that Gerson wrote for his college newspaper, praising Mother Teresa both for her opposition to abortion and for her charity to AIDS patients. A year into the job, Gerson moved on to work for Republican senator Dan Coats of Indiana, a fellow Wheaton alumnus who was interested in Gerson's ideas about poverty. Gerson once confided to Coats that he dreamed of being a speechwriter to a president. So, in the early 1990s, Coats gave him leave to write speeches for a few ill-starred Republican hopefuls— Jack Kemp, Steve Forbes, and Bob Dole—before passing his name to George W. Bush, for whom Coats himself hoped to be secretary of defense. Bush read some of Gerson's speeches, met with him at a Marriott hotel in Washington, D.C., and hired him on the spot.

Gerson took the Gospel seriously, as a guide to both personal living and political policy. A rare sort of Washington conservative, he believed that government had a moral duty to help the poor and cure the sick everywhere on Earth. Bush was famously a born-again Christian who credited God for saving him from a life of drugs and alcohol. As governor of Texas, he was also familiar with Colson's Prison Fellowship Ministries and its "faith-based" approach to cutting crime.

At their first meeting, the two talked mainly about race and poverty. This was consistent with Gerson's breakthrough moment, his drafting of Bush's acceptance speech at the Republican Convention, with its crossover message of "compassionate conservatism."

But in November 1999, two months after his speech on military policy at The Citadel, Bush was scheduled to speak at the Ronald Reagan Presidential Library in Simi Valley, California, and he asked Gerson to write him a suitable address on the broader issues of foreign policy and America's place in the post–Cold War world. Gerson knew little about foreign affairs. So he transposed his theology of social justice to fit the global arena. (Years later, he told a reporter that he viewed the ideas of the second inaugural address as compassionate conservatism writ large.)

The Reagan Library speech marked Bush's first expression of those grander ideas. "The most powerful force in the world," the speech stated, "is not a weapon or a nation but a truth: that we are spiritual beings and that freedom is the soul's right to breathe." It went on: "Some have tried to pose a choice between American ideals and American interests—between who we are and how we act. But the choice is false. America, by decision and destiny, promotes political freedom—and gains the most when democracy advances." American foreign policy, it concluded, "must have a great and guiding goal: to turn this time of American influence into generations of democratic peace."

The themes of the speech directly anticipated the second inaugural address of five years hence. But, among Bush's pre-9/11 pronouncements, it was a distinct anomaly.

In his one foreign policy debate with Vice President Al Gore, the Democratic candidate, Bush took a more mainstream Republican line, criticizing President Bill Clinton's—and, by extension, Gore's—frequent military interventions on behalf of humanitarian causes. Far from touting the power of freedom to change the world, Bush stressed that America should be strong but "humble" in its dealings with other nations.

During the 2000 campaign, Bush was advised by a mix of foreign-policy specialists. Some were "neoconservatives," mid-to-upper-level officials of the Reagan administration. These were policy intellectuals who had carried the spears in Reagan's moral-political crusade against Soviet Communism and who now yearned to wage the same sort of crusade against new threats in a demonstration of America's ascendant power.

Paul Wolfowitz, one of Bush's senior advisers, was the intellectual leader of this group. A former undersecretary of defense, he had gone into academic exile, as dean of the Johns Hopkins School for Advanced International Studies, when Bill Clinton entered the White House. But Wolfowitz kept politically active as a founding member of PNAC, the Project for a New American Century, an organization mainly of other Reagan exiles who advocated a remilitarized foreign policy that would promote democracy and topple "rogue regimes," especially Saddam Hussein's Iraq.

Yet Bush relied far more on another senior adviser, a less crafty, more studious professor from Stanford University, a black woman in her mid-forties named Condoleezza Rice.

• • •

Rice came highly recommended by Bush's father, who got to know her when she worked as a top aide to his national security adviser and longtime friend, Brent Scowcroft. It was Scowcroft who first took note of Rice at various arms-control seminars and who hired her when the first President Bush took office. Scowcroft was a protégé of Henry Kissinger, the ultimate theorist and practitioner of Realpolitik. Even more than Kissinger, Scowcroft scorned the idea that morality should play a big role in foreign policy. And Rice, at least at the time, was cast very much in the same mold.

A piano prodigy as a child, Rice switched studies and life plans while taking a class in international relations at the University of Denver from a charismatic professor and Czech émigré named Josef Korbel. Rice was Korbel's prize student in the mid-1970s and went on to graduate school at Denver, earning a Ph.D. under his tutelage. (Korbel was also the father of Madeleine Albright, who would go on to become President Clinton's secretary of state.)

Korbel was an international Realist in the tradition of Hans Morgenthau, George Kennan, and Reinhold Niebuhr. They all, from separate vantage points, witnessed the collapse of the world order between the twentieth century's two great wars. And they drew from it the lesson that nations could not rely on international law to keep the peace but must instead maintain a stable balance of power. Moral values may have a *place* in this scheme, but a nation's actions and policies must be determined principally by its vital *interests*.

In the 1960s, Korbel welcomed the rise of nonaligned and national-liberation movements in third-world nations that had only recently gained (or were still fighting for) independence from Europe's colonial rule. In one lecture from the era, he noted that the mounting demands for freedom played to America's strength because they created "a precious opportunity" to demonstrate "its superiority over the Communist policy" and might even, over time, "serve the policy of widening the cracks in the Iron Curtain."

However, Korbel emphasized, none of these developments altered the "few basic principles" of international relations, which were "as valid today as they were one hundred years ago." As long as we lived in a world of nation-states and ideological division, he emphasized, "we cannot afford, nor do we dare, to think of abandoning a diplomacy of balance of power." To do otherwise, he said, would be to indulge in "dreams."

In the fall of 1999, George W. Bush tapped Condi Rice, not Paul Wolfowitz, to write an article for a special "Campaign 2000" issue of *Foreign Affairs* magazine, outlining the Republican position on national-security policy. (It appeared in the January/February 2000 issue; three advisers to Al Gore wrote up the Democratic position for the following issue.) Rice's piece—which Bush read in advance and approved—was titled "Promoting the National Interest," and it could have come straight out of Korbel's, or Scowcroft's, lesson book.

"The crucial task for the United States," she wrote, "is to focus on relations with other powerful states," especially Russia and China. Many Americans are "uncomfortable with the notions of power politics, great powers, and power balances." But, she insisted, these are the central elements of national security.

As for the "rogue regimes" that obsessed her neocon colleagues, she thought they posed a problem with their "potential for terrorism and . . . weapons of mass destruction." Saddam Hussein was especially dangerous, so the United States should support the opposition groups that were trying to oust him. But, she added, regimes such as Iraq and North Korea "are living on borrowed time, so there need be no sense of panic about them. Rather, the first line of defense should be a clear and classical statement of deterrence—if they do acquire WMD, their weapons will be unusable because any attempt to use them would bring national obliteration."

The problem with Clinton's foreign policy, she continued, was its lack of focus on truly vital interests, its excessive kowtowing to multilateral organizations, and its scattershot "humanitarian interventions" in places of minimal strategic value, like Haiti and Somalia. "To be sure," she wrote, "there is nothing wrong with doing something to benefit all humanity, but that is, in a sense, a second-order effect."

She allowed that "American values are universal" and that "the triumph of these values is most assuredly easier when the international balance of power favors those who believe in them." However, she went on, sometimes this favorable balance of power takes a long time to achieve; and in the meantime, "it is simply not possible to ignore and isolate other powerful states that do not share these values."

Her essay was widely seen as a stunning rebuke to the neocons and a somewhat puzzling one as well. Even many Realists were beginning to wrestle with some of the new global problems that preoccupied some of the neocons—genocide, non-state-sponsored terrorism, the end of the Cold War and the security structure that went with it. But Rice wrote as if *nothing* had changed.

The article seemed to convey one clear impression: if Bush were president, he would be leery of adventurous wars in distant lands.

In the first few months of his administration, Bush said and did little to contradict this impression. His first inaugural address hardly dealt with foreign affairs, and to the extent that it did, Gerson's themes from the Reagan Library speech were nowhere to be found. Rather, it took a line, almost precisely, from Rice's *Foreign Affairs* essay: "America remains engaged in the world by history and by choice," he said, "shaping a balance of power that favors freedom." It was an invocation of Realpolitik ("a balance of power") with just a light touch of idealism ("that favors freedom"), so light that neither Rice's late professor from Denver nor her former boss in the first Bush White House would have found reason to disagree.

• • •

In their first few months in power, Bush and his top aides—Rumsfeld, Cheney, and Rice—made good on their derision of multilateralism, which they viewed as a vestige of Clinton's liberal sentimentality and, more than that, an unnecessary burden in an age of indomitable American power. The open intention to withdraw from the Anti-Ballistic Missile Treaty, the explicit scuttling of talks on missiles and nuclear weapons with North Korea, the brusque discarding of the Kyoto environmental accord—all signaled that a new, hard-nosed team was running the White House and, by extension, the world.

In short, one plank of neoconservatism was now policy. But the other plank—the idea of using American power to change the world by promoting democracy—was not yet on the agenda.

On May 31, 2001, as President Bush prepared for his first trip to Europe, Condi Rice arranged a meeting to discuss ideas about the nature of the international system. She invited a small group of friends from academia, journalism, and the diplomatic world: Felix Rohatyn, the financier and former ambassador to France; Tom Graham, a Republican specialist on Russia; Michael McFaul, a colleague of Rice's from Stanford who had advised prodemocracy organizations in post-Soviet Russia; Timothy Garton Ash, an Oxford historian who had chronicled the Eastern European democracy movements of the late 1980s; and Lionel Barber, editor of the *Financial Times*.

For two and a half hours, the five guests sat on two couches in the Yellow Oval Room, upstairs in the White House, with Bush, Cheney, and several midlevel officials. Rice moderated the discussion.

Bush asked a lot of questions, but they reflected an attitude very different from the one he would adopt after September 11. Little was said about freedom. When McFaul and Garton Ash advocated expanding NATO to include a democratic Russia, at least sometime in the future, Bush sympathized with the notion but for hardheaded strategic reasons. "Where else have they got to go?" Bush replied. His view was that America's competition with Russia was over; a competition with China might lie in the future, so a strategic partnership was needed with Russia to offset China.

This was very much the sensibility of the Bush administration's top tier; it reflected the sensibility of Rice's *Foreign Affairs* article—a focus on big-power politics.

September 11 changed that. Such a brazen attack was bound to send a shock. The shock was intensified by the fact that no one expected it—or at least none of the policymakers did, despite the "hair on fire" warnings all summer from CIA director George Tenet and White House counterterrorism chief Richard Clarke. It was the first time America had been attacked not just by foreign terrorists but by *any* foreign power since Pearl Harbor—in other words, the first time America had been attacked for as long as George W. Bush and most of his top advisers had been alive.

It was a natural impulse to believe that because their lives were now changed, the world had changed, too.

The first week after the attack, Bush and his advisers debated what to do, specifically whether to retaliate only against Afghanistan or to use the opportunity to go after suspected supporters of terrorism everywhere, starting with Iraq.

But also lurking on the agenda were broader questions of what 9/11 implied about the nature of the world, the requirements of national security, possibly the need for a whole new outlook in America's foreign policy.

The neocons felt redeemed and politically on the ascension—a trend confirmed and accelerated by the apparent lightning victory in Afghanistan.

• • •

In the late summer of 2000, as Condi Rice was writing her fairly traditional essay for *Foreign Affairs*, Paul Wolfowitz was putting together a more radical document—a report titled "Rebuilding America's Defenses," to be published by the Project for a New American Century. PNAC was founded in the mid-1990s mainly as a vehicle for petitioning Clinton to overthrow Saddam Hussein. Now that its members seemed on the verge of regaining power (nearly all the Iraq petition's signatories would get well-placed jobs in the George W. Bush administration), they decided to proclaim a broader agenda.

The PNAC authors were up front about their goals. They wrote in its introduction that the report was meant as "a blueprint for maintaining U.S. preeminence," for "shaping the international security order in line with American principles and interests." America, it stated, was now "the world's sole superpower," and the task of foreign policy should be "to secure and expand the 'zones of democratic peace' . . . deter the rise of a new great-power competitor . . . [and] preserve American preeminence through the coming transformation of war made possible by new technologies."

The PNAC report grew out of a classified document called the Defense Policy Guidance, which Wolfowitz had helped write back in 1992 when he was the undersecretary of defense for policy and Dick Cheney was secretary.

The Berlin Wall had just tumbled, the Gulf War had been won, and Andy Marshall and Andrew Krepinevich were laying out their concept of military transformation. The Defense Policy Guidance sought to place all these developments into a geopolitical grand statement.

"In the Middle East and Southwest Asia," the document said, "our overall objective is to remain the predominant outside power in the region and preserve U.S. and Western access to the region's oil." More provocatively, it stated that one goal of U.S. policy across the globe should be "to prevent any hostile power from dominating a region" and, even more, to discourage any "advanced industrial nations" from challenging American leadership.

This idea of *uncontested* American power grew out of a concept that Andy Marshall had been developing for years. Marshall took the phrase "arms *race*" seriously; he looked at international relations as extended *competitions*. Some defense analysts examined the capabilities of America's main foes and calculated how many of what kinds of weapons the United States would need to counter the threat. Marshall was more interested in analyzing America's strengths, other nations' weaknesses, and what the United States could do to maximize both.

For example, during the Reagan administration, Marshall thought the B-1 bomber was a useful weapon to buy, not so much because the United States needed a new bomber but because the Soviet Union spent nearly one-eighth of its military budget on surface-to-air missiles designed to shoot down American bombers. Spending a little money on B-1s would force the Soviets to spend a lot more money on air defense, which meant they would have less money to spend on offensive weapons.

Marshall's contribution to the Defense Policy Guidance—he helped with some drafts, as did Albert Wohlstetter and Richard Perle—was that the Pentagon should focus on weapons and strategies that would give the United States such overwhelming superiority that other countries wouldn't bother trying to compete. "We have to think about the potential emergence of major threats in the future and how we could postpone their emergence," Marshall wrote in his paper titled "Some Thoughts on Military Revolutions." This, as he saw it, was the main appeal of transformation—that it delayed the emergence of competitors and therefore maintained "our preeminent position."

The authors of the Defense Policy Guidance took this argument further. In their fervent promotion of American preeminence, they wrote that *all* industrial nations—adversaries and allies—should be discouraged from trying to put up a challenge. Marshall wasn't so extreme. He often told his aides that allies were "vital assets in our strategic portfolio." In his paper on military revolutions, he wrote, "We need to think through how to involve allies, what coalitions we want to form."

The Defense Policy Guidance went nowhere in large part because of this dismissal of allies. When news of its contents leaked to the press, the Western European governments were furious. President George H. W. Bush dissociated himself from it. A few months later, he lost his reelection bid to Bill Clinton. That buried the paper for good, or for eight years anyway.

The authors of the PNAC report, published in September 2000, wrote in their introduction that they saw it as "building upon the defense strategy outlined by the Cheney Defense Department," specifically the "Defense Policy Guidance drafted in the early months of 1992"—a paper that they hoped might find a "more receptive audience now."

Back in 1992, Dick Cheney had told Wolfowitz that he liked the Defense Policy Guidance, that it outlined a convincing rationale for an American global role. He still liked it in 2001, when he became vice president.

The main authors of the 1992 report were Wolfowitz and Lewis "Scooter" Libby. In the George W. Bush administration, Wolfowitz was back in the Pentagon. Libby, a former student of Wolfowitz's, was Cheney's chief of staff in the White House. The authors of the PNAC report included Wolfowitz and Libby, as well as Stephen Cambone and Abram Shulsky. Cambone became Rumsfeld's special assistant, then undersecretary for intelligence. Shulsky was placed in charge of the Pentagon's Office of Special Plans, which was tasked with finding any evidence that might suggest Iraq had weapons of mass destruction.

After September 11, the Bush White House was looking for new ideas to deal with this new threat, ideas that went beyond traditional Realism. The PNAC report seemed to fit the times, and the PNAC authors were well placed to argue its case.

On June 1, 2002, President Bush delivered the commencement address at West Point and laid out a new doctrine—a "Bush doctrine"—on national security. The doctrines of deterrence and containment, which served the nation well in the Cold War, were, he said, obsolete. "Deterrence—the promise of massive retaliation against nations—means nothing against shadowy terrorist networks with no nation or citizens to defend," the speech declared. "Containment is not possible when unbalanced dictators with weapons of mass destruction can deliver their weapons on missiles or secretly provide them to terrorist allies. . . . If we wait for threats to fully materialize, we will have waited too long. . . . We must take the battle to the enemy, disrupt his plans, and confront the worst threats *before* they emerge." That is, we must take "preemptive action."

The argument in Rice's *Foreign Affairs* article—that rogue regimes were living on "borrowed time" and that they can be dealt with through classic deterrence—fell by the wayside.

At this point, though, Bush had not yet drawn the link between security and freedom, the link that would animate his second inaugural address. That connection clicked three weeks later, on June 20, when Dick Cheney flew to a resort in Beaver Creek, Colorado, to chair the World Forum, the annual conference of the American

Enterprise Institute. The AEI was Washington's leading neocon think tank. It had served as a Republican cabinet-in-exile while Clinton was president, and it was riding high now that many of its denizens from those years were back in power.

At that conference, Cheney heard a galvanizing speech by Natan Sharansky.

•   •   •

Sharansky was a heroic figure to anyone who cared about human freedom and dignity. Within the neoconservative movement, he was an icon. In the time of the Soviet Union, he was a human-rights activist who worked closely with Andrei Sakharov, the physicist-philosopher who was the most renowned of all Soviet dissidents.

In 1977, Sharansky was arrested on charges of treason and spent the next nine years in the gulag as a political prisoner. Senator Henry Jackson was the most outspoken American politician calling for Sharansky's release. Richard Perle was Jackson's foreign-policy aide at the time. Through their connections, Sharansky became a cause célèbre. After his release in 1986, he and Perle and the burgeoning neocon community—Wolfowitz, Abrams, Libby, Feith, Shulsky, and others—became not just political allies but friends.

Sharansky had charismatic appeal. He was short, disheveled, and very funny, disarmingly, even self-deprecatingly so—the freedom fighter as Everyman. After he was let out of prison, he changed his first name from the Russian Anatoly to the Hebrew Natan. He emigrated to Israel, was greeted there as a hero, and was elected to the parliament. As a "minister without portfolio" in the Israeli government, he took a hard line on Palestinian issues—much harder than even that of Prime Minister Ariel Sharon—to the applause of the neocons, many of whom were Jewish and more hawkish on Israel than most Israelis.

Many of those at the AEI World Forum knew that President Bush was about to decide on an administration policy toward the Israeli-Palestinian conflict. Perle, who at the time was chairman of

Rumsfeld's Defense Advisory Board, had persuaded Sharansky to deliver the forum's keynote address, in hopes that he might have an impact.

Nine months had passed since the September 11 attacks, but they still shaped the way Americans thought about everything related to foreign policy. Sharansky knew this—he felt the same way—and he placed the topic of his speech in that context.

The Israeli-Palestinian conflict, he began, was "not a tribal war between Jews and Arabs in the Middle East," but rather a key battle in "the first world war of the twenty-first century, waged between the world of terrorism and the world of democracy." Just as the Cold War divided the world into democracy and Communism, so, after 9/11, have we returned "to the world of two poles"—this time, "democracy and terrorism." The West's key task, he said, was "to expand the world our enemies try to destroy"—that is, "to export democracy."

He urged America not to push for a Palestinian state—not yet. Yasser Arafat, the PLO chairman, was a dictator and a terrorist; the mere granting of statehood would not turn him into a responsible leader, because he would still be a dictator and, therefore, would still lead a terrorist state.

Sharansky presented his own plan for Middle East peace. There should be a three-year transition period, during which Israel and other nations would pour billions of dollars into the Palestinian territories *if* the Palestinians halted terrorist attacks, shut down propaganda bureaus, removed anti-Semitism from their textbooks, and opened up communications with the outside world. After the three years, free elections would be held. Sharansky said he was "confident" that the newly elected leaders would agree to a lasting peace—because they would be leaders who "depend on their people," not the other way around, and "because history has taught us that democracies will make the greatest efforts and deepest compromises to avoid the suffering of war."

Sharansky acknowledged that many people thought Arabs and democracy were incompatible, but he recalled that many people had said the same thing about Russians and, before that, at the end of World War II, about the Japanese. Yet democracy had triumphed in Russia and Japan, and it could triumph in the Middle East, too. "Democracy is for everybody!" he exclaimed. (The text of the speech printed the sentence in italics.) "What a powerful weapon, democracy! What a drug for the people!" Not only does it allow people the freedom to say and do as they pleased, but—because it makes leaders accountable to the people, and because people want to live in peace—it is also, Sharansky said, "the best guarantee of security."

A nation's interests and ideals, as one.

Cheney had spoken with Sharansky a few times over the years. They were scheduled to meet for a half hour after the speech. They ended up talking for an hour and a half. Cheney said he would pass Sharansky's comments on to the president.

Four days later, in the White House Rose Garden, Bush gave his much-anticipated speech about the Israeli-Palestinian conflict. Its theme came straight out of Sharansky's AEI address. The formation of an independent state and Israel's withdrawal from its territories, he said, should be preceded by—and explicitly linked to—the Palestinians' move toward democracy.

"I call on the Palestinians to elect new leaders, leaders not compromised by terror," Bush said. "I call upon them to build a practicing democracy, based on tolerance and liberty." These new leaders, Bush predicted (following Sharansky to a T), will be able to work out security arrangements with Israel. And after that, "the United States will support the creation of a Palestinian state."

Sharansky was on a plane heading back to Israel when Bush delivered the speech. Perle later called him on the phone to tell him about it. "He was speaking your words," Perle told him. Sharansky was thrilled. The news, he wrote later, was "almost too good to be true."

In Israel, Sharansky was widely viewed as an obstructionist to peace talks. Long before the AEI Forum, he had presented his plan to Ariel Sharon's government, which brusquely rejected it. There was no chance Arafat would step down or allow pluralism. Maybe Sharansky was right; maybe that meant there could be no peace as long as Arafat was in charge. But to make Palestinian democracy a precondition for talks was equivalent to saying there would be no talks, and not even Sharon was willing to go that far.

This political dynamic was well known to the American neocons. As they spelled out in the PNAC report, they were interested, above all, in preserving an international environment conducive to "American preeminence"—a goal consistent with preserving Israel's preeminence in the Middle East. Cheney was less a neocon than a classic nationalist conservative; his main goal was to protect and expand American power. On Middle Eastern issues in particular, his view and the neocons' view converged precisely.

President Bush wasn't a neocon, either—not yet anyway. As governor of Texas, he had never come under the sway of—or come into much contact with—that wing of the Republican Party. But he came into the White House determined not to repeat his father's political mistakes. As he and others saw it, one of those mistakes— made still worse by the fact that Clinton perpetuated it—was taking an expressly balanced position on the Israeli-Palestinian question. Early in his presidency, George W. Bush announced that he wouldn't send diplomats to mediate every little crisis in the Middle East; he wouldn't commit American prestige to a futile mission; he was more inclined to let the Israelis solve problems as they saw fit.

By the time of his Rose Garden speech, however, Bush was coming under pressure to do something. The violence was spiraling. The day before Sharansky's speech, a Palestinian suicide bomber blew up a crowded bus in Jerusalem, killing and injuring dozens. (One of those wounded was Sharansky's secretary.) Bush was in a quandary. Over and over, since September 11, he had publicly drawn a line between those who harbor terrorists and those who join the fight against terrorists. This was the struggle of our time, he had said. How could he not try to quell the violence in Israel? Yet how could he be neutral when Palestinians were engaging in such blatant acts of terror?

Sharansky's speech provided what seemed to be a solution: endorse Israeli withdrawals and a Palestinian state in principle, but demand that the Palestinians first change their behavior and oust their leaders. Since the demand was sure to be rejected, the formula would have no effect. But it made Bush appear bold without having to take any action or make any real choices. And Bush liked to sound bold; sometimes he seemed to think that bold talk from the president amounted to the same thing as bold action, and that by virtue of American power, saying something was tantamount to making it so.

• • •

On another level, though, the Rose Garden speech marked a pivotal moment in the Bush presidency. The growing alliance between the administration's neocons and its conservative nationalists now had the president's imprimatur. From this point on, nearly all of Bush's remarks on foreign policy emphasized the need to spread freedom and democracy, both for humanity's good and for America's interests.

And that meant, among other things, a larger portfolio for Mike Gerson.

Gerson was the vehicle through which Bush maneuvered alongside the neocon agenda, by linking its expansionist impulses with explicitly moral imperatives. In July 2002, Bush appointed Gerson to be a policy adviser, in addition to his duties as speechwriter. To the amazement of some White House officials, the two started spending time, one on one, discussing not just speeches but issues. Gerson was coming to be recognized—along with Cheney, Rice, and Karl Rove—as one of Bush's indispensable advisers. Gerson kept Bush grounded to his religious instincts, kept him convinced that his vision of the world corresponded to those instincts; he was the only member of Bush's entourage who could do so with authenticity.

Their relationship was cemented in the days after the 9/11 attacks. Gerson wrote the speech that Bush delivered to a joint session of Congress on September 20, the speech that impressed everyone for its plainspoken eloquence and that briefly convinced several skeptics that Bush might prove to be a leader after all.

When Bush thanked him after the speech, Gerson replied, "Mr. President, this is why God wants you here."

"No," Bush responded, "this is why He wants *us* here."

Bush's second State of the Union address, on January 28, 2003, was a far-flung, ambitious oration that pledged billions of dollars to fight AIDS in Africa (Gerson's passion, which, in the end, Bush didn't fully fund) *and* warned Saddam Hussein to disarm or face war (by this time, a fait accompli). In the speech's final line, he made a declaration that he would repeat many times—and that would guide his outlook—in the next few years: "Americans are a free people who know that freedom is the right of every person and the future of every nation. The liberty we prize is not America's gift to the world; it is God's gift to humanity."

. . .

On December 3, 2002, almost two months before this State of the Union address, Bush named Elliott Abrams to be the National Security Council's senior director for Near Eastern, South Asian, and North African Affairs, with special responsibility for Israeli-Palestinian issues.

Abrams had been hired to head the NSC staff's human-rights office in June 2001, a move that provoked some outrage because, as an assistant secretary of state in the Reagan administration, Abrams had been indicted on multiple felony counts for his involvement in the Iran-contra scandal. (He pled guilty to two misdemeanors, to avoid jail, and was eventually pardoned by Reagan's successor, George H. W. Bush.)

But the larger significance of Abrams's hire—and, even more, of his promotion—was his long and central affiliation with the neocons. The involvement was more intimate than that of most of his colleagues. His wife was Rachel Decter, whose mother, Midge, was married to Norman Podhoretz, the editor of *Commentary* magazine and the intellectual godfather of the neoconservative movement.

In the 1970s, Abrams had worked with Richard Perle in the office of Democratic senator Henry Jackson, whose advocacy of liberal domestic policies and hawkish foreign policies inspired Perle, Abrams, and their generation of neocons (and also turned them into Republicans after Jackson found himself a pariah in his own party, which the Vietnam War had pushed leftward). During his exile from government after the Reagan years, Abrams worked in several conservative think tanks, attended AEI conferences, and signed the PNAC petition. His friends in Rumsfeld's Defense Department—Wolfowitz, Perle, and others—had lobbied hard for Abrams to get the NSC job. He would be another point of alignment between the Pentagon and the White House.

But Abrams also made a tight, if unlikely, fit with Gerson. In the mid-1990s, Abrams, an observant Jew, set up the Ethics and Public Policy Center, an organization that sought to forge an alliance between American Jews and Christian evangelicals around the cause of strengthening support for Israel. Abrams feared that trends in Jewish-American secularization and intermarriage were shrinking Israel's natural base of support. "Tomorrow's lobby for Israel has got to be conservative Christians," Abrams once said, "because there aren't going to be enough Jews to do it."

Abrams, who was both religiously devout and politically shrewd, personally embodied both factions behind the administration's new policies—the moral crusaders and the power-centric nationalists.

On February 26, 2003, Bush gave a speech at the AEI's Washington headquarters, spelling out the linkage between freedom and security. "A liberated Iraq," he said, "can show the power of freedom to transform that vital region, by bringing hope and progress into the lives of millions." A new democratic Iraq "would serve as a dramatic and inspiring example of freedom for other nations in the region."

The invasion of Iraq lay only a few weeks away. Few would claim that the war was motivated chiefly by a desire to spread freedom; but many believed that a free and democratic Iraq might have a domino effect. Wolfowitz had said a free and democratic Iraq would "cast a very large shadow . . . across the whole Arab world." Perle claimed that a democratic Iraq might "transform the thinking of people around the world about the potential for democracy even in Arab countries, where people have been disparaging of their potential."

•   •   •

By coincidence, on the same day as Bush's AEI speech, the State Department's intelligence and research bureau put out a classified "assessment" that called Bush's analysis into question. Wayne White, the assessment's author, titled it, with deliberate dryness, "Iraq, the Middle East and Change." White's boss, Assistant Secretary of State Thomas Fingar, added a snappy subtitle: "No Dominos."

White argued that most Arab countries were racked with ethnic and sectarian tensions, which would impede the development of a national identity; that people in most of these countries did not view the idea of power sharing, so vital to a democratic system, as desirable or feasible; and that if democracy were to emerge, it "could well be subject to exploitation by anti-American elements."

His assessment foresaw much of what would happen in the coming years—in Iraq, in the Palestinian territories, and in Lebanon—but nobody paid much attention at the time.

•   •   •

The invasion of Iraq began March 19 and ended three weeks later in what seemed a lightning victory. The idea took hold that one remarkable event might follow another—that a democratic transformation was possible.

In the White House, Elliott Abrams became the point man for a project that came to be called the Greater Middle East Initiative. The idea was to put the words of the president's State of the Union address into action—to make the promotion of freedom the centerpiece of U.S. policy in the region.

The idea was fleshed out in a speech that Bush gave on November 6 before the National Endowment for Democracy. For sixty years, he said, Western nations had been "excusing and accommodating the lack of freedom in the Middle East"—and, as a result, had failed to contain, or even to notice, the looming security threats that produced 9/11. It was time, Bush said, for a new policy toward the region—"a forward strategy of freedom"—that would turn oppressive regimes into democratic governments and cauldrons of mass hatred into civil societies.

Bush told Rice, and Rice told the other players, that this was not mere rhetoric. Over the next two months, the NSC staff, mainly under Abrams's supervision, hammered out an eight-page draft of a document that Bush hoped to present as a proposal for a common policy at the upcoming G-8 summit of industrial nations.

The paper drew a brutal portrait of Arab governments and societies. It noted that three "deficits"—deficits of freedom, knowledge, and women's empowerment—had "contributed to conditions that threaten the national interests of all G-8 members." The combined gross domestic product of the twenty-two Arab League nations was less than that of Spain's. Forty percent of adult Arabs were illiterate. Less than 2 percent of the population—a lower percentage than in sub-Saharan Africa—had access to the Internet. Fifty million young Arab men would enter the labor market by 2010—100 million by 2020—with not nearly that many jobs awaiting them. "So long as the region's pool of politically and economically disenfranchised individuals grows," the paper predicted, "we will witness an increase in extremism, terrorism, international crime, and illegal migration."

It then laid out an ambitious program to fix these maladies, including free elections, independent media, women's leadership academies, literacy programs, textbook translations, development banks, and anticorruption laws—all to be facilitated by Western loans and expert assistance.

In early February 2004, a copy of the draft was leaked to the London-based Arab newspaper *Al-Hayat*, which published the text in full. Arab leaders were furious, in public and in private. Egyptian president Hosni Mubarak issued a statement, published in papers throughout the Middle East: "Whoever imagines that it is possible to impose solutions or reform from abroad, on any society or region, is delusional. All people by their nature reject whoever tries to impose ideas on them." The Bush White House, he said, was behaving "as if the region and its states do not exist . . . as if they had no sovereignty over their land."

European and Arab diplomats added in press interviews that the plan was off the table until the Bush administration made progress on Israeli-Palestinian peace talks; many saw the plan as a distraction from Bush's refusal to get seriously involved in those talks.

The fuss on all sides aggravated a pathology that had infected the region for decades. Few could dispute the White House paper's critique. Most Arab states were in a serious rut; their leaders had long used their territorial disputes with Israel as an excuse to ignore—and as a scapegoat they could blame for—their chronic internal problems. Yet the White House document also seemed to confirm the Arab world's deepest paranoia. It seemed to call for a Western takeover of the region in the name of democracy. The plan had been designed to quell anti-Americanism in the Arab world, but it was only aggravating the hostility.

It was time to send Colin Powell out on the road.

• • •

Bush's secretary of state was the moderate Realist in the administration. For that reason, he was often trotted out to put a reasonable face on unpopular policies—especially in front of America's traditional allies, who trusted Powell even as they had come to distrust Bush and loathe Rumsfeld. When Bush realized that he had to go back to the UN Security Council before invading Iraq, even if just for political show, he asked Powell to present the case for war (to Powell's ultimate discrediting). When Rumsfeld disparaged France and Germany as "old Europe" for opposing the Iraq war and touted Poland and Romania as part of a more friendly "new Europe" because they supported the war, Powell was dispatched to repair the damage.

So, in March 2004, Powell flew to Kuwait and Saudi Arabia to calm this new storm.

Powell ordinarily didn't travel much, but he wanted to make this trip. He regarded it as vital to America's long-term interests. He had been leery of the White House plan from the outset, knowing that it would be viewed by most Arab powers as condescending and dangerous.

Speaking privately with his aides, Powell said the White House was, in effect, telling the Arabs, "Get down out of those trees and be democrats." The United States had just toppled the governments of Afghanistan and Iraq with military force. Now, Powell said, we seemed to be ordering the Arab nations, "Line up, you're all next."

In Riyadh, Powell met with Saudi crown prince Abdullah and the foreign minister, Prince Faisal, both of whom he had known for years. At a press conference with Faisal afterward, Powell said, in his customarily diplomatic tone, that President Bush's freedom strategy recognized that "reform has to come from within the region; it can't be imposed from outside." He added, "Each nation has to find its own path and follow that path at its own rate of speed." The industrialized nations "stand ready to help" in this process, but only if the countries wanted help. It's "not something to be imposed," but "something to be partnered with our friends."

In a private conversation before the press conference, Faisal pointed out a political reality that Powell did not repeat publicly but knew was true—he knew it was the main reason Arab leaders were frightened by the White House paper, and the reason Western leaders, including American leaders, should be frightened by it, too.

If the Saudis were to hold elections the way President Bush seemed to desire, Faisal said, the winners would be the most radical Islamists. That would be terrible for Western interests. And those winners would make sure that there would never be another Saudi election. They would do everything they could to stay in power forever.

"You understand this, Colin," Faisal said. "But do your friends understand?"

For the rest of the year, nobody in the Bush administration said much about the freedom agenda. The president was preoccupied with the close reelection campaign against Senator John Kerry. His national-security team was absorbed by Iraq, where the battlefield victory was disintegrating into an insurgency war. In June, the G-8 summit, in Sea Island, Georgia, produced a very watered-down version of the NSC paper.

In September, Colin Powell organized a meeting of foreign ministers from twenty-eight Middle Eastern and northern African nations at the Waldorf-Astoria Hotel in New York to discuss "reform"—a palatable euphemism for democracy and free-market capitalism without the American slant or pressure. That session led to the Forum for the Future in Morocco, the purpose of which— according to the preparatory documents—was to begin "an open and enduring dialogue" on "reform efforts" that respond to "the needs of the region while respecting the unique character of each country."

The ambitious vision of spreading freedom, which Bush had laid out at the start of the year, seemed dead.

• • •

John Kerry conceded defeat to George W. Bush on Wednesday, November 3, the day after the election. The following day, Tom Bernstein, a former business partner of Bush's from his days as an owner of the Texas Rangers baseball team, dropped by the White House to offer congratulations and to give Bush a book. It was called *The Case for Democracy: The Power of Freedom to Overcome Tyranny and Terror.* The author was Natan Sharansky.

Bernstein was a lawyer active in human-rights causes. His father, Robert, had started Human Rights Watch and had met Sharansky while visiting Moscow in the late 1970s. At the time, Sharansky was the only English speaker in Andrei Sakharov's circle of dissidents, so he acted as his tour guide. Robert Bernstein was also the head of Random House, and in 1992, he had published Sharansky's memoir of his captivity in the Soviet gulag, *Fear No Evil.*

Both Bernsteins were friends with Peter Osnos, the founder of Public Affairs, which was publishing Sharansky's new book the following week. Osnos had given Bernstein an advance copy. He read it avidly, and thought Bush should read it, too.

Bush spent the following weekend at Camp David, relaxing, thinking about his next term, and reading Sharansky's book.

Sharansky and his coauthor, a *Jerusalem Post* columnist named Ron Dermer, had started working on the book the previous April, around the time Bush started backing away from the freedom strategy that had been inspired by Sharansky's speech at the AEI World Forum. Sharansky intended the book for an American readership, especially for American policymakers, in the hopes that it would stiffen their spines.

The book laid out ideas that Sharansky had been mulling and shaping for twenty years, going back to his days as a Soviet dissident. The world is divided, he wrote, "into two categories"—societies based on freedom and societies based on fear. There was "nothing in between." During the Cold War, the key borders were not East and West, or capitalist and Communist, but rather "those who were prepared to confront evil" and "those who were prepared to appease it."

The same divide exists today, he wrote. But "the free world continues to underestimate the universal appeal of its own ideas." He went on: "Rather than place its faith in the power of freedom to rapidly transform authoritarian states," the free world "is eager once again to achieve 'peaceful coexistence' and 'détente' with dictatorial regimes." In a passage that stirred Bush back to his own declarations earlier that year, Sharansky wrote, "I am convinced that *all* peoples desire to be free. I am convinced that freedom *anywhere* will make the world safer *everywhere*. And I am convinced that democratic nations, led by the United States, have a critical role to play in expanding freedom around the globe. By pursuing clear and consistent policies that link its relations with non-democratic regimes to the degree of freedom enjoyed by the subjects of those regimes, the free world can transform any society on earth, including those that dominate the current landscape of the Middle East."

Some policymakers, he wrote in a clear dig at State Department diplomats, believe that "the advent of democracy in some countries would only make the world more dangerous today." But Sharansky insisted this wasn't true. Dictators, he argued, are inherently aggressive because they need to create external enemies to justify the fear that keeps them in power. Democracies, on the other hand, are inherently peaceful because they must be accountable to their people, and free people want peace. At one point in the book, he went so far as to claim, in a breathtaking flight from real history, "Since all democracies strive for peace, there is no such thing as belligerent democracies." Therefore, he reasoned, "the democracy that hates you is less dangerous than the dictator who loves you." The very concept of a "friendly dictator" is "a figment of our imagination because the internal dynamics of non-democratic rule will always require external enemies." It was "folly" to believe "that a non-democratic regime will help preserve stability." A "genuine and lasting peace can be made only with democracies. The more free a society is, the less belligerent it is likely to be toward its neighbor."

In sum, Sharansky stated, "when it comes to promoting democracy and human rights across the globe, the values and interests of the free world are one and the same."

Books rarely change a president's mind, but they can confirm and legitimize his deep-rooted instincts. During the Cuban missile crisis of 1962, John F. Kennedy took extraordinary care to prevent escalation in part because he had read Barbara Tuchman's bestseller of the day, *The Guns of August*, which chronicled how the great powers of Europe spiraled uncontrollably from the assassination of Archduke Ferdinand to the outbreak of World War I. (At one point during the crisis, JFK told his brother Robert, "I don't want some future historian to write a book called *The Missiles of October*.") But Kennedy was open to Tuchman's influence because he was by nature a stickler about personal control, about not letting things get out of hand. In his first few years as president, Bill Clinton justified staying out of Slobodan Milosevic's brutal war in Yugoslavia by citing Robert Kaplan's book *Balkan Ghosts*, which argued that ethnic wars had consumed the region for centuries and there was nothing we could do about them. Later, as the crisis intensified and as Clinton grew more comfortable with international politics, he justified intervening after all by citing Michael Sells's *The Bridge Betrayed: Reform and Genocide in Bosnia,* which argued that ethnic conflict had ebbed and flowed through the ages and that Western help might make a difference.

George W. Bush saw Sharansky's book as validating his instincts about freedom. The experts, including some of his own experts, had dismissed these ideas as unrealistic. But here was a hero of freedom, who had lived under tyranny and now lived in democracy, saying that Bush's instincts were right.

Bush was already in a buoyant mood, emboldened by his reelection victory. Sharansky's book gave him the confidence to revive the freedom agenda, to make it the centerpiece of his foreign policy.

Back in the Oval Office, he told Condi Rice—who would soon be replacing Powell as secretary of state—that she had to read Sharansky's book, that it outlined exactly what he wanted to do in the second term. Tony Blair was visiting later in the week; Bush wanted an extra copy of the book to give him, too.

Elliott Abrams knew that Sharansky was in town, doing publicity for the book. The author, in fact, was speaking at the AEI's Washington headquarters. Maybe President Bush would like to meet with him.

On Thursday, November 11, at two o'clock, Sharansky and Dermer were in the Oval Office with President Bush, Abrams, White House Chief of Staff Andrew Card, and Deputy National Security Adviser Stephen Hadley (who would soon move up to fill Rice's post).

The meeting was scheduled to last forty minutes. It ended up going on for an hour and a quarter. A secretary came in to the office four times to interrupt; each time, the president waved her away.

Bush said that he had read up to page 210 (all but the last 69 pages) and that it expressed his views precisely. "I believe that freedom is a gift from God," Bush told Sharansky, repeating the line from his 2003 State of the Union address. "I firmly believe this."

Sharansky, a master at playing to people, gave Bush the ultimate compliment. "Mr. President," he said, "you are a real dissident." Unlike most democratic leaders in the world, he explained, you believe in the power of democracy. People call you naïve, but you stick with the idea. That's the mark of the dissident. Dissidents are usually alone in their struggle. It's very hard being a dissident, the most famous living Soviet dissident told the leader of the free world, "but ultimately, history is on their side."

Bush asked him what he should do to keep the struggle going. Sharansky invoked his own experience. The weapon that brought down the Soviet Union, he said, was the "moral clarity" of a few Western leaders—Ronald Reagan, Henry Jackson, and Margaret Thatcher—combined with the courage of dissidents who confronted the Moscow regime from behind the Iron Curtain. That same combination could alter the landscape of the Middle East.

The most effective way the president could promote democracy, he said, was to say clearly that America will stand with those who yearn for freedom and that it will no longer condone—that it will directly confront—regimes that oppress their own people.

Sharansky's view of history was, to say the least, askew. His Western heroes had certainly highlighted the Soviet Union's dismal record on human rights. The Helsinki Accords, which they championed, created an international forum where this record could be discussed. That, in turn, exposed the contradictions between Soviet rhetoric and reality and, no doubt, ratcheted up the tensions within the Kremlin. But it was a huge stretch to claim that those tensions set in motion the collapse of Soviet Communism. As with the historic arms reductions of the mid-to-late 1980s, none of the reforms would likely have taken place—certainly not as soon, or as peacefully, as they did—without the emergence of Mikhail Gorbachev as the Soviet premier and Communist Party chairman in March 1985. It was Gorbachev who, eleven months later, around the time of his first Party Congress, let Sharansky out of prison, as the first of many political prisoners Gorbachev let free. It was a move that none of Gorbachev's predecessors had been anywhere near taking, despite a decade of Western pressure.

The problem was, there were no Gorbachevs in any of the Middle East's ruling circles—no leaders who displayed any interest in following through on Western pressures or in joining Western economic institutions. Nor were there many Sharanskys or Sakharovs—highly educated "enemies of the state" who could act as popular role models or whose liberation might signal a new tolerance, much less an open embrace, of Western ideas.

Sharansky scoffed that many "experts" had dismissed the notion that Russians could quickly adapt to freedom and capitalism once the Communist Party's grip loosened, then collapsed. But Russia was an industrial society with a literate population and an educational system grounded in science. (Outside Russia's cities, Western ideas hardly took hold at all.) Millions of Russians who despised their leaders were well disposed to the West, especially to America. They had come of age during the Cold War, when the world was divided into the Soviet and American blocs. To be alienated from the former was, almost by definition, to be attracted to the latter, especially when the few available glimpses of the West—the jazz on Voice of America, the banned books and other goods on the black market—were so free and boisterous, the exact opposite of Soviet culture's rigid banality.

Yet Sharansky failed to detect that, even with this favorable climate, Russia was sliding back into authoritarianism. Gorbachev—and, even more, his successor, Boris Yeltsin—had blown the lid off Soviet tyranny, but democracy didn't come bubbling out. Yeltsin, in his years as Russia's first post-Communist president, refused to allow the creation of real political parties, property laws, independent governors, and the other entities and institutions that are required to sustain a democratic society. And when Vladimir Putin, an ardent nationalist and former KGB officer, rose to replace him, he suppressed free speech, at least tolerated the murder of certain critics—and yet was hailed by the vast majority of Russians, even those in the major cities, for restoring order. Democracy had not taken hold so firmly after all.

The Middle East's Muslims and Arabs, in the post–Cold War world, lived in a still less hospitable climate. To the extent the people hated their ruling elites, some might be attracted to the West, but more were likely to be attracted to Islamic fundamentalists or to no particular political view. There was, in any case, little evidence that loosening the leadership's grip would unshackle the forces of democracy.

Nor was there much reason to believe that if democracy did blossom in some of these lands, the new leaders would be pro-Western or peaceful. Mature democracies tend not to go to war against each other, though they do go to war. But *emerging* democracies—nations in transition from authoritarian rule—tend to be more warlike than all other types of regimes.

Sharansky acknowledged this point in his book. Well before the point where Bush stopped reading, he referred to "dangers involved in the *transition* to democracy" and noted that this transition "can be long and arduous." This was what Powell, among others, saw as the chief danger of bringing swift democracy to the Middle East. But Sharansky gave the idea just one sentence in his book and not even that in his meeting in the Oval Office.

His moral dictum—always side with freedom fighters, never with repressive regimes—also skirted one of diplomacy's perennial dilemmas: whether to support a nasty regime for the sake of a vital interest. It also ignored the fact that sometimes it was *moral* to support such a regime, for the sake of defeating a still nastier one. Sharansky acknowledged this, too, in a magazine interview after his book came out. "Of course, a time of war is different," he said. "No one would have expected Roosevelt and Churchill in 1943 to say to Stalin, 'You are not our ally because you have the gulag.'" But the United States was at war in 2004; Bush certainly thought so, and he might have benefited from the caveat.

Many books made these alternative points; they were based on historical data rather than ideology and hope. Some of Bush's advisers must have read a few of these books. But nobody passed them along to the president, or briefed him on their contents, or pointed out that Sharansky's views—however noble, inspiring, and rooted in his experience as a dissident—were far from commonly accepted.

The crucial thing was that his views fit. They provided an intellectual foundation, an air of legitimacy, for Bush's view of the world. In a pre-inaugural interview with the *Washington Times*,

Bush said, "If you want a glimpse of how I think about foreign policy, read Natan Sharansky's book, *The Case for Democracy*." On CNN, he elaborated on the plug. "Sharansky's book," he said, "confirmed . . . what I believe . . . that deep in everybody's soul—everybody's soul—is this deep desire to be free. That's what I believe. No matter where you were raised, no matter your religion, people want to be free. And that a foreign policy, particularly from a nation that is free, ought to be based upon that thought."

The policies that followed matched the policies advocated by the administration's dominant voices—the moralists, the neocons, and the conservative nationalists—whose voices would grow more dominant still in the second term. Abrams was promoted to deputy national security adviser. Gerson was named senior policy adviser to the president and was moved just two doors down from the Oval Office. Each was given a portfolio of issues that included the global spread of freedom.

Meanwhile, the cabinet member who was most skeptical of this view, Colin Powell, lost his job. And he was replaced as secretary of state by the woman who had access to Bush whenever she wanted—Condoleezza Rice.

When Sharansky came to see Bush that day in November 2004, Rice, who was still national security adviser, asked him to drop by her office first. Sharansky was apprehensive. He knew her background: her Realist article in *Foreign Affairs*, her time as top aide to Scowcroft and Bush's father. Sharansky had criticized both men for placing more value on Soviet stability than on the Russian people's freedom.

But during their forty-five-minute conversation, it became clear that Rice's thinking had changed. She said that American policymakers used to think that they could pursue stability at the cost of democracy but ended up getting neither—a line straight out of Bush's speech at the National Endowment of Democracy. Sharansky said that if they tried democracy, they might end up with both. To his surprise, Rice agreed.

Rice's shift stemmed from several influences, above all her position within the government and her relationship with Bush. Rice

was dismal at a national security adviser's main task—coordinating
the interagency decision-making process. Not a strong manager
to begin with, she was continually outmaneuvered, or brazenly
ignored, by the men she was supposed to be controlling, especially
Rumsfeld, a ruthless infighter, and Cheney, who had set up a parallel national-security apparatus inside the office of the vice president. So Rice focused on her job's other function—to be the
president's counselor on foreign affairs. And here she chose to be
more his facilitator—articulating his impulses and turning them
into sharply crafted arguments and doctrines.

When Sharansky came into her office, she greeted him holding a copy of his book, which she had just obtained. "I'm already
halfway through," she said. "Do you know why I'm reading it?"

"Because it's good?" Sharansky ventured with a self-effacing
smile.

"No," she replied. "I'm reading it because the president is reading it, and it's my job to know what the president is thinking."

That was the key phrase—to know what he was thinking, and
then to shape it into something coherent but still faithful. This fi-
delity bolstered his trust in her and, as a result, boosted her standing. This was the basis of her power: other powerful people, in the
American government and abroad, knew that when she spoke, she
was speaking on behalf of the president. Her bureaucratic rivals'
strong personalities worked against them in this regard; nobody
could be sure whether they were speaking merely for themselves.

But Rice also came to believe in the freedom agenda, a
process—a conversion—that was jolted into motion by 9/11.

• • •

The worldview of international Realism—which focused on sovereign nation-states acting to maintain a balance of power—was the
dominant theory in academia and in previous administrations, but
at first blush it seemed to offer little insight into why the attacks of
9/11 took place or how the United States should respond. September 11 seemed triggered by a fault line not in the balance of power

among nations but rather in the balance of power *within* certain nations. The terrorists came of age in Middle Eastern nations, mainly Saudi Arabia and Egypt, which seemed "stable" but were in fact seething with discontent. Moreover, the local governments had no ability to deal with the discontent—except by suppression, which bred still more discontent—because they lacked the democratic institutions that might mediate internal conflicts peacefully.

In other words, issues of war and peace might be affected by the character of a regime, not just by its place on the international chessboard. From this insight, it was no enormous leap to the view that it might sometimes be a good idea, for the sake of national security, to change a regime, to try and turn it into a democracy.

There was also a personal dimension to Rice's conversion. To friends who asked about the change in her thinking, she would say, "Remember where I come from."

Rice was born in Birmingham, Alabama. She was eight years old in 1963, when racists bombed a local black Baptist church. She was friends with one of the four girls who were killed in the bombing. Her family moved to Denver not long after, mainly so she could grow up in a less racially charged environment. The fields in which she came to thrive—competitive ice skating, classical music, and finally international relations and arms control—were not thickly populated with African Americans.

The parallels between the American South and the Muslim Middle East were dubious, to say the least. But when Bush started talking about freedom, especially in Mike Gerson's stirring rhetoric, it seemed to have struck a chord; it resonated with her own experience and reawakened an aspect of her life that had long lain dormant.

As Bush's second term began, the world seemed briefly to be spinning on a whole new axis. The Iraqi elections, the Orange Revolution in Ukraine, the Cedar Revolution in Lebanon—Rice felt vindicated in her new thinking and emboldened by the events.

On February 25, 2005, she canceled a long-scheduled trip to Egypt, in protest of President Mubarak's arrest of Ayman Nour, the leader of a major opposition party. She rescheduled her trip in

June, after Mubarak released Nour on bail, and she used the occasion to deliver a rousing speech at the American University in Cairo, demanding that Mubarak give his people liberty.

"We are all concerned for the future of Egypt's reforms when peaceful supporters of democracy—men and women—are not free from violence," she said, reviving the language of the Greater Middle East Initiative.

"For sixty years," she said, invoking a still-earlier Bush line and making public what she had told Sharansky in the White House, "my country . . . pursued stability at the expense of democracy in this region . . . and we achieved neither. Now we are taking a different course. We are supporting the democratic aspirations of all people."

Breaking into her own variation on the second inaugural address, employing an almost gospel cadence, she proclaimed, "The day is coming when the promises of a fully free and democratic world, once thought impossible, will . . . seem inevitable. . . . Ladies and gentlemen, across the Middle East today, millions of citizens are voicing their aspirations for liberty and for democracy. . . . To these courageous men and women, I say today: All free nations will stand with you as you secure the blessings of your own liberty."

Many times Bush had said that freedom was "on the march." During the spring of 2005, several hard-bitten skeptics, including Condi Rice, thought it might be true.

By the fall, the march had sputtered to a crawl, then erupted into chaos.

5

The Dreams Dissolve
into Nightmares

Just a few days after the war in Iraq began, Wayne White started to suspect it might go badly. The alarm bells rang during the first battle, in Umm Qasr, a major Iraqi port just across the Kuwaiti border. The U.S.-led coalition's war plan called for the British marines to take the port as the first step toward controlling all of southern Iraq. They took it, but then had to take it again, and again, as Iraqi resistance fighters kept coming at them in waves.

Umm Qasr was supposed to be an easy win. If the Iraqi people were expected to greet the "coalition forces" with flowers and candy, the residents of southern Iraq—mainly Shiites who had been persecuted by Saddam Hussein for decades—should have rolled over with glee. What was going on?

White was deputy director of the State Department's intelligence and research bureau. In the 1990s, he had been the bureau's director of Middle East and South Asian affairs, and, for seven years before that, its chief analyst on Iraq. He knew that Saddam had placed several thousand Sunni Arabs in Umm Qasr, so that they, and not politically unreliable Shiites, could run and protect the port. Now they were coming out to fight for the regime. If Sunnis were putting up sustained resistance in an area where they were a tiny minority, what was going to happen farther north and west, where they comprised a majority?

That weekend, White wrote an internal memo warning that Umm Qasr was an ominous sign that the war might foment a sectarian insurgency.

As the American-led invasion picked up speed, White's warning was dismissed. One higher-up in the State Department who was briefed on his memo sent back a message: "Can somebody tell Wayne that we're winning the war?"

A mere three weeks later, American soldiers and marines plowed into Baghdad, as Saddam fled and his regime collapsed. But order and security collapsed as well. Looting broke out, not only in museums, factories, and government ministries, but also in ammunition dumps—thousands of them, all across Iraq.

Under a more traditional battle plan, some American units might have been diverted to guard the ammo dumps while others dashed toward Baghdad. But Donald Rumsfeld's battle plan was designed to vindicate the theory of transformation—to show friends and foes that America could topple a regime quickly with a light, lithe force. One side effect of this plan was that there weren't enough troops to guard the dumps.

In the first few months after the toppling of Saddam, looters made off with a quarter-million tons of heavy ordnance—bombs, artillery and tank shells, mines, and rockets—and many of these weapons would be used to maim and kill American troops in the coming insurgency war that Wayne White foresaw.

Even so, the insurgency might have been curtailed, to some degree, had it not been for two additional crucial missteps.

On May 14, not quite two months after the fall of Saddam, L. Paul (Jerry) Bremer arrived in Baghdad to assume his post as head of the Coalition Provisional Authority, in essence the viceroy of Iraq. The next day, he released CPA Order Number 1, "De-Baathification of Iraqi Society," barring members of Saddam's ruling Baath Party from all but the lowliest government posts. The day after that, he issued CPA Order Number 2, disbanding the Iraqi Army.

Those two orders all but guaranteed the subsequent years of strife and chaos.

Blacklisting Baath Party members meant putting at least fifty thousand Iraqis out of their jobs, leaving them angry at the American occupiers—angry enough to give insurgents aid and comfort or to turn a blind eye to their activities or in some cases to join the insurgency themselves. Some of them had been Saddam stooges or outright war criminals, but most were ordinary people who had had to join the party to get a job. More than that, these were the people who knew how to make the wheels of governance spin.

Disbanding the Iraqi Army had still graver consequences. The move put around a quarter-million young Iraqi men out on the streets, most of them with guns and ammo and access to much more.

Many of the war's critics, including some erstwhile supporters, soon realized that these two directives marked the beginning of the end for Iraq. But more telling, and alarming, was the way the directives were put in place—and what that revealed about the breakdown of the decision-making machinery not in Baghdad but in Washington.

● ● ●

Bremer's orders took nearly everyone by surprise, including most of George W. Bush's top advisers. On March 10, a week before the invasion, the National Security Council had held a Principals' meeting, attended by the president, the vice president, the national security adviser, the director of Central Intelligence, the secretaries of State and Defense, the Joint Chiefs of Staff, and the top aides to all these officials. They decided that after the war, a Truth and Reconciliation Commission would be set up—similar to such panels in South Africa and post-Communist Eastern Europe—to ferret out the undesirable Baathists from those who could reliably work for a post-Saddam government. A rough calculation indicated that only about 5 percent of the party—the leaders—would have to be removed, and even they would have the right to appeal.

On March 12, at another Principals' meeting on what to do about the Iraqi military, the top administration officials decided to disband the Republican Guard—Saddam's elite corps and body-guards—but to call the regular army's soldiers back to duty and to reconstitute their units after a proper vetting of their likely loyalty to a new regime.

Both decisions were unanimous. NSC staff members had briefed officials on the plans before the meetings, up and down the chain of command, and they encountered no substantive dissent.

In short, Bremer's first two orders, issued during his first two days on the job, violated decisions made at the highest level of the U.S. government—and not routine decisions, but decisions of staggering importance that would shape the future of Iraq's security, society, and politics.

Most high-ranking officials back in Washington had not been notified of Bremer's directives; they heard about them the way everybody else did—through the newspapers. Colin Powell, who had maintained his contacts with the active-duty officer corps, called General Peter Pace, vice chairman of the Joint Chiefs of Staff, and asked if he had known about these orders. Pace replied that he had not, that none of the Chiefs had been consulted.

Bremer didn't draft the orders himself; he would not have had the time. He later wrote in his memoirs that he was handed the documents by Douglas Feith, the undersecretary of defense for policy, and was told to sign and implement them as quickly as possible. "We've got to show all the Iraqis that we're serious about building a New Iraq," Feith told him. "And that means that Saddam's instruments of repression have no role in that new nation."

Feith was an unusually arrogant member of the Pentagon's in-ner circle. He was the one who usually delivered the most unpleas-ant messages to the officer corps and the permanent bureaucracy, and he relished the task. But Feith was no independent agent; he was merely serving as a messenger, albeit an enthusiastic one, for his bosses, Rumsfeld and Wolfowitz.

In February, a month before the invasion, Feith told his counterparts on the NSC staff that Rumsfeld wanted the Defense Department to be in charge of postwar Iraq. By rights, this should have been the State Department's mission, but Powell had no problem with the request; he knew that State had too few resources for such a massive undertaking. But Rumsfeld's motive soon became clear: he wanted to control postwar policy in Iraq so that there would essentially *be* no postwar policy.

Rumsfeld wanted to get into Iraq, crush Saddam's army, overthrow his regime, then get out. The whole point of military transformation, as he saw it, was to demonstrate that America could project power and topple rogue regimes with a small, light force and that, therefore, it could do so repeatedly, anytime, anywhere, at low cost and little effort. To get involved in a serious postwar occupation—stabilization, security, nation-building, and all the rest—would nullify the concept; it would bog down lots of troops for a long time.

In short, Rumsfeld did not miscalculate how many troops would be needed to stabilize Iraq after the war, as some critics later charged; he understood the calculations all too well. Rather than ratchet up the troop levels to meet that mission, he simply sidestepped the mission. He wasn't interested in it, didn't think postwar stabilization was what a modern military—especially a transformational military—ought to be doing. He focused on the distant horizon: the impact of quick, easy victory on the image of American armed power in the long run—the imperative, as Andy Marshall had put it in his paper on military revolutions, to maintain "our preeminent position." Rumsfeld was less interested in the tangible realities on the ground in Iraq: the consequences, and further requirements, of the war that he helped to start.

Some of Rumsfeld's top aides—especially Wolfowitz, Feith, and Richard Perle—thought that they had a solution for whatever postwar troubles might arise: an Iraqi exile named Ahmad Chalabi. The plan was that Chalabi, accompanied by a planeload of the militia that he had organized, called the Free Iraqi Forces, would be flown into Baghdad and installed as the head of government around the same time that the U.S. military toppled Saddam.

Chalabi was a suave London banker and also a mathematician trained at MIT and the University of Chicago. While at Chicago, he befriended Albert Wohlstetter, the former RAND strategist. In the mid-1980s, Wohlstetter introduced Chalabi to one of his young protégés, Richard Perle. In the 1990s, after the first Gulf War left Saddam in power, Perle brought Chalabi into the burgeoning neocon circle. At AEI seminars and in less formal sessions, Chalabi emerged as a rallying force behind the lobbying campaign to overthrow Saddam.

In 1996, the CIA lent its resources to an insurrection that Chalabi tried to organize from the northern Kurdish territories. The plot backfired, got a lot of rebels killed, and earned Chalabi the agency's eternal enmity. The State Department cut him off as well, after receiving reports of Chalabi's dubious political and financial dealings from officials throughout the Middle East, including several who otherwise supported his aims.

After George W. Bush was elected, and the neocons took high posts in the White House and the Pentagon, Chalabi's influence once again grew. When reports trickled in that Saddam might be building weapons of mass destruction, Chalabi provided sources to confirm them. When conversation turned to post-Saddam Iraq, Chalabi offered firm assurances that the Iraqi people would greet American soldiers as liberators. He also told them, in confident tones, that though the majority of Iraqis were Shiite Muslims, they were basically a secular people, like him; there would be no cravings for an Iranian-style Islamic Republic. Especially if he took control, the new Iraq would be a Western enclave. He would recognize Israel, grant drilling rights to American oil companies, and let the U.S. military set up bases and thus expand its foothold in the region. Between Israel on the region's west flank and this new Iraq on the east, the flames of Western-style freedom—and American material interests—could spread across the Middle East.

Those with expertise in the region scoffed at this dream. In the late 1990s, Wayne White spent an evening in one-on-one conversation with Chalabi and came away comparing him to a "used-car salesman." General Tony Zinni, who was the head of Central Command around the same time and who had spent years negotiating with Arab leaders, dismissed Chalabi and his entourage as "silk-suited, Rolex-wearing guys in London" who had no real constituency in the cities and villages of Iraq. Richard Armitage cut off the State Department's funding of Chalabi's exile group, citing the lack of receipts for money already spent—a move that sharpened the disdain, even hatred, between the Pentagon and Foggy Bottom.

Chalabi's friends in the Pentagon believed him, mainly because they wanted to believe him. Not believing him would mean that they would have to think about post-Saddam Iraq—maybe deploy extra troops to impose order and security—and that was the last thing they wanted to do.

Together, they formed a mutual-enabling society. If Chalabi was going to take command, that gave Rumsfeld another reason to believe he could get by with a small invasion force. Chalabi's ambitions for power and Rumsfeld's devotion to the doctrine of transformation reinforced each other.

Here, though, Rumsfeld's plan hit two roadblocks. The first, unexpectedly, was President Bush. At an NSC meeting in February, a few weeks before the invasion, Feith mentioned in passing Chalabi's impending government. Bush interrupted him. We're not choosing anybody as Iraq's leader, he said. That's for the Iraqi people to decide. A few days later, Wolfowitz, who had not been at the earlier meeting and apparently had not been briefed on it by Feith, brought up Chalabi again. Bush lashed out. This is about democracy, Bush said. He had nothing for or against Chalabi, but the United States was not going to put its "thumb on the scale."

Now Rumsfeld and his assistants were in a spot. The invasion was about to go forward with the small force that Rumsfeld had demanded. He was convinced it would be enough to beat the Iraqi Army and topple Saddam; in that, he turned out to be right and the generals turned out to be wrong. But his solution for postwar order—his excuse for not thinking about, much less authorizing a plan for, Phase IV—had just been overridden by the president.

Some defense secretaries might have hurriedly prepared a new plan. Rumsfeld prepared an end run. Right after Saddam's regime fell and American troops took the capital, Wolfowitz supplied Chalabi and more than six hundred of his Free Iraqi Fighters with a transport plane to Nasiriya.

Then came the second roadblock—the Iraqi people. After a brief flurry of excitement, Chalabi never sparked popular support. He allied himself with one political party after the next, ran some ministries in transition governments, and headed a de-Baathification board for a while. But he alienated the various party chiefs. By the time parliamentary elections took place, he ran on his own ticket—and didn't attract enough votes to win a seat.

The only option left for Rumsfeld, at this point, was denial. The Department of Defense had executive authority over postwar Iraq. But by June 2003, just a couple months into the occupation, it was clear to several officials who watched him at NSC meetings on the subject that the secretary of defense had lost interest.

•   •   •

Frank Miller was the NSC's point man on Iraq planning. A former Pentagon official for the previous two decades, Miller had spent the eight months leading up to the war organizing the vital logistical politics of preparing an invasion: securing basing rights and over-flight rights, drafting evacuation procedures, taking 150 separate actions. After the war, he tried to put together the nuts and bolts of Iraqi reconstruction—obtaining and setting up electrical power generators, oil pipelines, water filters, and infrastructure—but he kept meeting resistance from the Pentagon.

NSC meetings were held, decisions were made, but still the Defense Department, which was formally in charge of the program, refused to budge.

Condi Rice was concerned, too. In December 2002, three months before the war, she and Miller had asked General Tommy Franks about plans to secure the Iraqi towns that U.S. troops would be bypassing as they rolled toward Baghdad. Franks had told them not to worry, that "lord mayors" would be installed in every city. A month later, Rice asked Franks again, and he bristled. "I told you!" he said. "It's all covered!"

Now it was clear that nothing was covered. The whole mission of postwar security had fallen through the cracks.

At least twice, Condi Rice told President Bush privately that Rumsfeld wasn't doing what the NSC—in some cases, what the president himself—had ordered him to do. But Bush never intervened. Instead, he told Rice to call a meeting with Andrew Card, the White House chief of staff; Andy would settle the dispute. But Card wasn't a head-knocker, especially when the head to be knocked was as determined and crafty as Rumsfeld's. So nothing got done. Essential services were not provided; police were not trained. Iraq was falling apart.

By July 2003, attacks on coalition forces grew more frequent and more violent, and the American officers in Iraq didn't know who was shooting at them or why. Central Command asked Washington for a National Intelligence Estimate to find out.

At the first meeting of the intelligence agencies' coordinating committee, which would produce the NIE, Wayne White—the State Department analyst who had warned of a possible insurgency in the opening days of the war—said that the insurgency was now under way. Analysts from the other intelligence agencies disagreed; they were inclined to view the violence as random or as the final throes of Saddam's henchmen. But White saw it as broader and deriving strength from a variety of economic, political, and military sources: the disbanding of the army; the bitterness over de-Baathification, compounded by the aggressive door-bashing tactics of American soldiers; and especially the looting, which ruined whole industries (and thousands of jobs that went with them), unlocked heavy weapons from the unguarded ammo dumps, and thickened the atmosphere of disorder.

Over the next three months, as arguments played out and drafts were revised, and especially as the violence in Iraq began to soar, the consensus shifted toward White's view. The NIE's final draft, finished on Halloween, concluded unanimously that Iraq was now in the grip of an insurgency war and that the violence and instability were likely to get worse.

One implication of this assessment was that Rumsfeld had planned for the wrong war. Iraq was supposed to be the first war of the twenty-first century (Afghanistan, in this sense, was a small-scale preview), the premier showcase for America's new, assured style of rapid dominance. But now it was proving to be more like the grunt battles of old. The satellite-guided bombs and other high-tech weapons, which performed so well at hitting crucial targets on the battlefield, were of little use against urban guerrilla fighters armed with rifles, grenades, and improvised explosive devices.

Back in February 2003, General Eric Shinseki, the Army's chief of staff, had said in hearings before the Senate Armed Services Committee—reluctantly, only after repeated questioning—that "something on the order of several hundred thousand soldiers" would be needed "to maintain a safe and secure environment" in postwar Iraq. Wolfowitz was promptly dispatched to testify that Shinseki's estimate was "wildly off the mark." It was "hard to believe," Wolfowitz said, that more troops would be needed to stabilize Iraq after the war than to remove Saddam from power.

Had Wolfowitz studied some history, he would have seen that the idea wasn't at all far-fetched, that in fact it was par for the course. Shinseki wasn't pulling a number out of the air when he said the job would take so many soldiers; he was extrapolating from historical data on actual wars.

• • •

In the previous dozen years, the United States had taken part in five major postwar exercises, four of them in predominantly Muslim nations. There was a record of what worked and what didn't. Wolfowitz had a colleague named James Dobbins who had compiled and analyzed this record; he could have called Dobbins, but he didn't. Dobbins had been Bush's special envoy to post-Taliban Afghanistan. Through the 1990s, under Clinton and Bush's father, he had overseen postwar reconstruction in Kosovo, Bosnia, Haiti, and Somalia.

At the time Wolfowitz testified, Dobbins was policy director at the RAND Corporation's Washington office, working on a study of America's experience in postwar operations since World War II. Dobbins concluded that the successful cases of achieving post-war stability and democracy all had one thing in common: foreign occupiers who dedicated a high "level of effort"—a lot of money, a lot of time, and a lot of troops.

The best gauge of how many troops were needed, he found, was as a percentage of the occupied country's population. By that mea-sure, to achieve the same level of security as that in postwar Kosovo, there would have to be 520,000 foreign troops in Iraq for at least three years. Bosnia-level security would require 258,000 troops for five years, at which point they could be reduced to 145,000 troops.

In Iraq, the United States and its coalition partners had barely fielded 145,000 troops from the beginning.

Dobbins made another discovery that might have interested Rumsfeld and Wolfowitz. The more troops there were in the occu-pation, the fewer of them got killed. During the long and massive postwar occupations in Germany, Japan, and Kosovo, American troops suffered *no* combat deaths.

No high-level officials consulted Dobbins in the lead-up to the Iraq war. They weren't interested in this sort of mission, these sorts of calculations. They weren't interested in the lessons of history.

They were making the mistake that Huba Wass de Czege had warned about in pre-invasion war games, a mistake that anyone who had read Clausewitz might have noticed from the outset. They neglected to consider that wars are fought for political objectives and that, therefore, wars aren't won until those objectives have been achieved. The minimal objective in the Iraq war was to over-throw Saddam and to provide security while a new state took power. As Bush's second term began, the problem wasn't that he and Rumsfeld had won the war but not the peace; it was that they had not yet won the war, in part because they hadn't understood the war or what they needed to do to win it.

At this point, there was little they could do. Neither the U.S. Army nor the U.S. Marines had another hundred thousand troops to send over. So the strategy of denial was continued. In November, shortly after the NIE came out, President Bush told his cabinet members not to use the word "insurgency" when describing the war. Rumsfeld kept up the pretense for the next two years; as late as November 2005, he mused at a press conference that the armed factions in Iraq didn't deserve the term "insurgency" because they "don't have a legitimate gripe."

Meanwhile, the war's foundations were crumbling. In January 2004, David Kay, director of the Iraq Survey Group, the Pentagon-CIA team of 1,500 inspectors and analysts who had spent over half a year searching for Saddam's weapons of mass destruction—interviewing hundreds of officials and scientists, checking every lead, probing every suspect site—concluded that there were no such weapons or even serious weapons programs. The imminent threat of Iraqi chemical, biological, and nuclear weapons was the public rationale for invading Iraq—and the basis for the claim that Saddam had violated UN Security Council resolutions calling on him to disarm. It was a terrible blow to the legitimacy of the war that it turned out Saddam had no arms to dismantle.

Figuring Kay must be wrong, President Bush appointed a new director to continue the hunt. Kay's replacement, Charles Duelfer, had been deputy director of the UN's inspection team in Iraq after the first Gulf War, back in 1991. Duelfer probably knew more about how to conduct this sort of search than anybody in the U.S. government. His report, issued in October 2004, concluded even more firmly than Kay's that Iraq had no weapons of mass destruction and that even if Saddam had remained in power, he had no way of getting such weapons anytime soon. All of Iraq's chemical-weapons facilities had been destroyed back in 1991, and no production had since resumed. The biological-warfare program had been "put on the shelf" after UN inspectors destroyed the final lot in 1996. And Iraq's "ability to reconstitute a nuclear weapons program" had "progressively decayed" over the years.

Another blow came when the CIA concluded, and Rumsfeld (but not Cheney) acknowledged, that Saddam Hussein never had any connections to al-Qaeda or to the attacks of September 11.

• • •

The next month, President Bush won reelection and read Natan Sharansky's book, which sparked the second inaugural address and the resurrection of the freedom agenda. The idea of a democratic Iraq, which might serve as a beacon for freedom across the Middle East, was only one of several rationales for going to war, and far from the most compelling or widely held; even Paul Wolfowitz, who embraced the view most deeply, would later say that if it had been the only reason for going to war, it would not have justified the loss of American soldiers. But as the fighting slogged into its third year, with no end in sight, the idea took on a much larger role. Bush wasn't going to give up on the war; he *knew* that he was right to stay the course. If the war's other rationales were discredited, he would boost his devotion to this one.

Increasingly, he saw Iraq as the central battleground in the larger war between the forces of freedom and the forces of terror. It was "the decisive ideological struggle of the twenty-first century," he said in many speeches (and repeated in private meetings), no less vital than the nation's earlier struggles against Nazism and Communism. He came to see all conflicts through this lens. It gave him a view of the world that was crystal clear—but it was also distorted, stripped of color and detail, precluding a deep understanding or shrewd response.

Viewed through Bush's lens, the insurgents were enemies of freedom, plain and simple. The complexities of sectarian tension, the disputes over control of oil revenue, the grievances embittered by the transfer of power, the chaos unleashed by the dissolution of authority—these were seen as, at most, footnotes to the underlying clash of civilizations.

Bush had never come to grips with Iraq's sectarian nature; perhaps he had never been briefed on it. During Super Bowl weekend

2003, two months before the invasion, he met in the Oval Office with three Iraqi exiles. The most prominent was Kanan Makiya, a professor at Brandeis University and the author, a dozen years earlier, of *The Republic of Fear*, which had exposed the totalitarian horrors of Saddam's regime as vividly as Aleksandr Solzhenitsyn had described the horrors of Soviet Communism in *The Gulag Archipelago*. After the 1991 Gulf War, Makiya and a group of other exiles drafted a manifesto for a democratic, secular Iraq called Charter 91, modeled after Vaclav Havel's Charter 77 in Soviet-dominated Czechoslovakia.

Sitting in the Oval Office that January day, excited that Saddam might soon be gone, Makiya cautioned the president that toppling the dictatorship might be the easiest part of the war, that the new government would have to dampen the historic tensions between the country's Sunni and Shiite Arabs, which were sure to flare after Saddam's lid was blown off. It soon became clear that Bush didn't know what Makiya was talking about; he seemed not to have heard about the two kinds of Iraqi Arabs or the tensions between them.

The exiles spent much of their remaining time with the president explaining these realities, but the lecture didn't seem to take. For the first few years of the occupation, Bush described the insurgency as consisting mainly of foreign terrorists, not as the natural outgrowth of long-held animosities within Iraqi society. With few exceptions, American military commanders tried to defeat the insurgents the way they had defeated other enemies: with massive firepower rather than by isolating them from—and otherwise winning over—the Iraqi population. They didn't view the struggle as a counterinsurgency war, in part because the White House and the Pentagon persistently denied there was an insurgency to counter.

Bush put great stock in Iraq's first national election, held on January 30, 2005, and at first he seemed vindicated by the results. Despite insurgents' threats to kill those who dared go to the polls, eight million Iraqis turned out to vote. In a televised address, just hours after the polls closed, President Bush declared, "The world is hearing the voice of freedom from the center of the Middle

East. . . . By participating in free elections, the Iraqi people have . . . taken rightful control of their country's destiny . . . and they have chosen a future of freedom and peace."

His words were premature; the final count revealed that voting was heavy in the Shiite south and the Kurdish north but almost nonexistent in the Sunni-dominated western districts. Since the insurgency was mainly Sunni, it was not at all clear that democratic politics could bring peace or settle disputes.

A follow-up election eleven months later, on December 15, proved more hopeful, at least initially. Many Sunni leaders had concluded that they had made a mistake in boycotting the earlier election, and this time they encouraged their people to vote. Turnout soared to twelve million. But the violence only escalated.

For several months afterward, as the insurgency morphed into sectarian civil war between Sunnis and Shiites, President Bush invoked the elections to dispute that anything of the sort was happening. "I hear a lot about 'civil war,'" he said at one press conference. "The Iraqis want a unified country. . . . Twelve million Iraqis voted. . . . It's an indication about the desire for people to live in a free society."

But it indicated no such thing. Had Bush looked at his own country's history, he would have seen that the election sporting one of the highest turnouts ever, with 81 percent of the eligible population voting, was the election of 1860—the election right before the American Civil War. He would have seen, in other words, that high turnouts don't necessarily reflect great harmony, that they can also presage implacable conflict and impassioned violence.

In the 2005 Iraqi election, Sunnis voted almost entirely for Sunni parties, Shiites voted almost entirely for religious Shiite parties (the explicitly secular Shiite candidates won only a handful of seats), and the Kurds ratified a nonbinding referendum to secede from Iraq altogether. The Iraqis didn't vote for a free society; rather, each ethnic or religious group voted for a society in which it would dominate the rival groups. And the act of voting that way—the politicization of social tensions—hardened their mutual hostilities.

• • •

Bush and Rice would often chide critics for assuming that Arabs or Muslims were unsuited for democracy. But that was a red herring. The issue was whether a nation—Iraq or any other—had democratic institutions that could mediate political conflicts and resolve them in a way that all parties would respect. Iraq had no such institutions; the government had no widespread legitimacy.

Sharansky had made this point in his book. Elections, he wrote in a passage that Bush must not have read closely enough, "are not a true test of a democracy." They "are never the beginning of the democratic process. Only when the basic institutions that protect a free society are firmly in place—such as a free press, the rule of law, independent courts, political parties—can free elections be held." Until then, "elections are just as likely to weaken efforts to build democracy as they are to strengthen them."

Sharansky had made this same point to Bush more directly in May 2005, after resigning in protest from the Israeli government. Prime Minister Ariel Sharon was enacting his policy of "disengagement," unconditionally withdrawing from a small number of settlements in Gaza. Sharansky wrote an open letter to Sharon, denouncing the policy as a "tragic mistake" and arguing that "any concessions in the peace process must be linked to democratic reforms within Palestinian society."

Sharansky wrote a private letter to President Bush, making the same points and hoping that he too would oppose Sharon's move. Bush wrote him back a private letter, saying that he supported Sharon's policy. Disengagement, the president argued, would create a vacuum, which the natural forces of freedom would fill; Gaza would become a democracy almost of its own accord. Sharansky may have had a rosy view of freedom's adaptability, but he held no illusions, as Bush did, that it was mankind's natural state; he viewed freedom as a delicate phenomenon, which the free world had a responsibility to cultivate and preserve. He feared that a vacuum in Gaza, left to itself, would be filled by more chaos and terror.

Another test of democracy came on January 26, 2006, when the Palestinian territories held their first parliamentary elections. Bush was expecting further vindication; he had encouraged the Palestinian leaders to hold the elections. A year earlier, in an election to replace Yasser Arafat as president, Palestinian voters had given a decisive majority to Mahmoud Abbas, the leader of the Fatah party and a moderate who favored recognition of Israel. But the radical parties, Hamas and Islamic Jihad, had boycotted that election. They were not boycotting this one; they were actively campaigning for candidates.

Six weeks before the parliamentary elections, Dennis Ross was on one of his frequent trips to Israel and the territories. Ross had been the special Middle East envoy for President Clinton and for the first President Bush; he had more experience at negotiating with Israelis and Palestinians than anyone in the U.S. government. He was no longer in government—he had left when Clinton did, and he was now a senior analyst at the Washington Institute for Near Eastern Policy—but he still knew all the players at least as well as anybody anywhere.

Ross was leery of these elections. In general, he thought, democratic institutions should precede elections (on this point, he was in agreement with Sharansky). As for these elections in particular, Hamas was a militia that rejected Israel's right to exist and embraced the tactics of terrorism; whatever their ideology, militias should not get to run in elections as parties; they should have to choose between joining the system and waging violence against it. Ross didn't think Hamas would win the election outright, but he figured that Hamas would definitely be a power broker in the winning coalition, that its leaders would emerge from this election stronger than they had been before.

Moderate Palestinians, mainly members of Abbas's Fatah party, came up to Ross and asked if he could quietly urge the Israelis to block the election. An odd alignment was taking shape; Ross had never seen anything like it. Fatah and Israel were against holding the election; Hamas and the United States were in favor. "What's wrong with this picture?" he asked himself.

Robert Zoellick had the same concerns. Zoellick had been deputy chief of staff in the White House of Bush's father, as well as counselor to James Baker, the elder Bush's secretary of state. A loyal Republican of a pragmatic bent, he was the U.S. trade representative in the younger Bush's first term. Rice asked him to be deputy secretary of state in the second term. (He lasted eighteen months on that job before quitting to become a vice president at Goldman Sachs; later, in May 2007, Bush named him to the job he'd always wanted, president of the World Bank.)

Like Ross, Zoellick didn't expect Hamas to win the election, but he thought the Bush administration could do things to improve Abbas's image and thus widen his margin of victory. For instance, the Israelis could be nudged to ease up on border crossings in the Palestinian territories and to let Abbas take credit for the improvements. Zoellick advised Rice to push for such moves. She wouldn't. It was as if democracy—specifically, elections—were a magic potion for curing political ills, and the United States, having delivered or blessed it, should sit back and let the historical forces flow.

Natan Sharansky was in Washington the day of the elections. He dropped by the White House to visit his friend Elliott Abrams, and predicted, woefully, that Hamas would win.

Hamas did win, capturing 74 of the parliament's 132 seats—a solid majority—to Fatah's mere 45. Bush and Rice made efforts to support and strengthen Abbas, who by law would remain the Palestinian president for another two years, but it was too late. Hamas held the new center of power, and the more Abbas was embraced by the Bush administration, the more tainted he appeared.

Bush's view of the world—that freedom was on the march, liberty a universal desire, and democracy an unambiguous force for peace and U.S. security—took a huge hammering from this election. Yet five days later, he delivered his sixth State of the Union address and budged not an inch from his beliefs. He stood at the podium contented and confident, as if his imploded North Star were still sparkling in the sky.

• • •

If Bush stuck to his convictions, Rice redoubled hers. A month earlier, shortly before Iraq's elections, she published an op-ed piece in the *Washington Post* that marked a deepening of her belief. "The fundamental character of regimes matters more today than the international distribution of power," she wrote, in a repudiation of everything she had learned in graduate school and in her subsequent career. "Democracy is the only guarantee of lasting peace and security between states," she continued, "because it is the only guarantee of freedom and growth within states."

In March 2006, despite the continuing decline of Iraq and the baleful results of the Palestinian elections, the White House released a revised edition of *The National Security Strategy of the United States of America*, which restated this theme and pushed it still further. "In the world today," it stated, "the fundamental character of regimes matters as much as the distribution of power among them," adding, "It is the policy of the United States to seek and support democratic movements and institutions in every nation and culture, with the ultimate goal of ending tyranny in our world." This idea was now the official manifesto of U.S. foreign policy. "The more countries demonstrate that they treat their own citizens with respect and are committed to democratic principles, the closer and stronger their relationship with America is likely to be."

There were at least three fallacies with this statement. First, a growing number of national leaders no longer cared as much as they once did about their relationship with the United States. Second, nobody really believed what Bush was saying. Bush, after all, was still consorting with the likes of the crown prince of Saudi Arabia and the presidents of China and Pakistan. Nobody took umbrage at this; it was understandable that Bush needed the Saudis for an assured supply of oil, the Chinese to bail out American debt, and the Pakistanis to help fight terrorists (even if with just one hand). But these courtships suggested he wasn't serious about his demand that a nation must be "committed to democratic principles" in order to be friends with the United States.

Third, there was the case study of Iraq. Whenever the administration or local activists tried to pressure a Middle Eastern government to adopt reforms, the government's leaders would reply, "You want us to have democracy like the kind they have in Iraq?" The fear tactic was a ploy, a transparent excuse for them to avoid reform. But it was also genuine; it was based on real fear.

• • •

On the morning of July 12, 2006, Hezbollah militiamen stationed in southern Lebanon fired Katyusha rockets at Israeli military positions. But this was a diversionary tactic for what came next. A separate Hezbollah unit stole across the border, kidnapped two Israeli soldiers, and killed three others. After a failed rescue attempt, which resulted in five more soldiers' deaths, the Israeli government retaliated not with a "proportionate" tit for tat—as it had done after a similar rocket barrage in May and an attempted kidnapping of soldiers the previous November—but, instead, with massive artillery and air strikes. Hezbollah fired more rockets into northern Israel. The Israeli Defense Force widened the air strikes—against highways, bridges, TV towers, suspected militia hideouts—and mobilized ground forces to occupy a narrow swath of southern Lebanon. Hezbollah guerrillas fought back against the ground troops and fired still more rockets. The two countries—or, rather, the state of Israel and Hezbollah's state-within-a-state inside Lebanon—were at war.

Three days after the war started, the Arab League, meeting in an emergency summit in Cairo, released a statement—authored by Saudi Arabia but supported by Egypt, Jordan, the Palestinian Authority, and the United Arab Emirates—criticizing Hezbollah for committing "unexpected, inappropriate, and irresponsible acts."

It was an astonishing statement. All of these Arab leaders were naturally leery of Hezbollah; they were Sunnis, while Hezbollah was not only Shiite but allied with Iran, whose expansionist ambitions they feared. Even so, no Arab power had ever publicly criticized any entity for attacking Israel. The official stance of most of these states was that Israel had no right to exist; yet here they were, upholding Israel's right to coexist in peace and to defend itself from attack.

Dennis Ross received a call from a midlevel State Department official he knew, asking what he thought the Bush administration should do in response to this development. Ross said that Rice should get on a plane and fly to the Middle East right away. The Saudi statement marked a strategic shift, a potential turning point. Here was a rare, if not unprecedented, opportunity to forge a new alignment between the Arabs and Israelis, not only on Lebanon but perhaps on the gamut of contentious issues. The Saudis needed to coordinate a common Arab position on Israeli-Lebanon security. The Israelis needed to rethink their military tactics, to calibrate them to feasible political objectives; this would mean, among other things, toning down their air attacks, which were already beginning to kill Lebanese civilians and which would soon alienate their new supporters.

But neither the Saudis nor the Israelis could do this on their own; they had no diplomatic relations, and it would have been too politically risky for either to make the first move. They needed the United States as a go-between. The whole point of "shuttle diplomacy," as practiced in the past by Henry Kissinger and James Baker in particular, was to carry messages back and forth among various governments that couldn't speak to one another directly. This was a prime moment to revive shuttle diplomacy. But, Ross emphasized, it was just a moment; it wouldn't last much longer.

Quite separately, Philip Zelikow, Rice's counselor at the State Department, had a similar idea. Rice and Zelikow had worked together in the NSC under the first President Bush. Afterward, they coedited a book on German reunification, and over the years they remained friends. During George W. Bush's first term, Zelikow went off to teach history at the University of Virginia, then served as staff director of the 9/11 Commission. But Rice hired him as a member of her inner circle when she became secretary of state in the second term.

Rice and Bush were attending a G-8 summit in St. Petersburg when the war broke out. Zelikow, back in Washington, wrote Rice a memo, encouraging her to do two things. First, she should go to Israel right away, preferably to Haifa, the northern city where several Hezbollah rockets were exploding, to display American solidarity. Then she should go to Tel Aviv and pressure Israeli officials, asking them what they were trying to accomplish with these air strikes, how they thought the conflict would play out, nudging them and the region's other powers into a settlement that would keep the war from escalating while securing Israel's borders.

Neither Ross nor Zelikow had any impact. On Monday, July 17, Bush and Tony Blair, still at the G-8 summit, had a private lunchtime conversation (which was picked up by an open microphone). Blair noted that the conflict could quickly "spiral out of control." Bush interrupted him. "Yeah," he said, "she's going. I think Condi's going to go pretty soon."

But Rice didn't go to the Middle East for another week. First, she and Bush were disinclined to push the shuttle-diplomacy button because that was what previous administrations did, and they weren't like previous administrations. Second, they wanted to wait a while, to give Israel a chance to demolish Hezbollah.

This latter hope was a delusion. To have any chance of destroying Hezbollah, Israel would need to send a massive invasion force into southern Lebanon. Yet very few Israelis had the stomach for that option; they had recently ended an eighteen-year occupation of Lebanon, and they didn't want to begin another one. The Israeli military's chief of staff, General Dan Halutz, was an air force officer who had convinced his inexperienced cabinet ministers that he could defeat Hezbollah with air power alone.

Halutz had emulated one of the greatest miscalculations of recent American strategy—that air power alone can work magic—and here too failure was certain. Hezbollah was integrated into Lebanese society. To destroy Hezbollah's infrastructure meant destroying Lebanese society's infrastructure—roads, bridges, houses, power plants—and it is impossible to destroy guerrilla groups from the air, in any case. Hezbollah survived the attack. But Lebanon was severely damaged, and Lebanese civilians emerged from the fray more sympathetic to Hezbollah and more hostile to Israel.

By the time Rice finally got on a plane, Israel had stepped up its bombing and shelling so drastically—and had, in the process, displaced and killed so many Lebanese civilians—that the Arab powers backed away from their condemnation of Hezbollah and began to criticize Washington for failing to put restraints on Israel. (Even some Israeli newspaper columnists, who had initially supported their government's strong response, were criticizing the subsequent escalation as "disproportionate.")

After her first stop, in Israel, Rice had wanted to meet with European and friendly Arab diplomats in Cairo, but Egypt's president, Hosni Mubarak, refused. No Arab leader wanted to host such a session and risk looking like a handmaiden to American one-sidedness. Instead they met in Rome—neutral territory—and, predictably, accomplished nothing.

The whole trip was useless, not least because Bush was adamant that Rice not meet with anyone from Syria or Iran—Hezbollah's main allies and suppliers and, therefore, the two powers that could have exercised some leverage over its actions.

At a press conference on July 21, two days before she left for the region, Rice was asked why she wasn't going to talk with the Syrians. "Syria knows what it needs to do," Rice replied.

That may have been true, but Syria did not know what the United States or any other power was willing to give in exchange for their doing it. That's what diplomacy might have clarified.

But Bush, as a matter of ideological principle, wasn't interested in talking with Syria or with Iran. His refusal stemmed from the same "moral clarity" that stiffened his resistance against talking with North Korea. "We don't negotiate with evil," Cheney had once said, "we defeat it." Iran and North Korea were part of the axis of evil; Syria was, at the very least, a junior partner in evil with Iran. So there was to be no talking, no dealing, with either.

When asked at her press conference why she hadn't embarked on shuttle diplomacy already, Rice replied, "I could have gotten on a plane and rushed over and started shuttling," but "it wouldn't have been clear what I was shuttling to do." She added, "I have no interest in diplomacy for the sake of returning Lebanon and Israel to the status quo ante. I think that would be a mistake."

Then came the remark that dropped jaws and made headlines. "What we're seeing here," she said, "is, in a sense, the growing— the birth pangs of a new Middle East. And whatever we do, we have to be certain that we're pushing forward to the new Middle East, not going back to the old Middle East."

Bush and Rice were hardly the first Western leaders to sally forth into the desert with bright eyes and blueprints for a "new Middle East." But they seemed unaware of how many hopeful predecessors had bogged down in the dunes, blistered by sunstroke and bitten by scorpions. Or maybe they thought the world had changed so much that this history held no useful lessons.

Rice said she would accept only a "real and lasting peace," which "must address the root causes of the violence." Yet, as anyone who had so much as waded into the morass of Middle Eastern politics well knew, the opposing players disagreed about "the root causes of the violence" as intensely as about any other issue; it was what often inflamed the violence and made a "lasting peace" so hard to define, much less achieve.

A cease-fire without a political solution, she said, would mean she would be back "in six months again or in nine months or in a year, trying to get another cease-fire." But that's what the region sometimes required. When Dennis Ross was special envoy, he would occasionally get a phone call at night or during the weekend from some Israeli security officer at a Palestinian checkpoint. A fistfight was about to break out, and the officer wanted Ross to help stop it. That had been one of Ross's jobs: to put out fires the instant someone lit a match, because fires in the Middle East can spread far if the flames aren't doused quickly. When opportunities for positive change materialized, they should be grabbed at once, before they evaporated. In the meantime, there were worse things than preserving, or restoring, the status quo.

And in the summer of 2006, one thing that seemed worse than the status quo was the "birth pangs of a new Middle East." If something new was indeed slouching toward Bethlehem to be

born, it was a rough beast that no one who valued stability or freedom should have welcomed.

But by this time, Bush and Rice were convinced that stability in
the Middle East was itself a delusion—that for sixty years, as they
had said many times, the United States sought stability at the expense of democracy and got neither. They believed that reversing
priorities—pursuing democracy at the expense of stability—would
yield both; but there was nothing beyond faith to support this belief. Maybe democracy would ease the prospects for stability; but
in the absence of stability, the seeds of democracy could not sprout.

The puzzling thing was, when a chance to build democracy presented itself, Bush and his advisers did next to nothing. In a press
conference on August 7, at his ranch in Crawford, Texas, Bush said
of the fighting in Lebanon, "We want the Siniora government to
survive and be strengthened." He added, "What Condi and I are
working on is to remind people about the stakes in the Middle East.
And those stakes include . . . helping the Lebanese government
firm up its democracy."

But when the UN Security Council passed a cease-fire resolution five days later—after Bush and Rice finally realized that Israel
wasn't going to win the war or stop it on its own—Bush did nothing
to strengthen the government of Lebanon's prime minister, Fouad
Siniora, or to strengthen its wobbly democracy. He announced a
$230 million aid package, to help repair the war's damage. This was
better than Rice's initial promise of $50 million, but it was a pit-
tance against the $1 billion-plus that Iran and Syria poured in—
and their aid was distributed with great fanfare by Hezbollah.

• • •

In terms of Western interests, the war was a disaster. Israel didn't
lose, but it didn't win, either, and that's what it had to do to maintain its image of invincibility—an image that had gone a long way
over the years toward deterring its hostile neighbors from contem-
plating aggression. Hezbollah didn't win, but all it had to do was not
lose, and it clearly achieved that goal, enhancing its reputation on

"the Arab street" as the power that had stood up to the Zionists and faced them down. Now the peace was turning no less disastrous, with Hezbollah—the party that started the war—emerging as the savior of reconstruction.

Back in that hopeful spring of 2005, when the uprisings in Beirut forced the Syrian army to leave Lebanon, many analysts warned that the expulsion would leave a vacuum that Hezbollah would fill unless Western countries moved quickly to bolster the new independent government.

Lebanon had never managed to stay peaceful for long without foreign intervention. The country was always a patchwork of rival ethnic and religious groups that readily devolved into factions, then hardened into militias—Sunnis, Shiites, and several Christian factions, with Communists and other fringe groups thrown in for good measure. In 1975, these tensions exploded in civil war, which raged off and on for fifteen years, clamped only by Syria's occupation in the north and the PLO's, then Israel's, occupation in the south.

The Israelis withdrew in 2000, and after that, the Syrians expanded their presence. When the Syrians withdrew in 2005, those familiar with the country's history knew that some abstract concept called "freedom" wasn't going to take over; the flesh-and-blood Lebanese people were. Those people may have been united in their opposition to Syria, but their deep-seated tensions would flare at the first spark.

President Bush touted that brief moment of unity, along with the emergence of Siniora's government, as Exhibit A in his case that freedom was on the march. But he did nothing to preserve that unity or to bolster Siniora. Hezbollah won a large number of seats in the new parliament, as had been predicted; it also openly armed its militia, engaged in increasingly provocative behavior, and—at the same time—stepped up social services to the Lebanese population, with, again, the help of the Iranians. Siniora couldn't do much to counter or co-opt this growing influence: his government lacked the resources; the Western nations didn't give him more; the results were all but inevitable.

It may well be that Bush believed he didn't need to do anything to help. He had said as much back in May 2005 in his letter to Sharansky about democracy filling vacuums. If freedom is "God's gift to humanity"—if it is, in effect, humanity's default mode—then, once a tyrant's lid is blown off, and once free elections are held, the other ingredients fall into place naturally.

Bush's faith on this issue fed his tendency to view all conflicts as manifestations of the global struggle between freedom and tyranny, and this led him to misread most of the world's conflicts and most of the world's politics.

• • •

At a press conference on August 21, nine days after the UN cease-fire resolution passed but before it went into full effect, Bush made a revealing observation. "What's very interesting," he said, "about the violence in Lebanon and the violence in Iraq and the violence in Gaza is this—these are all groups of terrorists who are trying to stop the advance of democracy."

Yet Hamas, which was responsible for much of the violence in Gaza, had won the Palestinian parliamentary elections. Hezbollah, which had started the war in Lebanon, held a substantial minority of seats in Lebanon's parliament and would probably have won many more seats if a new election were held on that day. Many of the militants waging sectarian battle in Iraq had representation in Baghdad's government.

In short, all these hostile groups had been strengthened by the advance of democratic processes. Democracy and terrorism are not opposites. They can, and sometimes do, coexist in the same country. One is not a cure for the other. The emergence of democracy marks the starting point of politics, not its end. Politics by nature involves conflicts. A democracy thrives or crumbles on how well it deals with those conflicts, on whether the resulting government can mediate conflicting claims without violent rancor. There is nothing inherently civilizing about holding elections—nothing unusual, much less contradictory, about a putatively democratic government embroiled in war or chaos.

• • •

Back in April 2005, a mere three months after he proclaimed that promoting democracy would be the centerpiece of American foreign policy, George W. Bush invited Saudi prince Abdullah to the Crawford, Texas, ranch—the highest token of honor and friendship that this president bestowed on leaders from abroad—and the two strolled through the bluebonnets, hand in hand, before an array of cameras and reporters.

The point of the visit was not to discuss the royal family's execrable human-rights record or its snail-paced crawl toward long-promised local elections, but to ask if the crown prince might do something to lower oil prices.

Even in President Bush's mind, access to cheap oil sometimes trumped the promotion of democracy. Similarly, when he dealt with Chinese president Hu Jintao, the need for China to keep buying dollars and floating the U.S. debt overrode whatever concerns he might have had with Beijing's jailing of dissidents.

In May 2006, Vice President Dick Cheney embarked on a rare foreign trip to Vilnius, Lithuania, where he denounced Russian president Vladimir Putin for having "unfairly and improperly restricted the rights of the people." The next day, Cheney flew on to the former Soviet republic of Kazakhstan, where he expressed "admiration" for the "political development" achieved by its president, Nursultan Nazarbayev, who had recently won reelection by fraudulent ballots and whose rule was far more tyrannical than Putin's.

The real issue—and the barely disguised reason for Cheney's trip—was not democracy but, again, the politics of energy. Putin had recently cut off natural gas supplies to Ukraine and backed out of a prospective partnership with American oil companies. In Vilnius, Cheney also denounced Putin for using energy access as a tool of "intimidation or blackmail." In Kazakhstan, Cheney and

Nazarbayev's ministers talked about constructing a pipeline to Turkey (and, from there, further west) via Azerbaijan, bypassing the existing route through Russia. A week before Cheney's trip, Bush held a state dinner at the White House for Azerbaijan's president, Ilham Aliyev, who had ordered the beating of protesters after his most recent election, then banned mass demonstrations altogether.

In short, contrary to the clever syllogism in Bush's second inaugural address, American ideals and American interests still sometimes clashed with each other. This tension was nothing new. During the Cold War, presidents tried to undercut Communism and pressure the Kremlin to ease up on human rights—but they tried even harder to avoid World War III. Across the vast range of issues in foreign policy, dilemmas routinely imposed themselves; basic choices had to be made. So it was now, even with a president who tried to pretend that such dilemmas had been transcended, that ideals and interests were now one. In the basic workings of politics among nations, little had changed after all.

Bush must have been aware of the occasional contradiction between his words and his deeds on the subject. But he may not have thought it mattered; he may not have thought it through. He regarded himself, especially after 9/11, as a president of big ideas. He did so in conscious opposition to his father, who had once shrugged that he lacked "the vision thing" and may have lost his reelection as a consequence.

The younger Bush viewed his job as pointing the nation in what he saw as the right direction and staying out of the thicket of details. But sometimes principles or impulses led in opposite directions, and it was in the details that the untangling would have to occur. During the first term, Colin Powell sometimes drew attention to these anomalies—as when he noted that instant democracy in Saudi Arabia would put the most hostile radicals in power. But Bush never liked to tangle with these sorts of choices, and in the second term he rarely had to. Powell was gone, and anyone who saw the contradictions was glad to ignore them. Cheney and Rumsfeld in particular saw the rhetoric about spreading freedom as a palatable cover for their desire to expand American power. If the two agendas clashed now and then, why spoil things by pointing out the inconsistencies?

Besides, it could be reasoned, if American interests and ideals were identical, then a contradiction was logically impossible. Policies that promoted U.S. security by definition promoted global freedom. The logic fed, and fed off, the perception that America was the sole superpower, the indispensable bulwark against evil and chaos. By definition, what was good for America was good for the world.

However, out in that world, the view was very different. Against the backdrop of Bush's rhetoric about freedom, his maneuverings for material interest appeared more venal than usual; and against those maneuverings, his lofty rhetoric rang especially hollow.

For two brief periods—just after Saddam Hussein was toppled, when American power seemed supreme, and during the Orange and Cedar Revolutions, when it seemed that freedom might really be "on the march"—some leaders in the Middle East wondered if their days of unfettered power were numbered, if they might have to adopt political reforms to survive.

But before long, they concluded that Bush's calls for reform were bogus, a cynical veneer for big-power domination. They saw the war in Iraq as purely a play for Middle Eastern oil or as a crusade against Islam or simply as a sign of incompetence. And as American troops became bogged down in Iraq, it became clear that Bush had little leverage to press the issue in any case. Because they thought Bush didn't believe his rhetoric about democracy, they didn't have to take it seriously either. They could clamp down on their oppressed people even more, without consequence.

In their attempt to pass off America's ideals and interests as one and the same, President Bush and his advisers damaged both.

• • •

After the attacks on September 11, most of the world famously reached out to America in friendship. The French newspaper *Le Monde*, never one for transatlantic sentimentalism, proclaimed,

"We are all Americans." The band outside Buckingham Palace played "The Star-Spangled Banner" during a changing of the guard, as thousands of tearful Londoners waved small American flags. Most significant, the European leaders of NATO, for the first time in the organization's history, invoked Article 5 of its charter, calling on its nineteen member nations to treat the attack against America as "an attack against them all"—a particularly moving gesture, as Article 5 had been intended to guarantee American protection in the event of an attack on Europe.

Ever since the crumbling of the Soviet Union, foreign-policy specialists had been wondering how to create a new world order—or at least how to preserve alliances—in an era that lacked a common enemy. Here was a moment when the world viewed America with more empathy than at any time in the previous half-century. An American leader could have taken advantage of that moment and forged new alliances, strengthened old ones, and laid the foundations for a broad-based system of international security—much as Harry Truman and George Marshall had done in the months and years following World War II.

But George W. Bush, Dick Cheney, Donald Rumsfeld, and Condoleezza Rice did not take that path. And Colin Powell, who was more a problem-solver than a strategic thinker, brought no alternative grand ideas to the table. Apart from letting a handful of NATO's AWACS radar planes help patrol American skies, Bush's response to the Europeans' offer was a terse "Thanks, but no thanks."

The common view, in the White House and along the upper corridors of the Pentagon, was that it's better to go to war alone, that allies only constrain America's tactics and flexibility.

The effect was to alienate America's allies just as they were rediscovering their affections. As London's conservative *Financial Times* put it, "A disdainful refusal even to respond to a genuine offer of support from close allies, at the time of America's most serious crisis in decades, spoke volumes about its attitude to the alliance."

On the attack's first anniversary, the Europeans were willing to keep the door open. French president Jacques Chirac recited the famous *Le Monde* headline as if its words were his own and added, "When the chips are down, the French and Americans have always stood together and have never failed to be there for one another."

Two months later, in November 2002, NATO held a summit in Prague, mainly to expand its membership to include several nations of the former Warsaw Pact, but also to devise, as the summit's planning documents put it, "a comprehensive package of measures" to combat terrorism and other common threats.

A week before, Lord George Robertson, NATO's secretary general, gave a glowing speech about its prospects. The summit, he said, will "debunk the myth that has crept into the trans-Atlantic relationship after 9/11—the myth that the U.S. and its allies are no longer able or willing to cooperate as a military team. . . . It will demonstrate that Europe and America are on the same wavelength, both mentally and militarily."

But the summit did no such thing. Bush's delegates used it purely as a vehicle to rally support for the impending war against Iraq, the planning for which was by then in full steam. Rumsfeld aggravated the growing rift by touting the new members of the alliance—the small nations of the former Soviet empire, whose leaders tended to endorse the war—over the traditional, much stronger Western allies, whose leaders tended to oppose it.

"Rarely has a NATO summit been dominated by the United States as much as in Prague," editorialized the centrist *Der Tagesspiel* of Berlin. *De Financieel-Economische Tijd of* Brussels lamented, "More and more, the Americans view NATO as a useful toolbox," choosing their partners on the basis of "their loyalty and obedience."

By the summer of 2003, as the war in Iraq devolved into a violent occupation, it could fairly be said that most of the world hated the United States or at least the administration in power. A poll by the BBC revealed that the vast majority of Jordanians and Indonesians regarded the United States as more dangerous than al-Qaeda. Majorities in India, Russia, South Korea, and Brazil viewed America as more dangerous than Iran. A poll by the Pew Research Center reported that over 70 percent of citizens in such generally friendly countries as Spain, France, Russia, and South Korea thought that the U.S. government didn't take others' interests into account. Two years earlier, three-quarters of Indonesians had had a positive view of America; now, more than four-fifths had a negative view. In the summer of 2002, just a year earlier, two-thirds of the French and Germans viewed America favorably; now the share had dropped to half. Bush and those around him were aware of the country's declining image. Shortly after 9/11, many Americans wondered why anyone would attack them. "Why do they hate us?" asked a cover of *Newsweek*. The Bush administration dealt with the problem by trying to alter the image.

One month after the attack, Bush hired Charlotte Beers, a canny Madison Avenue advertising executive, to "rebrand" America. She got run out of town within a year, after her marketing campaign, a propaganda film showing American Muslims lavishing praise on their country, prompted howls and jeers from preview audiences. Bush then turned to Margaret Tutwiler, James Baker's former press secretary from his father's presidency, who dug into the job with customary can-do gusto and fled six months later to take refuge as vice president of the New York Stock Exchange.

As Bush's second term began, he appointed Karen Hughes to the job, which he elevated to the status of undersecretary of state for public diplomacy. Hughes postponed her acceptance of the job until September, after her son had left home for college. (The six-month delay was an ominous sign of the mission's priority in the eyes of the White House.) She then took a hands-on approach, traveling to the Middle East as the public diplomat herself, after just weeks on the job.

In Saudi Arabia, Hughes assured a room of women that they too would someday drive cars; they told her they were actually quite happy now, thank you. In Turkey, she met with a group of women—handpicked by an organization that supported women running for political office—who brusquely told her that she had no credibility as long as U.S. troops occupied Iraq.

Her trip was a fiasco, but the only surprise was that anyone might have predicted otherwise. If some Muslim leader had wanted to improve Americans' image of Islam, it's doubtful that he would have sent as his emissary a woman in a black chador who had spent no time in the United States, possessed no knowledge of its history or movies or pop music, and spoke no English beyond a heavily accented "Good morning." Yet this would have been the counterpart to Karen Hughes, with her lame attempts at bonding ("I'm a working mom") and her tin-eared assurances that President Bush too is a man of God (one could almost hear the Muslim women thinking, "Yes, we know; that's why he has relaunched the Crusades").

The fault wasn't with Hughes personally, or with Beers or Tutwiler, but rather with the assumption that led Bush to regard their credentials as suitable in the first place. The assumption was that a clever slogan and a smiling face could sell America in much the same way that they can sell Coca-Cola. And the premise underlying that assumption was that people everywhere wanted the same things that Americans wanted, had the same tastes, the same interests; that if only the essence of America could be properly packaged, people everywhere would crave and embrace it.

However, in consumer marketing, it's not just the slogan that counts; it's ultimately how the product tastes, feels, or looks. The same is true with public diplomacy. America's image is ultimately shaped by what America *does*.

When Karen Hughes was appointed to the job in March 2005, Condoleezza Rice introduced her at a press conference, saying, "We must do more to confront the hateful propaganda, dispel dangerous myths, and get out the truth."

A few months earlier, Charles Wolf, a longtime analyst at the RAND Corporation, wrote a paper on the subject entitled "Public Diplomacy: How to Think About It and Improve It." Almost twenty years earlier, Wolf had served with Andy Marshall on the panel that foresaw the economic downfall of the Soviet Union. Now, Wolf wrote, referring to the declining image of the United States, "*Misunderstanding* of American values is not the principal source of anti-Americanism." Many foreigners understand America quite well; they simply don't like what they see. It isn't myths, Wolf noted, but rather "some U.S. policies" that "have been, are, and will continue to be major sources of anti-Americanism."

· · ·

Bush and his top advisers began their administration believing that America was so peerlessly strong it could impose its will unilaterally. This may have been their gravest miscalculation. Like all great powers, America had always worked its will through alliances, even if sometimes by manipulating them. As the Cold War ended, and the East and West blocs dissolved, America turned out to need allies more than ever; it lacked the wealth and muscle to run the world alone. Even in a small country like Iraq, it was taking more troops than the U.S Army and Marines possessed to impose order, much less foster freedom.

The realization of these limits came toward the end of Bush's reign, at first in trickles and, for the most part, too late.

After the 2006 midterm elections, when the Democrats won back both houses of Congress, Bush finally fired Donald Rumsfeld. Two of Rumsfeld's top aides, Paul Wolfowitz and Doug Feith, had departed already. Now others, including Stephen Cambone, exited along with their boss.

At the start of 2007, not only did Bush acknowledge that the Iraq war was going badly, he named General David Petraeus as the new commander of U.S. forces there. Three and a half years earlier, as commander of the 101st Airborne Division, Petraeus had run a successful counterinsurgency operation in the northern Iraqi city of Mosul, before he ran out of money and the administration refused to give him more.

In the interim years, he had been in charge of the Army's Command and General Staff College at Fort Leavenworth, where, a quarter-century earlier, Huba Wass de Czege revolutionized the teaching of warfare. Petraeus spent his time there putting together a new field manual on counterinsurgency, the Army's first in decades. The manual, jointly published by the U.S. Army and Marine Corps in December 2006, amounted to a scathing critique of the administration's entire conduct of the war. At one point, it listed practices that have proved successful and unsuccessful in past counterinsurgency campaigns. Though the authors didn't say so, the list came from a memo written two years earlier by Kalev Sepp, a professor at the Naval Postgraduate School in Monterey, California, who at the time was advising General George W. Casey Jr., then the commander of coalition forces in Iraq.

It must have been obvious when he wrote it that U.S. forces had committed at least half of the "unsuccessful practices," among them: "Overemphasize killing and capturing the enemy rather than securing and engaging the population. . . . Concentrate military forces in large bases for protection. . . . Focus military forces primarily on raiding. . . . Ignore peacetime government processes, including legal procedures."

It would also have been clear that U.S. commanders had ignored or violated nearly all the principles of "successful" counterinsurgency, especially in the occupation's crucial early phases: "The more force is used, the less effective it is. . . . An operation that kills five insurgents is counterproductive if the collateral damage or the creation of blood-feuds leads to the recruitment of fifty more. . . . Only attack insurgents when they get in the way. . . . Provoking combat usually plays into the enemy's hands. . . . A defection is better than a surrender, a surrender better than a capture, and a capture better than a kill."

One page of the manual summarized Napoleon's occupation of Spain in 1808:

Conditioned by the decisive victories at Austerlitz and Jena, Napoleon believed the conquest of Spain would be little more than a "military promenade." [He achieved] a rapid conventional military victory over Spain's armies but ignored the immediate requirement to provide a stable and secure environment for the populace. . . . The French failed to analyze the history, culture, and motivations of the Spanish people, or to seriously consider their potential to support or hinder the achievement of French political objectives. Napoleon's cultural miscalculation resulted in a protracted occupation struggle that lasted nearly six years and ultimately required approximately three-fifths of the Empire's total armed strength, almost four times the force of 80,000 Napoleon originally designated.

Again, the authors didn't mention it, but no reader could miss the parallel to Bush and Rumsfeld in Iraq.

Now, Bush gave Petraeus a fourth star and sent him back to Iraq with a mandate to put his theories into practice. The problem was that by this time, Iraq was no longer just a war of an insurgency challenging a weak government. The war had splintered into multiple wars: not only an insurgency but also several sectarian civil wars of Shiites versus Sunnis, Kurds versus Arabs, and, in some areas, Sunnis versus Sunnis and Shiites versus Shiites. The government's army itself—predominantly Shiite—was a player in the sectarian conflict. And though Bush mobilized 30,000 additional American troops to help Petraeus impose order on Baghdad, the calculations in his own field manual suggested that they wouldn't be enough. At least five times as many troops would be necessary just to bring the insurgency under control; and the U.S. military didn't have that many extra combat troops to deploy.

Around the same time that Bush brought back Petraeus, he finally allowed the State Department's diplomats to hold bilateral talks with their North Korean counterparts. Meeting in Berlin, they reached a deal in a matter of days. Kim Jong Il's emissaries agreed to freeze Pyongyang's nuclear weapons program, shut down its main reactor and reprocessing plant, and let international inspectors back in to monitor them. In exchange, the United States agreed to give Pyongyang a million tons of heavy fuel oil, to unfreeze some foreign bank accounts, and to hold further talks on normalizing political and economic relations. In Beijing, the other powers quickly approved the deal.

In its basic approach, the deal was strikingly similar to Bill Clinton's Agreed Framework, which Bush and his top aides had been pillorying for years. It was even less restrictive than the Agreed Framework, because during the years of Bush's no-negotiations policy, the North Koreans had churned out enough plutonium to build at least half a dozen atom bombs and had tested one of them.

John Bolton, who had been removed as UN ambassador a few months earlier, criticized the deal, saying, "It contradicts fundamental premises of the President's policy . . . for the past six years." He was right about that. The most remarkable thing about the deal was that by giving it his approval, Bush put arms control above regime change; he accepted the continuation of Kim Jong Il's regime—or, in any case, acknowledged America's inability to bring down his regime—in exchange for a freeze of his nuclear weapons program.

As for the freedom agenda, it had pretty much vanished. Nowhere in the world could anyone claim that America was advancing, or much trying to advance, democracy.

At the end of 2005, Condi Rice wrote an op-ed piece for the *Washington Post*, decrying previous administrations for valuing stability over democracy in the Middle East. "Had we believed this, and had we done nothing," she wrote, "consider all that we would have missed in just the past year: a Lebanon that is free of foreign occupation and advancing democratic reform; a Palestinian Authority run by an elected leader who openly calls for peace with Israel; an Egypt that has amended its constitution to hold multiparty elections; a Kuwait where women are now full citizens; and, of course, an Iraq that in the face of a horrific insurgency has held historic elections, drafted and ratified a new national charter, and will go to the polls in coming days to elect a new constitutional government.

"At this time last year," she concluded, "such unprecedented progress seemed impossible. One day, it will all seem to have been inevitable."

Yet by the end of 2006, except for women's rights in Kuwait (a development that was under way in any event), all these dreams lay shattered. Lebanon was in shambles, with Hezbollah asserting more control. The Palestinian territories elected Hamas, which advocated terror against Israel; within a few months, it and Fatah would be embroiled in their own civil war. Outside the Middle

East, in Ukraine, the Orange Revolution was sputtering out; the reform party shattered into factions, and Viktor Yanukovich, the Russian-backed politician who had won the fixed presidential election back in December 2004, formed a majority coalition in parliament, became prime minister, and blocked or reversed the reforms.

The ultimate retreat took place in January 2007, when Rice journeyed to Cairo and said at a press conference, "I especially want to thank President Mubarak for receiving me and for spending so much time with me to talk about the issues of common interest here in the Middle East. Obviously, the relationship with Egypt is an important strategic relationship—one that we value greatly."

Just two years earlier, Rice had canceled a trip to Cairo after Mubarak arrested Ayman Nour, the leading opposition candidate. It was one of her first acts as secretary of state. Now, though Nour was back in prison, Rice was kowtowing to Mubarak, in the tradition of previous U.S. diplomats whom she had once criticized for doing so. She needed Egypt's help to bolster Israel and to help contain Iran's expansive ambitions.

Suddenly, the international balance of power meant more than the internal character of regimes after all. But these steps marked not so much a return to Realism as a retreat to randomness. The grand vision was shattered by reality, but no new concept rose up in its place. Policies were devised piecemeal; actions were scattershot, aimless.

Then again, the policies stemming from the grand vision were abstractions all along. Bush and his aides and enablers set forth a new way of fighting battles—but withheld the tools for winning wars. They aimed to topple rogue regimes—with scant knowledge of the local culture and no plan for what to do after the tyrant fell. They dreamed of spreading democracy around the world—but did nothing to help build the democratic institutions, without which mere elections were moot or worse. In their best-intentioned moments, they put forth ideas without strategies, policies without process, wishes without means.

The 2006 edition of the White House document *The National Security Strategy of the United States of America* included an introduction signed by President Bush. It read, in part: "We seek to shape the world, not merely be shaped by it; to influence events for the better instead of being at their mercy."

To a degree, this statement was a truism, a defining feature of a global power. But pressed too far, as Bush and his top aides tended to do, it verged on not merely hubris but fantasy, a mistaken notion that the end of the Cold War left America in control of the world— when, in fact, it left much of the world beyond anyone's control. And when America's leaders acted as if things were otherwise, as they often did in the first years of the twenty-first century, they only trumpeted their reduced powers—and, as a result, they weakened their nation still further.

6

Waking Up to Reality

When Condoleezza Rice became secretary of state, she hung a portrait of Dean Acheson in her office. As she explained in an op-ed piece for the *Washington Post*, Acheson worked in that office at the start of the Cold War "as America sought to create the world anew." His portrait was to serve as a reminder that we too "live in an extraordinary time," that "the terrain of international politics is shifting beneath our feet," and we must "transcend the doctrines and debates of the past" to "transform volatile status quos that no longer serve our interests."

George W. Bush liked to invoke the same era of history. In the fall of 2006, after the Republicans lost both houses of Congress, mainly as a result of growing opposition to the war in Iraq, Bush was said to be reading biographies of Acheson's president, Harry Truman. At a meeting of Republican congressional leaders, he noted that Truman's policies were unpopular in their day but were vindicated by history. The implication was that history would vindicate Bush's policies, too.

Bush had drawn the same parallel the previous May in a commencement address at West Point. "By the actions he took, the institutions he built, the alliances he forged, and the doctrines he set down," Bush told the graduating cadets, "President Truman laid down the foundations for America's victory in the Cold War.

Today, at the start of a new century, we are again engaged in a war unlike any our nation has fought before—and, like America in Truman's day, we are laying the foundations for victory."

But the comparisons that he and Rice invited were far from flattering. Where were Bush's new institutions and alliances, his Marshall Plan or NATO? Which of his doctrines would survive the year, much less the ages?

Truman and Acheson's creations set the policies of the Cold War. These policies, as they evolved, were hardly perfect. They tended to overemphasize military power, bolster brutal dictators, and embroil the United States in trivial but deadly wars, all in the name of anti-Communism.

Yet their main legacies—the strategies of deterrence and containment—prevented much larger wars and well served the interests of the West and the world. The strategies endured and, on their own terms, succeeded, because they fit the basic realities of their time. They were grounded in an understanding of history, technology, and the culture of America's allies and adversaries.

George Kennan, the State Department policy planner who wrote the 1946 "Long Telegram," which laid out the ideas for containment, was a scholar of Russian history and a seasoned observer of Soviet politics.

The pioneering nuclear strategists who spelled out the requirements of deterrence were versed in the power—and the limits—of nuclear weaponry.

The officials and advisers who built the institutions that revived Western Europe's prosperity and freedom—the Marshall Plan, the Bretton Woods agreement, the World Bank, the International Monetary Fund—were economists and bankers who understood the mechanics of finance.

Finally, the decision makers—especially Acheson and, before him, George Marshall, who translated these ideas into policies and integrated the policies into strategy—understood that to be a global power, America needed strong allies, not puppets, and an international order with rules that it too would have to follow, if only to promote the compliance of others.

By contrast, Bush's strategies neither succeeded nor endured—not even through the two terms of his presidency—because they did not fit the realities of his era. They were based not on a grasp of technology, history, or foreign cultures but rather on fantasy, faith, and a willful indifference toward those affected by their consequences.

Those in charge of his policies cared little about the details of warfare, knew little about the realities of the Middle East, and had not thought through what made freedom work in their own country, much less what might make it work elsewhere.

Acheson somewhat haughtily titled his memoir *Present at the Creation*, but he might have shuddered at Rice's inference that he had "sought to create the world anew." When he came to office, the world was already convulsed and transmogrified by world war, the atom bomb, and the crumbling of old empires. He realized that although many things about the world had changed, the way the world worked—the nature of politics among nations, the basic motivations of human beings—had not. What he helped create was not a "world anew" but a set of strategies and institutions through which the emerging American superpower could advance its interests without triggering World War III.

To do that, he began not with an abstract vision or a rigid concept of moral clarity, but rather with empirical observations. Communism tended to thrive amid poverty and chaos; so part of Acheson's strategy was to help make the West's war-ravaged nations more prosperous and stable. The atom bomb was imponderably destructive; so he helped build a security framework that contained Soviet expansion while also keeping the rivalry from spiraling out of control.

If America's Cold War presidents had adopted Bush's strategic outlook, they would have attacked the Soviet Union at some point during the long standoff, on the grounds that Communism was the "root cause" of many problems. (And there were outspoken officers and fringe politicians—antecedents to the neocons—who advocated "preventive war" against Moscow.)

If Franklin Roosevelt and Winston Churchill had thought the way Bush did while planning the strategy for World War II, they would not have formed an alliance with the Soviet Union in order to beat Nazi Germany, because Communism—especially Josef Stalin's version of it—was evil, too. They might even have declared war on both Russia and Germany—and, in their high moral dudgeon, suffered catastrophic defeat.

The great divide in thinking about American foreign policy today is not so much between Realists and Neoconservatives; it's between realists (with a small *r*) and fantasists. The split lies not in what is desirable over the long run but in what is possible here and now. It is a debate about not so much what America should do as what it can do—about the limits of American power in the post–Cold War world, about whether there are limits, about the way the world works.

In these opening years of the twenty-first century, the United States has been led by fantasists—by the sort of people that T. E. Lawrence decried as "dreamers of the day." Most people, he wrote, "dream by night in the dusty recesses of their minds" and "wake in the day to find that it was vanity." By contrast, the daydreamers "are dangerous men, for they may act their dream with open eyes, to make it possible."

Lawrence acknowledged that he was one of those dangerous men, acting the British Empire's dream of remaking Arabia at the turn of the twentieth century. So too are America's present-day aspiring empire builders, who dream of remaking not just the Middle East but the world.

They believe that America emerged from its Cold War victory as not only the most powerful nation but the only nation whose power deserved heeding. From there, it was a short leap—and a leap consistent with a common parochialism—to view America's values and interests as identical with those of the world; to assume that, deep inside, everyone would want to live the way Americans live, if only they were set free from tyranny.

Combine these notions with America's technological superiority—which played some role in winning the Cold War and which took amazing leaps and bounds in the microprocessor revolution just after—and the stage was set for the delusions that followed.

The high-tech wonder weapons developed in the 1990s—especially the smart bombs and the computerized intelligence networks—certainly gave the U.S. military an unrivaled edge on the open battlefield. But they don't win wars; they can't achieve the political objectives that inspired the war in the first place. They're useful for toppling a regime, but of no use in imposing order afterward. In the end, the old verities—boots on the ground, shrewd strategy and tactics, knowledge of the local language and culture—remain key.

Advances in missile-defense technology have produced dazzling choreographed tests, which show that a bullet *can* hit a bullet. But it's another matter for several bullets to hit several bullets, in the span of a few minutes, with no advance warning of where they're coming from or going to—and another thing still to do all this if the enemy builds missiles that unfurl decoys as well as warheads, or if he outmaneuvers the defenses by exploding nuclear bombs from something other than ballistic missiles. It's natural to wish for a magic potion that makes the nuclear nightmare vanish. But we're stuck with the more mundane, if imperfect, methods of damping its fevers: deterrence, diplomacy, disarmament talks, aggressive intelligence-gathering, and a strenuous global campaign to keep the materials for nuclear bomb-making under wraps.

Finally, the world might be a more peaceful place if every nation were free and democratic (or all alike in some other way). It's merely utopian to believe that this someday may happen; it's folly to base policies on the premise that utopia is imminent.

If freedom is mankind's natural state, it's worth asking why it took until the eighteenth century—several millennia into civilization's development—for the concept to gain philosophical traction. Even in America, the first country to encode its principles in a constitution, it wasn't until the 1920s that women's rights were remotely recognized and not until the 1960s that blacks in the South could sit at the front of a bus or vote without paying a prohibitive poll tax. In modern times, in many nations—Germany, Italy, Greece, France, Russia, to name a few—democratic liberties have been adopted and allowed to flourish, in some cases for years, only to be eroded, curtailed, or wiped out in a flash by internal or external pressures.

In short, history suggests that freedom—social and political freedom—is not at all a natural impulse; to the contrary, it's difficult to cultivate and still harder to sustain.

There is no Universal Man marching inexorably down a common path to freedom. Real human history is molded, not fated; and its raw materials are the culture, geography, traditions, and past events of particular areas. It is not only naïve but reckless to believe that blowing off a tyrant's lid will unleash the geyser of liberty. It will unleash only whatever social forces have been teeming or festering underneath. If those forces are favorably disposed to democracy, as in some of the central European nations after the Soviet empire fell, democracy will have a good chance of flourishing. If they're not so well disposed, as in, for example, Iraq, the chances for democracy will be dim.

All this may seem the stuff of common sense, except that it's so uncommon in American political circles—and not just in the Bush White House, among the hard-core neocons, or within the Republican Party.

George W. Bush violated these commonsense precepts to an unprecedented degree and at staggering cost. But leading Democrats have not presented an alternative approach.

They may lament the skyrocketing defense budget, but they rarely cut or challenge specific weapons systems. They veer away from military strategy, and though many doubt the plausibility of missile defense, they scarcely touch the program's $10 billion yearly allotment, for fear of prompting accusations that they're "soft" on homeland security.

They criticize the war in Iraq, but mainly for the way Bush and his aides have conducted it. Few explicitly challenge the wisdom of regime change or the advisability of exporting democracy.

They criticize Bush's unilateralism, but only rhetorically. They stop short of acknowledging that America's interests might differ from those of prospective allies and that, therefore, building alliances often requires serious compromise.

In short, they don't dispute Bush's principles, at least not openly or directly, but instead claim that they would observe them with greater competence. That would be an improvement. But it sidesteps the central challenge of foreign policy in a fractured world—facing up to the limits of America's power while preserving its stature and influence.

Bush's mix of neoconservatism and evangelism has wreaked such disaster that those seeking substantial change in policy might be lured by two drastic alternatives—retreating into isolationism or reverting to the severe brand of Realism associated with Henry Kissinger.

Neither alternative is practical; nor would either elevate America's standing.

Pulling back from the world is not an option, and few serious analysts or politicians pretend otherwise. From a purely material standpoint, America's resources, finances, and well-being crucially depend on other countries and, by extension, those countries' security.

On a more strategic level, a world without blocs or clear power centers could easily devolve into anarchy, in which no country or group of countries can amass the strength and legitimacy to reward the good, deter or punish the bad, and impose rules and order. In such a world, the shrewd assertion of American power remains essential because America is the only nation theoretically capable of global leadership—because it is, for now, the only nation that possesses global reach, politically, economically, and militarily.

And yet, far more than during the Cold War, America has to earn the mantle of leadership, not merely declare or assume it. This is why, though realism (with a small *r*) is essential, Kissingerian Realism (with an emblazoned capital *R*) is not quite adequate.

The neocons were right about one lesson of September 11: the internal character of a regime does matter to some degree. Condoleezza Rice went too far in claiming that it matters as much as or more than the balance of power among nations. But the Kissinger-style Realists go too far the other way when they argue that America should pay no attention to an oppressive regime's domestic policies.

The question raised by the neocons (and, from a different angle, some human-rights groups) is this: if a country is ruled or taken over by extremists who promote terrorism, or who torture and slaughter civilians, should they be allowed to get away with their behavior—should their regime be allowed to continue existing—just because they claim the immunity and privileges of a sovereign state?

Afghanistan is cited as a classic case in point, but it doesn't really address the question because, in overthrowing the Taliban regime, the United States was invoking the traditional right of self-defense. By providing a base for al-Qaeda, which launched the attacks of September 11, the Taliban had declared war on America; and America—by any standard, justifiably—fought back.

But what about the case for overriding sovereignty in order to invade Iraq or attack Iran? What about the case for intervening to stop the ghastly civil wars in Bosnia or (to cite wars in which America did, or as yet has done, nothing) Rwanda or Sudan? And are there distinctions to be drawn? Is there a difference, in principle, between President Clinton's "humanitarian intervention" in Bosnia and President Bush's "regime change" in Iraq?

A classic Realist would argue (and some did) that there is no meaningful difference and no good reason to intervene militarily in any of those cases. But for those of a different mind, it's a disturbing question. At least one prominent liberal advocate of using force in Bosnia suffered a crisis of conscience after finding himself opposed to using force in Iraq. He dealt with the apparent contradiction by abandoning his earlier stance and concluding that the very concept of "humanitarian intervention" was a ruse for neo-colonialism.

It may be hard to devise an ideological argument for embracing one type of intervention and protesting the other. But it is not so hard to make distinctions on practical grounds. It is eminently reasonable to base a foreign policy chiefly on traditional concepts of national interests—and still sometimes go out of the way, maybe go to war, in order to help a ravaged people or oust a monstrous tyrant, even when those interests are not directly at stake, especially if the job can be done at low risk or little cost.

Yet it's difficult to predict risks and costs, harder still to weigh them against benefits.

A better, more tangible litmus test for getting involved in "wars of choice"—wars that might be compelling but don't involve imminent threats to vital interests—is whether other powers or international bodies endorse and join the fight.

This is not to make a moral pitch for multilateralism, but it is to make a realistic case. The purpose behind wars of choice is to enforce international norms. One central fact of our time is that the U.S. government can no longer claim that it embodies these norms—that it holds the right to be judge, jury, and executioner on matters of when, where, and how to enforce them.

The U.S. government's recent actions—the willful disregard of international treaties, the documented instances of torture at Abu Ghraib prison, the often-arbitrary detentions at Guantánamo Bay, the illegal "renderings" of suspected terrorists on foreign soil, the harsh treatment of civilians under the occupation of Iraq, in the eyes of some the fact of the occupation itself—have undermined America's authority as a moral or legal arbiter.

Quite apart from questions of war, these actions have also tarnished America's stature as a beacon of democracy. In many parts of the world, especially in the Middle East, the word "democracy" is now discredited. Sadder still, the smattering of individuals and movements struggling for Western-style reforms shun association with the United States, knowing it would only hurt their cause.

America's record in this respect was hardly perfect during the Cold War, an era that some have nostalgically romanticized. Even so, America as a model was clearly preferable to the alternative superpower. And when the Soviet Union fell, those who had lived under its yoke all those decades celebrated and cherished America's embrace—at least initially.

That is not remotely the case with those whose hearts and minds the U.S. government—which represents only one of many alternatives—is attempting to win over now.

As a result, to the extent America might want to go to war for moral purposes—or wants to conduct foreign policy with a moral dimension—it needs other, less tainted powers to come along. It needs these allies, in part, to share costs and burdens, because it lacks the money and manpower to do much on its own. But more vitally, it needs allies to provide legitimacy.

The war in Bosnia was successful, in part, because it was—and, just as important, was seen as—a joint effort by the nations of the North Atlantic Treaty Organization to quash tyranny and ethnic violence in the heart of Europe, the alliance's area of operation and therefore a mission of common interest.

The first war against Iraq, in 1991, succeeded in large measure because it was waged by a genuine coalition, which included prominent Arab nations—Egypt, Saudi Arabia, even Syria—that not only openly supported the war but sent divisions of soldiers and squadrons of jet fighters. American diplomats labored strenuously to create this coalition and to hold it together. The Arab forces didn't make a vital military contribution, but their presence was vital to the war's broader political aims—one of which was to make clear that this was not a Western crusade, that pushing the Iraqi Army out of Kuwait was widely seen as a proper enterprise, even in the eyes of other Arabs and Muslims.

In April 1991, the month after the first Gulf War ended, Dick Cheney, then the first President Bush's secretary of defense, said it would have been a mistake for American or coalition forces to go all the way to Baghdad and overthrow Saddam Hussein, because they then would have had to form a new government and keep troops there for years to protect it. "It would have been a mistake," he said, "for us to get bogged down in the quagmire inside Iraq."

Surely Cheney hadn't forgotten this remark by the spring of 2003; it had been quoted back to him many times over the years. What was different was that he, and many of those around him, believed that the world had fundamentally changed. They thought that the lack of Arab allies—who had constrained the mission in the earlier war—freed the second Bush administration to muse more grandly about what war could accomplish. And they thought that the collapse of the Soviet Union—which had opposed the first Gulf

War—removed constraints definitively; that America now had the power to make all its musings come true.

Bush, Cheney, and the others didn't realize that many things about the world, especially the basic things, had not changed. More disastrous, some things that they thought were no longer important—for instance, the value of allies—had grown more important still.

A future president who recognizes this reality must also accept the fact that in the coming years, wars of choice will be a less open option. Achieving major goals, whether military or otherwise, requires allies, and allies are no longer guaranteed. An alliance depends on common goals. Persuading reluctant powers to go along on risky missions requires appealing to their interests, and this sometimes entails modifying the mission's goals or the means to achieve them. It is hard to convince a number of countries that some specific threat, conflict, or injustice can be dealt with only through war.

Frustrating as these restraints may be, one consequence of ignoring them will be that the United States suffers more defeats. Whatever policies a nation wants to pursue, its ambitions should not far exceed its abilities. Short of a dire threat to national survival, Americans are not likely to bring back the military draft or redouble military spending; there will not be a two-million-man army or a two-trillion-dollar defense budget. It will therefore be impossible to vanquish all foes, capture all terrorists, or topple all tyrants through American power alone.

America needs to advance its interests more through diplomatic routes, not because (or not just because) diplomacy is preferable to war, but because there is no alternative. This doesn't mean that America should be less assertive about its interests; since global power is so dispersed, its leaders must actively lead. But to do that, they must prove they're worth following. Leadership is about inspiring some combination of fear and respect. The limits of power and the quagmire in Iraq have made America less fearsome; the next president must restore its respect.

The neocons have no exclusive claim on the idea of standing up for freedom; it is an idea deeply ingrained in America's history, and it must continue to be if its foreign policy is to muster popular support. But it is one thing to defend free nations that are under attack or in danger of collapse; it is another thing to act as if freedom can be imposed at will, anywhere, by sword and fire.

Ironically, in one of his debates with Al Gore during the 2000 presidential campaign, George W. Bush said that the United States should "project strength" but also humility. "If we're an arrogant nation, they'll resent us," he said when asked about other countries' perception of America. "If we're a humble nation but strong, they'll welcome us."

"Humble" may have gone too far. Wily, shrewd, calculating, manipulative—these, too, are qualities that a world power must occasionally harness in pursuit of its interests; and every savvy leader knows this. But if candidate Bush meant that America doesn't always know what's in other nations' interests, and can't impose its will at whim, then he wasn't off the mark. He would have done well to hang on to that insight and to explore its implications, as the crises of his presidency exploded and his advisers' dreams and ambitions summoned his darker and holier instincts.

What was abandoned in the subsequent pursuit of absolute power and universal values was the concept of statecraft—the art of conducting the affairs of state. The term has always implied the meshing of interests and ideals with reality, while navigating the shoals of a dangerous world. On this voyage, which determines life and death for millions, moral clarity can be an aid, but it's not a goal, much less a strategy. It's one thing to be a visionary, another to have visions. At serendipitous moments, a particularly powerful nation can try to reshape an agenda. But it can't toss away maps or ignore laws of physics just because they impose unpleasant restrictions. Those limits have to be taken into account, even if doing so means setting aside a great dream. Whatever their ultimate hopes, the leaders of nations have to survive and thrive among the common elements. They have to deal with the world as it is.

Acknowledgments

This book is *not* a compilation of previously published material, but many of its ideas were developed in the "War Stories" columns that I have been writing regularly for *Slate* magazine since the fall of 2002. For hiring me and encouraging all my pursuits, I thank the editor-in-chief, Jacob Weisberg. For sharpening my focus and keeping me honest through these past few years, I thank *Slate*'s foreign editor, June Thomas; deputy editor, David Plotz; the whole crew of punctilious copy editors; and the entire staff, especially Jack Shafer for his longtime friendship and advice.

In the course of researching and reporting this book, a number of past and present officials, as well as other "characters" in this story, agreed to be interviewed, some on the record, some at least in part on background. For their cooperation and insights, I thank Richard Armitage, Thomas Bernstein, Barry Blechman, Stephen Cambone, Thomas Christie, Eliot Cohen, Mitch Crosswaite, Lieut. Gen. David Deptula, Ron Dermer, Robert Einhorn, Thomas Erhard, Timothy Garton Ash, Richard Garwin, Newt Gingrich, Marc Grossman, Andrew Krepinevich, Andrew Marshall, Michael McFaul, Franklin Miller, Larry Miller, Lieut. Col. John Nagl, Tony Namkung, Greg Newbold, Gen. David Petraeus, Colin Powell, Charles Pritchard, Donald Rice, Dennis Ross, Natan Sharansky, Wendy Sherman, James Wade, Huba Wass de Czege, Barry Watts, Wayne White, Lawrence Wilkerson, Philip Zelikow, and Robert Zoellick.

I thank my literary agent, Rafe Sagalyn, who also handled my last book a quarter-century ago, remained good-naturedly patient while awaiting this one, and offered his customarily sage advice after the notion finally took hold.

I thank Eric Nelson at John Wiley & Sons, who took on the project with welcome enthusiasm and edited the manuscript with extraordinary care, providing shrewd suggestions and cogent criticism at every step.

Thanks as well to the entire team at Wiley—especially Laura Cusack, Connie Santisteban, and John Simko—for bringing the book to life with such diligence and dedication.

I am grateful to all my friends who offered support, especially to those in the same line of work—journalism, policy analysis, or history—with whom I frequently discussed the issues while writing this book (though, of course, they bear no responsibility for the results): Deb Amos, Bill Arkin, Ethan Bronner, Bill Burr, Phil Carter, R. C. ("Rick") Davis, George Packer, John Pike, Barry Posen, Peter Pringle, Gideon Rose, Laura Secor, Dan Sneider, and Scott Snyder.

As for my wife, Brooke Gladstone, I fell for her the night of September 19, 1978, and I've been tumbling ever since. Besides doing many of the things for which authors thank their spouses, she has also been my third eye, tuned ear, ideal reader, and insistent conscience.

I cannot say enough about our two daughters, Maxine and Sophie, whose integrity, love, and tuition bills have been constant sources of inspiration.

Finally, I thank my mother, Ruth Kaplan Pollock, for a lifetime of patience and moral support.

Notes

In addition to the documents cited below, I have relied on material from daily news media and from interviews with thirty-seven people—most of them former officials—who play a role in this story. They are listed, and thanked, in the acknowledgments. Some of what they told me was on the record; much of it was "on background." I have footnoted the former, but not the latter. If a passage is based in part on documents, in part on a "background" interview, I have cited the document, then added "and interview(s)."

Introduction

4   *"vulcans"* or *"neoconservatives"*   See James Mann, *Rise of the Vulcans* (New York: Viking, 2004); Francis Fukuyama, *America at the Crossroads: Democracy, Power, and the Neoconservative Legacy* (New Haven: Yale Univ. Press, 2006).

1. The Mirage of Instant Victory

7   *Bush had given a speech*   Gov. George W. Bush, "A Period of Consequences," speech, The Citadel, Sept. 23, 1999.

8   *at the RAND Corporation*   See my book, *The Wizards of Armageddon* (New York: Simon & Schuster, 1983; reprinted Stanford Univ. Press, 1990), chaps. 4–7 and chaps. 12–17.

9   *consultant at the National Security Council*   Some accounts put Marshall in the White House in 1973, but declassified NSC documents reveal that he was a consultant to national security adviser Henry Kissinger as early as 1971. Along with a few others on the NSC staff, he tried to create a new office called the Net Assessment Group, which he would chair. The idea was that he would "review the intelligence community's output" and sum up the consensus and dissenting views in reports for the president. The idea didn't go far,

probably because of objections from the intelligence community. When James Schlesinger became Secretary of Defense in 1973, he brought Marshall across the river to create a different sort of Net Assessment Office in the Pentagon. See Draft Memorandum, Wayne Smith and Andrew Marshall to Kissinger, "Intelligence Reorganization: More Limited Options," July 30, 1971, and Minutes of Meeting, NSC Intelligence Committee, Dec. 3, 1971, both in U.S. State Department, *Foreign Relations of the United States, 1969–1976, Vol. 2: Organizational Management of U.S. Foreign Policy* (Washington, D.C.: U.S. Government Printing Office, 2006), 522, 563.

11 *commissioned a secret study*   Defense Advanced Research Projects Agency and Defense Nuclear Agency, *Summary Report of the Long Range Research and Development Planning Program*, Feb. 7, 1975, DNA-75-03055 (declassified Dec. 31, 1983).

11 *he was the chief mentor*   See Kaplan, *Wizards of Armageddon*, esp. chaps. 6–10.

14 *brainchild of John Foster*   Richard H. Van Atta et al., *Transformation and Transition: DARPA's Role in Fostering an Emerging Revolution in Military Affairs, Volume 1—Overall Assessment*, IDA Paper P-3698 (Alexandria, Va.: Institute for Defense Analyses), 40.

16 Discriminate Deterrence, *was an elaboration*   Commission on Integrated Long-Term Strategy, *Discriminate Deterrence* (January 1988).

17 *bombing of the Thanh Hoa Bridge*   Barry Watts, *Six Decades of Guided Munitions and Battle Networks* (Washington, D.C.: Center for Strategic and Budget Assessments, 2007), 185ff.; Kenneth Werrell, "Did USAF Technology Fail in Vietnam?" *Airpower Journal*, Spring 1998.

18 *For the rest of the decade*   Watts, *Six Decades*, 193ff.

19 *Billy Mitchell, the aviator*   Many air power purists were also enthralled by the theories of Italian aviator Giulio Douhet. See Perry Anderson Smith, *The Air Force Plans for Peace, 1943–45* (Baltimore: Johns Hopkins Univ. Press, 1970), 8.

19 *the first official statement*   Maj. Barbara J. Faulkenberry, *Global Reach—Global Power: Air Force Strategic Vision, Past and Future* (Maxwell Air Force Base: Air Univ. Press, Feb. 1996), 46.

19 *The paper was completed*   Dept. of the Air Force, *The Air Force and U.S. National Security: Global Reach—Global Power, A White Paper*, June 1990.

20 *Reagan ordered an air raid*   U.S. Air Force, *The Air Force and U.S. National Security*, white paper, June 1990, at http://www .afa.org/magazine/June2005/0605keeper.asp.

20 *scheduled a large military exercise*   Faulkenberry, *Global Reach—Global Power*, 30.

20 *"five-rings" strategy*   Michael R. Gordon and Bernard E. Trainor, *The Generals' War* (New York: Little, Brown, 1995), chap. 4; and interviews.

21 *air strikes alone*   Ibid., 187.

22 *Warden drew up a chart*   Ibid., 189.

23 *"the lethality and precision"*   An unclassified version of *The Gulf War Air Power Study: Summary Report* was published as Thomas Keaney and Eliot Cohen, *Revolution in Warfare? Air Power in the Persian Gulf* (Annapolis: Naval Institute Press, 1995). Insiders noticed two bits of eyebrow-raising significance: first, the question mark in the title, implicitly challenging the notion that a "revolution in military affairs" had taken place; second, the fact that it was published not by the Air Force but by the *Naval* Institute Press. Don Rice had commissioned the study. When it was complete, several of his staff advised him not to release it. To his credit, he ignored their advice. For quote, see pages 59–60.

23 *just 9 percent were smart bombs*   Ibid., 191.

24 *His paper for Marshall*   A decade later, the paper was declassified, and Krepinevich, who was by then president of a Washington think tank, published it as a 53-page monograph. See Andrew F. Krepinevich Jr., *The Military-Technical Revolution: A Preliminary Assessment* (Washington, D.C.: Center for Strategic and Budgetary Assessments, 2002). Marshall wrote a foreword, recalling the report's background.

26 *"major reductions"*   Testimony, Senate Armed Services Committee, January 31, 1992. That Cheney resisted comes from interviews.

26 *In August 1993 he wrote*   Memorandum for the Record, "Some Thoughts on Military Revolutions—Second Version," Aug. 23, 1993 (provided to author).

27 *"We are on the cusp"*   National Defense Panel, *Transforming Defense* (Dec. 1997), iii. Information on the origins of the panel comes from interviews.

28 *He formed the panel*   Harlan Ullman and James Wade, *Shock and Awe: Achieving Rapid Dominance* (Philadelphia: Pavilion Press, 1998).

28 *"shock and awe" the enemy*   Michael R. Gordon and Bernard E. Trainor, *Cobra II: The Inside Story of the Invasion and Occupation of Iraq* (New York: Pantheon, 2006), 35.

29 *The meeting didn't last long*   Karen DeYoung, *Soldier: The Life of Colin Powell* (New York: Knopf, 2006), 300–301; and interviews.

29 *denounced Kissinger's school of thinking*   Mann, *Rise of the Vulcans*, 75.

30 *The next QDR*   DoD, *The Quadrennial Defense Review Report*, Sept. 30, 2001, 6, 23, 37, 44; and interviews.

31 *"legacy systems"*   Ibid., 36, 46, 47.

34 *But by the time of Kosovo*   Lieut. Col. Sean M. Frisbee, *Weaponizing the Predator UAV* (School for Advanced Air and Space Studies, Air University, Maxwell Air Force Base, June 2004), chap. 4.

35 *A few miles outside the village*   This tale has been reported widely. For more details, see Max Boot, *War Made New: Technology, Warfare, and the Course of History, 1500 to Today* (New York: Gotham, 2006), 369–73; William Arkin, quoted in Fred Kaplan, "High-Tech US Arsenal Proves Its Worth," *Boston Globe*, Dec. 9, 2001.

37 *Rumsfeld was overstating his case*   Stephen Biddle, "Afghanistan and the Future of Warfare," *Foreign Affairs*, Mar./Apr. 2003; Sean Naylor, *Not a Good Day to Die: The Untold Story of Operation Anaconda* (New York: Berkley Books, 2005); and interviews.

38 *without Rumsfeld's explicit permission*   Naylor, *Not a Good Day to Die*, 56–57.

42 *"killed and wounded more enemy"*   West Point oral history at http://www.west-point.org/users/usma1958/22097/3tactics.html; interviews with Wass de Czege and others.

43 *School of Advanced Military Studies*   Letter, Lt. Gen. Carl Vuono to Gen. Richardson, Commander, TRADOC, July 1983, in "Priority Initiatives of the Combined Arms Center—SG: CC/FLVN 83, CMD GP-003/101" folder; "The Operational Level of War and the School of Advanced Military Studies" (unknown author and date), "CGSC-Departments-School of Advanced Military Studies (SAMS)" folder; at Combined Arms Command Archive, Fort Leavenworth, Kansas; and interviews.

43 *classes in a converted gymnasium*   Fact Sheet, Maj. Sudnik, Apr. 27, 1983, "Gen Vuono Transition Book—SG: CAC & FLVN 83, CMD GP-008" folder," Combined Arms Command Archive, Fort Leavenworth, Kansas.

43   *read one hundred fifty books*   "Advanced Studies," *Soldier*, July 1986.

43   *"We need to begin"*   Huba Wass de Czege, "How to Change an Army," *Military Review*, Nov. 1984.

44   AirLand Battle   FM 100-5 (Revised), U.S. Army, 1981.

44   *recruited four Jedi Knights*   Their role in Desert Storm is mentioned in Gordon and Trainor, *The Generals' War*, but not their SAMS roots. For more, see Richard M. Swain, *Lucky War: Third Army in Desert Storm* (Fort Leavenworth, Kans.: U.S. Army Command & General Staff College Press, 1994), chap. 3.

44   *officer named John Boyd*   I knew Boyd well when I was a congressional staffer in the late 1970s and Pentagon reporter for the *Boston Globe* in the 1980s. I talked with him many times and heard a three-hour version of his "Patterns of Conflict" briefing. See also Robert Coram, *Boyd: The Fighter Pilot Who Changed the Art of War* (New York: Little, Brown, 2005).

45   *Boyd made a deeper impression*   Though he was an Air Force officer, his papers are at the Marine Corps archives at Quantico.

48   *Wass de Czege wrote*   Memo provided to author; a close published version is Huba Wass de Czege, "Wargaming Insights," *Army*, March 2003.

49   *They cautioned that*   Ullman and Wade, *Shock and Awe*, 6, 40–41; Brig. Gen. David A. Deptula, *Effects-Based Operations: Change in the Nature of Warfare* (Arlington, Va.: Aerospace Education Foundation, 2001); and interviews.

50   *"after-action report"*   Reprinted by the invaluable Global Security Web site. See www.globalsecurity.org/military/library/report/2003/3id-aar-jul03.pdf, especially pages 17–18. For more on the military disasters of the Iraq war, see Gordon and Trainor, *Cobra II*; Thomas Ricks, *Fiasco: The American Military Adventure in Iraq* (New York: Penguin Press, 2006); for a chronicle of conceptual mishaps, see George Packer, *The Assassins' Gate: America in Iraq* (New York: Farrar, Straus, and Giroux, 2006).

2. The Fog of Moral Clarity

Much of this chapter is based on reporting I did for several *Slate* columns and especially for an article titled "Rolling Blunder" in the *Washington Monthly*, May 2004. Much of its conceptual framework is inspired by Scott Snyder, *Negotiating on the Edge: North Korean Negotiating Behavior* (Washington, D.C.: U.S. Institute of Peace Press, 1999), and by conversations with Snyder.

54 *"comprehensive engagement"*   Joel Wit, Daniel Poneman, and Robert Gallucci, *Going Critical: The First North Korean Nuclear Crisis* (Washington, D.C.: Brookings Institution Press, 2004), 7ff. The authors were State Dept. and NSC officials in the Clinton administration who were intimately involved in the crisis and negotiations.

55 *"nuclear war game"*   Ibid., 24.

55 *Clinton's generals' drew up plans*   Ibid., 164, 205.

55 *"red line," which, if crossed*   Ibid., 171.

55 *heightened danger of war*   Ibid., 129.

55 *On May 19, Clinton*   Ibid., 177ff.

56 *Jim Laney*   Ibid., 200–243; Snyder, *Negotiating on the Edge*, 72.

58 *"Agreed Framework"*   *Agreed Framework between the United States of America and the Democratic People's Republic of Korea*, Geneva, Oct. 21, 1994 (U.S. State Department).

58 *ship the fuel rods*   U.S. State Dept., Robert Gallucci, press conference, Oct. 25, 1994. The specific terms were laid down in a contract between North Korea and the Korean Peninsula Energy Development Organization (KEDO), the international consortium created to manage the light-water reactors, in *Agreement on Supply of a Light-Water Reactor Project to the Democratic People's Republic of Korea between the Korean Peninsula Energy Development Organization and the Government of the Democratic People's Republic of Korea*, Dec. 15, 1995 (www.kedo.org/pdfs/supplyAgreement.pdf), especially Article VIII and Annex 3.

60 *Powell held a press conference*   "Bush to Pick Up Clinton Talks on North Korean Missiles," *Washington Post*, Mar. 7, 2003.

60 *"too forward in my skis"*   Colin Powell, interview with Andrea Koppel, CNN, Mar. 14, 2003.

61 *"I loathe Kim Jong Il!"*   Bob Woodward, *Bush at War* (New York: Simon & Schuster, 2002), 340.

61 *"pygmy," . . . "spoiled child"*   Howard Fineman, "I Sniff Some Politics," *Newsweek*, May 27, 2002.

62 *Kim Jong Il also sent*   Wit et al., 378.

62 *the evidence on that point*   *The Nelson Report*, March 1, 2007.

66 *"regime change" in North Korea*   David Rennie, "Rumsfeld Calls for Regime Change in North Korea," *London Telegraph*, Apr. 22, 2003.

66 *Wolfowitz bitterly decried*   Wit et al., *Going Critical*, 8.

66 *"American policy must be"*   Testimony, Senate Foreign Relations Committee, Feb. 7, 2002, reprinted at http://www.yale.edu/lawweb/avalon/sept_11/kristol.htm.

67 *"a shrimp among whales"*   Snyder, *Negotiating on the Edge*, 20.

67 *"drama and catastrophe"*   Ibid., 43.

67 *mount a coup against*   Bruce Auster and Kevin Whitelaw, "Pentagon Comes Up with a Provocative Plan to Face Down North Korea," *U.S. News & World Report*, July 21, 2003; and plans described on Global Security's Web site, e.g., http://www.globalsecurity.org/military/ops/oplan-5027.htm.

68 *chemical warheads or shells*   See the database at www.globalsecurity.org.

69 *Krypton-85*   Rob Edwards, "Krypton Clue to North Korean Nuclear Progress," *New Scientist*, July 2003.

71 *"Joint Statement"*   U.S. Dept. of State, *Joint Statement of the 4th Round of the Six-Party Talks, Beijing, September 19, 2005*.

72 *"North Koreans have made agreements"*   President George W. Bush, press conference, Vienna, June 22, 2006.

73 *They'd alerted Russia*   Siegfried S. Hecker, Stanford University, "Report on North Korea Nuclear Program," Nov. 15, 2006 (http://www.keia.org/3 Programs/HeckerReport.pdf).

74 *"The Iraq war teaches us a lesson"*   Korean Central News Agency, DPRK, Apr. 18, 2003.

74 *Gallucci suddenly realized*   Wit et al., *Going Critical*, 97.

75 *made note of distinct patterns*   Snyder, *Negotiating on the Edge*, passim, esp. chaps. 3 and 6.

3. Chasing Silver Bullets

77 *"At the earliest possible date"*   Gov. George W. Bush, "A Period of Consequences," The Citadel, Sept. 23, 1999.

77 *"The Contract with America"*   The bill passed the House 241–181 on Feb. 16, 1995. It had no enforcement clause, however. "At the earliest *possible* date" allowed much leeway.

78 *"I think those who oppose"*   President Bush, speech, Ridley, Pa., Aug. 17, 2004.

80   *Thumper, Hermes, Terrier*   BDM Corp., *History of Strategic Air and Ballistic Missile Defense* (Army College of Military History, 1975), IV-68 to IV-72. (Formerly secret. Declassified by National Security Archive, George Washington Univ.)

80   *drop their ABM programs*   Ibid., IV-73.

80   *Lieutenant General James Gavin*   Ibid., IV-80.

81   *Air Force chiefs made McElroy aware*   Ibid., IV-81.

81   *Reentry Body Identification Group*   Fred A. Payne (deputy director, Defense Research & Engineering), "A Discussion of Nike-Zeus Decisions," a lecture at Brookings Institution, Oct. 1, 1964. Provided to author. (On file at National Security Archive, George Washington Univ., along with many other documents that I was able to get declassified or otherwise obtain while researching my book *The Wizards of Armageddon*.)

81   *ARPA's missile-defense unit*   BDM Corp., *History of Strategic Air and Ballistic Missile Defense*, IV-82.

81   *Nike-Zeus not be built*   "Report of the AICBM Panel," May 21, 1959, White House Office File, Office of Special Assistant for Science & Technology, Box 4, AICBM (1), Dwight D. Eisenhower Library. (Also in Kaplan Files at National Security Archive.)

82   *subcontracts to thirty-seven states*   BDM Corp., IV-92 to IV-93.

82   *Kennedy was also briefed*   Kaplan, *Wizards of Armageddon*, 345.

83   *came to be called the "whiz kids"*   Ibid., esp. chap. 16.

84   *ABMs would cost too much*   *Damage Limiting: A Rationale for the Allocation of Resources by the U.S. and the U.S.S.R.*, prepared for the DDR&E, Jan. 21, 1964 (obtained through Freedom of Information Act, on file in Kaplan Files, National Security Archive); see also Kaplan, *Wizards of Armageddon*, 320–25. For that section of *Wizards*, I also interviewed Robert McNamara, Gen. Glenn Kent, Harold Brown, Jack Ruina, George Rathjens, Jerome Wiesner, Paul Warnke, Morton Halperin, and others.

85   *"China bomb, Bob?"*   Kaplan, *Wizards of Armageddon*, 346–48.

85   *thirteen carriers that the Navy wanted*   William Kaufmann told me this story in 1978. Kaufmann was the special assistant to Schlesinger (and to secretaries of defense in every administration from Kennedy's to Carter's), as well as a professor of defense studies at MIT, where I attended graduate school at the time.

85   *In October 1965*   Strategic Military Panel of the President's Science Advisory Council, "Report on Proposed Army-BTL Ballistic-Missile-Defense System," Oct. 29, 1965 (National Security Archive,

Electronic Briefing Book, "Missile Defense 30 Years Ago: Déjà Vu All Over Again?" Document 1).

86   *"almost broke our arms"*   Richard Garwin, "Scientist, Citizen, and Government—Ethics in Action (or Ethics Inaction)," speech, May 4, 1993 (www.fas.org/rlg/930504-imsa.htm); information about the 1967 AAAS conference comes from Garwin interview. Marvin Goldberger of Cal Tech also spoke on the panel with Bethe and Garwin but decided not to take part in writing the article.

87   *Bethe and Garwin were making*   Hans Bethe and Richard Garwin, "Anti-Ballistic-Missile Systems," *Scientific American*, May 1968.

87   *it marked the first time*   See Kaplan, *Wizards of Armageddon*, chap. 24.

87   *Foster came up with*   Ibid., 350–55.

88   *"We must get PSAC"*   Memo, Laurence Lynn to Henry Kissinger, "PSAC Strategic Military Panel Comments on Minuteman ABM Defense," Jan. 5, 1970 (Electronic Briefing Book, National Security Archive, "Missile Defense 30 Years Later," Document 6).

88   *Bell no longer wanted*   Memo, Henry Kissinger to President Nixon, "Contractor Doubts About Safeguard," Apr. 15, 1970, attached to Memo, Laurence Lynn to Kissinger, "Bell Labs on Safeguard," Apr. 14, 1970 (National Security Archive, Ibid., Document 10).

89   *Nixon and Soviet premier*   The formal titles are *Interim Agreement between the United States of America and the Union of Soviet Socialist Republics on Certain Measures with Respect to the Limitation of Strategic Offensive Arms* and *Treaty between the United States of America and the Union of Soviet Socialist Republics on the Limitation of Anti-Ballistic Missile Systems*, both signed May 26, 1972.

89   *Gerald Ford met with Brezhnev*   *Protocol to the Treaty between the United States of America and the Union of Soviet Socialist Republics on the Limitation of Anti-Ballistic Missile Systems*, July 3, 1974.

90   *Reagan wrote that final sentence*   Paul Lettow, *Ronald Reagan and His Quest to Abolish Nuclear Weapons* (New York: Random House, 2005), 112.

91   *Reagan himself abhorred nuclear weapons*   Ibid., passim; cf. also Fred Kaplan, "Ron and Mikhail's Excellent Adventure," *Slate*, June 9, 2004.

92   *"line of defense"*   Lettow, *Ronald Reagan*, 41.

92   *On December 22, 1982*   Martin Anderson, *Revolution: The Reagan Legacy* (Stanford, Calif.: Hoover Institution Press, 1990), 97. In

her otherwise excellent book, *Way Out There in the Blue: Reagan, Star Wars and the End of the Cold War* (New York: Simon & Schuster, 2000), Frances FitzGerald argues, on page 197, that this meeting never took place, in support of her contention that the idea for SDI came from the Joint Chiefs, not from Reagan. However, Lettow convincingly argues that it did take place, citing internal records and official photos that were not available when FitzGerald wrote her account. See Lettow, *Ronald Reagan*, 86–88, and associated footnotes on 268–69.

93 *The group met again*   Lettow, *Ronald Reagan*, 99.

93 *resigned over the issue*   Ibid., 104–5.

93 *The SDI Office issued*   Based mainly on my reporting at the time as Pentagon reporter for the *Boston Globe*.

95 *70 percent of Soviet worldwide propaganda*   Lettow, *Ronald Reagan*, 140.

96 *"we will be pulled into an arms race"*   Declassified documents quoted by Vladislav M. Zubok, "Gorbachev's Nuclear Learning: How the Soviet Leader Became a Nuclear Abolitionist," *Boston Review*, April–May 2000.

96 *Reagan replied*   Declassified minutes at www.cnn.com/SPE CIALS /cold.war/episodes/22/documents/reykjavik/.

99 *Gates wrote that on balance*   CIA, *NIE 95-19: Independent Panel Review of "Emerging Missile Threats to North America During the Next 15 Years,"* Dec. 23, 1996 (www.fas.org/irp/threat/missile/oca961908.htm).

99 *The commission's chairman was*   *Executive Summary of the Report of the Commission to Assess the Ballistic Missile Threat to the United States*, July 15, 1998; interviews with Richard Garwin, Barry Blechman, Stephen Cambone, and others.

100 *favored scrapping the ABM Treaty*   For example, Stephen Cambone, testimony, House National Security Committee, Mar. 21, 1996, reprinted at www.globalsecurity.org/space/library/congress/1996_h/ h960321c.htm.

101 *commissioners met forty-eight times*   Of these, thirty-eight were in sessions, and ten were visits to outside sites. All were summarized at the end of the report's executive summary.

103 *"God bless you, Kim Jong!"*   Quoted in "Missile Wars," *Frontline*, PBS, 1992 (www.pbs.org/wgbh/pages/frontline/shows/missile/etc/script.html).

103 *The CIA had been wrong*   Interviews with Cambone, others.

103 *Rumsfeld created his own*   Eric Schmitt and Thom Shankar, "Threat and Response: A CIA Rival; Pentagon Sets Up Intelligence Unit," *New York Times*, Oct. 24, 2002. Doug Feith, who ran the unit, known as the Office of Special Plans, was later chastised by the Defense Department's inspector general, who called its operations "improper." See DoD, Inspector General, *Report on Review of the Pre-Iraqi War Activities of the Office of the Under Secretary of Defense for Policy* (Report No. 07-INTEL-04), Feb. 9, 2007 (declassified Apr. 2007).

104 *CIA released a revised NIE*   "Missile Wars."

105 *Coyle wrote*   Director, Operational Test & Evaluation, Dept. of Defense, *Report in Support of the National Missile Defense Deployment Readiness Review*, Aug. 10, 2000, at www.cdi.org/news/missile-defense/coyle.pdf.

106 *transfer $600 million*   Barton Gelman, "A Strategy's Cautious Evolution," *Washington Post*, Jan. 20, 2002.

106 *"the threats and problems"*   Robin Wright, "Top Focus Before 9/11 Wasn't on Terrorism," *Washington Post*, Apr. 1, 2004.

108 *Christie on the witness list*   Interviews with Thomas Christie, others.

109 *Christie submitted his first report*   Fred Kaplan, "Shoot-Down: The Pentagon Trashes Bush's Missile Defense Plan," *Slate*, Feb. 21, 2003.

110 *"To deter such threats"*   http://www.fas.org/irp/offdocs/nspd/nspd-23.htm.

4. Breaking the World Anew

114 *Bush spent nearly half his time*   Joe Conason, in "Bush Must Explain Why Washington Slept," *Salon*, Apr. 14, 2004, calculates that before 9/11, Bush spent 54 days at his Crawford ranch, 38 days at Camp David, and 4 at Kennebunkport, Maine, for a total of 96 days away—or 41 percent of his 234 days in office up to that point.

115 *"God's gift to humanity"*   He first says this publicly in his second State of the Union address, Jan. 28, 2003.

116 *"cowboy instincts"*   Powell claims no memory of this, but Wilkerson recalls—and has notes of—a conversation in which Powell made these remarks shortly before he traveled to Africa with President Bush in July 2003.

116 *Gerson was thirty-four*   Carl M. Cannon, "Soul of a Conservative," *National Journal*, May 14, 2005; Jeffrey Goldberg, "The Believer," *New Yorker*, Feb. 13 and 20, 2006.

117 *The Reagan Library speech*   Reprinted at www.mtholyoke.edu/acad/intrel/bush/wspeech.htm.

118 *strong but "humble"*   Transcript, "The Second Gore-Bush Presidential Debate," Oct. 11, 2000 (Commission on Presidential Debates).

118 *Rice came highly recommended*   James Mann, *Rise of the Vulcans,* 168.

119 *Rice was Korbel's prize student*   Michael Dobbs, "Josef Korbel's Enduring Foreign Policy Legacy," *Washington Post*, Dec. 28, 2000.

119 *indulge in "dreams"*   "Tools of Diplomacy," lecture, Nov. 24, 1963, and "Freedom and Diplomacy," n.d., Josef Korbel Papers, Univ. of Denver Archival Library; lecture, June 1964, tape aired on *All Things Considered*, NPR, Oct. 4, 2006.

120 *"it is simply not possible"*   Condoleezza Rice, "Campaign 2000: Promoting the National Interest," *Foreign Affairs*, Jan./Feb. 2000.

123 *"Rebuilding America's Defenses"*   PNAC, *Rebuilding America's Defenses: Strategy, Forces, and Resources for a New Century*, Sept. 2000.

124 *"In the Middle East"*   Patrick Tyler, "US Strategy Plan Calls for Insuring No Rival Develops in a One-Superpower World," *New York Times*, Mar. 8, 1992.

125 *Albert Wohlstetter and Richard Perle*   Mann, *Rise of the Vulcans*, 205–6.

125 *Marshall wrote in his paper*   See chap. 1 of this volume.

125 *Cheney had told Wolfowitz*   Mann, *Rise of the Vulcans*, 207.

126 *Cheney flew to a resort*   Natan Sharansky, *The Case for Democracy: The Power of Freedom to Overcome Tyranny and Terror* (New York: Public Affairs, 2004), 240–42. (Page numbers for all references refer to the 2006 paperback edition.)

129 *"the best guarantee of security"*   Text is at http://www.aei.org/publications/pubID.15187/pub_detail.asp.

129 *"I call on the Palestinians"*   President George W. Bush, speech, June 24, 2002.

129 *"almost too good"*   Sharansky, *The Case for Democracy*, 242; and interviews.

132 *"this is why God wants you here"*   Gerson told this story at a dinner of past and present White House speechwriters. A former

Clinton speechwriter reacted by stage-whispering, "God must *hate* Al Gore." Recounted in Goldberg, "The Believer."

133   *"Tomorrow's lobby for Israel"*   Michael Dobbs, "Back in Political Forefront: Iran-Contra Figure Plays Key Role on Middle East," *Washington Post*, May 27, 2003.

133   *Wolfowitz had said a free*   Bill Keller, "Sunshine Warrior," *New York Times*, Sept. 22, 2002.

133   *Perle claimed that*   Quoted by Greg Miller, "Showdown with Iraq: Democracy Domino Theory 'Not Credible,'" *Los Angeles Times*, Mar. 14, 2003.

134   *"No Dominos"*   Ibid.; and interviews.

136   *"as if the region and its states"*   Stories by Glenn Kessler and/or Robin Wright, *Washington Post*, Feb. 9, Feb. 22, Feb. 28, and Mar. 20, 2004; and interviews.

137   *Powell met with Saudi crown prince*   U.S. State Dept., press conference, Mar. 19, 2004; and interviews.

138   *Forum for the Future*   U.S. State Dept., Chairman's Summary: Preparatory Meetings for Forum for the Future, Sept. 24, 2004.

139   *"into two categories"*   Sharansky, *The Case for Democracy*, 41.

139   *"those who were prepared"*   Ibid., 4.

139   *"the free world continues"*   Ibid., 13.

139   *"I am convinced"*   Ibid., 17.

139   *"the advent of democracy"*   Ibid., 69.

140   *"Since all democracies"*   Ibid., 95.

140   *It was "folly" to believe*   Ibid., 93.

140   *"genuine and lasting peace"*   Ibid., 90, 92.

140   *"when it comes to promoting"*   Ibid., 72.

140   *"I don't want some"*   Robert F. Kennedy, *Thirteen Days: A Memoir of the Cuban Missile Crisis* (New York: W.W. Norton & Co., 1973), 49, 97–98.

140   *Clinton justified staying out*   For Robert Kaplan connection, see Elizabeth Drew, *On the Edge: The Clinton Presidency* (New York: Touchstone, 1995), 157. For Sells, see Al Kamen, "The Book on Kosovo," *Washington Post Magazine*, July 18, 1999.

141   *"you are a real dissident"*   Sharansky, *The Case for Democracy*, preface to paperback edition; and interviews.

144   *But* emerging *democracies*   This is the conclusion of Edward Mansfield and Jack Snyder in *Electing to Fight: Why Emerging Democracies Go to War* (Cambridge, Mass.: MIT Press, 2005). I

summarized their points in "Elections Aren't Enough," *Slate*, Dec. 15, 2005.

144 *"dangers involved in the* transition" Sharansky, *The Case for Democracy*, 75.

144 *"Of course, a time of war is different"* Sharansky conceded this at Tel Aviv University on Feb. 23, 2005, at a forum to discuss his book. Transcript at http://hnn.us/articles/13658.html.

145 *"If you want a glimpse"* "Excerpts: Bush to Remain 'Committed' to War on Terrorism," *Washington Times*, Jan. 12, 2005.

145 *"Sharansky's book"* President Bush, transcript, conversation with young German business leaders, CNN, Feb. 23, 2005.

145 *during their forty-five-minute conversation* Joel Rosenberg, "Two Great Dissidents," *National Review*, Nov. 13, 2004; and interviews.

146 *The worldview of international Realism* The classic books propounding international Realism, which most students of international relations read in the 1960s and 1970s, are Hans Morgenthau, *Politics among Nations: The Struggle for Power and Peace* (first published in 1948, with many revised editions, most recently one edited by Kenneth Thompson, published by McGraw Hill); and Kenneth Waltz, *Man, the State, and War* (New York: Columbia Univ. Press, 1965).

147 *resonated with her own* She talked about this on CBS's *60 Minutes*, Nov. 19, 2004; and interviews.

5. The Dreams Dissolve into Nightmares

149 *White started to suspect* Interview with Wayne White.

150 *CPA Order* These have been discussed in nearly all the critical books about the Iraq war, but it's not yet entirely clear who ultimately is responsible for them. In his memoir, *My Year in Iraq* (New York: Simon & Schuster, 2006), on page 39, Bremer tags Doug Feith, but who told Feith? Wolfowitz had to have been involved, and this means Chalabi was probably involved. Chalabi has always been a proponent of radical de-Baathification, and he aspired to make his militia the foundation of a new Iraqi Army. But was Rumsfeld involved? Bob Woodward, in *State of Denial: Bush at War, Part III* (New York: Simon & Schuster, 2006), 194, quotes Rumsfeld as saying the order came from elsewhere. Does that mean it came from the White

House? If so, did it come from Cheney or from Bush directly? Given how many decisions were made in phone calls between Rumsfeld and Cheney, and in one-on-one meetings between Cheney and Bush, we may never know—unless someone had a tape recorder running.

153 *point of military transformation*   This is confirmed by Newt Gingrich, who, as a longtime acquaintance and an active member of the Defense Advisory Board, talked with Rumsfeld at great length about the subject. They agreed firmly that the successful use of small, light, agile forces was important for America's ability to project power for the next several decades.

153 *"our preeminent position"*   See chap. 1 of this volume.

154 *one of his young protégés*   Perle dated Wohlstetter's daughter in high school; they first talked about strategy out by the pool. Wohlstetter later hired Perle to work with him and Paul Nitze in a group formed to criticize the ABM critics during the congressional debate. On that basis, he was hired by Senator Jackson. See Kaplan, *Wizards of Armageddon*, 387–88; Robert Kaiser, "Senate Staffer Richard Perle: Behind-Scenes Power Over Arms Policy," *Washington Post*, June 26, 1977.

154 *"used-car salesman"*   Interview with Wayne White.

155 *"silk-suited, Rolex-wearing"*   Quoted in Seymour M. Hersh, "The Iraq Hawks," *The New Yorker*, Dec. 24, 2001.

158 *"something on the order of"*   Gen. Eric Shinseki, testimony, Senate Armed Services Committee, Feb. 25, 2003; Wolfowitz testified in rebuttal on Feb. 27.

159 *Dobbins made another discovery*   It was published as James Dobbins, *America's Role in Nation-Building: From Germany to Iraq* (Washington, D.C.: RAND Corp., 2003).

160 *Bush told his cabinet members*   Bob Woodward, *State of Denial*, 266.

160 *Rumsfeld kept up the pretense*   U.S. Defense Dept., Donald Rumsfeld, transcript, press conference, Nov. 29, 2005.

160 *David Kay*   James Risen, "Ex-Inspector Says CIA Missed Disarray in Iraq Arms Program," *New York Times*, Jan. 26, 2004; Fred Kaplan, "The Art of Camouflage: David Kay Comes Clean, Almost," *Slate*, Jan. 26, 2004.

160 *Charles Duelfer*   The official title was *Comprehensive Report of the Special Adviser to the Director of Central Intelligence on Iraq's*

Weapons of Mass Destruction, Sept. 30, 2004; for summary, see Fred Kaplan, "War without Reason," *Slate*, Oct. 8, 2004.

161   *Another blow came*   Kaplan, "War without Reason."

162   *three Iraqi exiles*   George Packer, "Dreaming of Democracy," *New York Times Magazine*, Mar. 2, 2003.

163   *"I hear a lot about 'civil war'"*   President Bush, press conference, Aug. 21, 2006.

163   *American Civil War*   In the 1860 American presidential election, 81.2 percent of the eligible population voted. This was a very close second to the 1876 election, in which 81.8 percent turned out. See http://www.presidency.ucsb.edu/data/turnout.php.

164   *"are not a true test of a democracy"*   Sharansky, *The Case for Democracy*, 72.

164   *Sharansky wrote an open letter*   Reprinted in http://www.onejer usalem.org/newsletters/sharanskyletter.htm.

165   *"What's wrong with this picture?"*   Interview with Dennis Ross.

167   *she published an op-ed piece*   Condoleezza Rice, "The Promise of Democratic Peace: Why Promoting Freedom Is the Only Realistic Path to Security," *Washington Post*, Dec. 11, 2005.

167   National Security Strategy   White House, *National Security Strategy of the United States of America*, March 2006, 1, 7.

168   *On the morning of July 12*   For an excellent general account, see Max Rodenbeck, "War within War," *New York Review of Books*, Sept. 21, 2006.

168   *the Arab League*   Full statement is at http://www.saudi-us-rela tions.org/articles/2006/ioi/060718-lebanon-crisis.html.

169   *But, Ross emphasized*   Interview with Dennis Ross.

169   *Zelikow, back in Washington*   Interview with Philip Zelikow.

170   *But Rice didn't go*   Zelikow confirmed this reason; others did, too, on background.

171   *escalation as "disproportionate"*   Ze'ev Schiff, "A Strategic Mistake," *Ha'aretz*, July 20, 2006.

171   *"We don't negotiate"*   Quoted by Knight-Ridder news service, Dec. 19, 2003.

176   *denounced Russian president Vladimir Putin*   White House, Vice President's Remarks at Vilnius Conference, May 4, 2006.

176   *expressed "admiration"*   White House, Vice President's Press Availability with Nursultan Nazarbayev, May 5, 2006.

179 *"We are all Americans."* Jean-Marie Colombani, "Nous sommes tous americaines," *Le Monde*, Sept. 12, 2001.

179 *invoked Article 5* Statement by the North Atlantic Council, Sept. 12, 2001, at http://www.nato.int/docu/pr/2001/p01-124e.htm.

179 *"A disdainful refusal"* Gerard Baker, "Not Dead But Missing in Action," *Financial Times*, Nov. 21, 2001.

180 *"When the chips are down"* Interview with Jacques Chirac, *New York Times*, Sept. 8, 2002.

180 *"a comprehensive package"* Prague Summit Declaration, Nov. 21, 2002, at http://www.nato.int/docu/pr/2002/p02-127e.htm.

180 *"debunk the myth"* Lord George Robertson, speech to NATO Parliamentary Assembly, Nov. 15, 2002, at http://www.nato.int/docu/speech/2002/s021115a.htm.

180 *"Rarely has a NATO summit"* Quoted at http://www.globalsecurity.org/military/library/news/2002/11/mil-021127-wwwh21127.htm.

180 *A poll by the BBC* BBC News, "Poll Suggests World Hostile to US," June 16, 2003.

180 *A poll by the Pew Research Center* Cited in *New York Times*, June 4, 2003.

181 *"Why do they hate us?"* Fareed Zakaria, "Why Do They Hate Us?" *Newsweek*, Oct. 15, 2001.

182 *"Public Diplomacy: How"* Charles Wolf Jr. and Brian Rosen, "Public Diplomacy: How to Think About It and Improve It," occasional paper, RAND Corp., 2004.

183 *new field manual* U.S. Army and Marine Corps, *Counterinsurgency Field Manual (U.S. Army Field Manual No. 3–24, Marine Corps Warfighting Publication No. 3–33.5)* (Chicago: University of Chicago Press, 2007), 47–52; Napoleon parallel, 138; Petraeus's calculations, 22–23.

185 *U.S. military didn't have* For more elaborate analysis, see Fred Kaplan, "The Army, Faced with Its Limits," *New York Times* (Week in Review), Jan. 1, 2006.

186 *John Bolton* Transcript, CNN, Feb. 12, 2007.

186 *"Had we believed this"* Rice, "The Promise of Democratic Peace."

187 *"I especially want to thank"* U.S. State Dept., Condoleezza Rice, press conference, Cairo, Jan. 15, 2007.

188 *"We seek to shape the world"* White House, *National Security Strategy of the United States*, March 2006, Introduction.

6. Waking Up to Reality

189   *"as America sought to create the world anew"*   Condoleezza Rice,
"The Promise of Democratic Peace: Why Promoting Freedom Is the
Only Realistic Path to Security," *Washington Post*, Dec. 11, 2005.

189   *Bush liked to invoke*   Michael Abramowitz, "Truman's Trials
Resonate for Bush," *Washington Post*, Dec. 15, 2006.

189   *"By the actions he took"*   President Bush, commencement
address, West Point, May 27, 2006.

190   *"Long Telegram"*   Reprinted at http://www.gwu.edu/~nsarchiv/
coldwar/documents/episode-1/kennan.htm; see also X, "The Sources
of Soviet Conduct," *Foreign Affairs*, July 1947. (Kennan wrote the
article under the pseudonym "X" because he was an official at the
time.)

190   *The pioneering nuclear strategists*   Especially Bernard Brodie
and Albert Wohlstetter. See Kaplan, *Wizards of Armageddon, passim.*

191   *Acheson somewhat haughtily*   Dean Acheson, *Present at the
Creation: My Years in the State Department* (New York: Norton,
1969).

192   *The great divide*   For an excellent attempt at a modern realism
with a moral core, see Anatol Lieven and John Hulsman, *Ethical
Realism* (New York: Pantheon, 2006).

192   *"dreamers of the day"*   T. E. Lawrence, *Seven Pillars of Wisdom*
(New York: Doubleday, 1935; Anchor paperback ed., 1991), 24.

196   *At least one prominent liberal advocate*   David Rieff, *At the
Point of a Gun* (New York: Simon & Schuster, 2005).

198   *The war in Bosnia*   See Wesley Clark, *Waging Modern War:
Bosnia, Kosovo, and the Future of Combat* (New York: Public Affairs,
2001).

198   *a genuine coalition*   http://www.globalsecurity.org/military/ops/
desert_storm-allied.htm.

198   *"It would have been a mistake"*   Richard Cheney, speech,
Washington Institute for Near East Policy, Mar. 29, 1991.

200   *"If we're an arrogant nation"*   Transcript, "The Second Gore-
Bush Presidential Debate," Oct. 11, 2000 (Commission on Presidential Debates).

Bibliography

Government Documents

Agreed Framework between the United States of America and the Democratic People's Republic of Korea. Geneva, Oct. 21, 1994.

Agreement on Supply of a Light-Water Reactor Project to the Democratic People's Republic between the Korean Peninsula Energy Development Organization and the Government of the Democratic People's Republic of Korea. Dec. 15, 1995.

Interim Agreement between the United States of America and the Union of Soviet Socialist Republics on Certain Measures with Respect to the Limitation of Strategic Offensive Arms (SALT I). Geneva, May 26, 1972.

North Atlantic Treaty Organization. Atlantic Council statement, Sept. 12, 2001.

———. Lord George Robertson, speech to NATO Parliamentary Assembly, Nov. 15, 2002.

———. Prague Summit declaration, Nov. 21, 2002.

Protocol to the Treaty between the United States of America and the Union of Soviet Socialist Republics on the Limitation of Anti-Ballistic Missile Systems. Vladivostok, July 3, 1974.

Treaty between the United States of America and the Union of Soviet Socialist Republics on the Limitation of Anti-Ballistic Missile Systems (ABM Treaty). Geneva, May 26, 1972.

U.S. Air Force. *The Air Force and U.S. National Security: Global Reach— Global Power, A White Paper* (Deptula Report). June 1990.

U.S. Army. *Army Field Manual FM 100–5* (Operations). Washington, D.C.: U.S. Government Printing Office, 1976.

———. *Army Field Manual FM 100–5* (Operations). Washington, D.C.: U.S. Government Printing Office, 1982.

U.S. Army and U.S. Marine Corps. *Army Field Manual No. 3–24, Marine Corps Warfighting Publication No. 33–5 (Counterinsurgency)*. Washington, D.C.: U.S. Government Printing Office, 2006.

U.S. Central Intelligence Agency. *Comprehensive Report of the Special Adviser to the Director of Central Intelligence on Iraq's Weapons of Mass Destruction* (Duelfer Report). Sept. 30, 2004.

———. *NIE 95–19: Independent Panel Review of "Emerging Missile Threats to North America during the Next 15 Years"* (Gates Report). Dec. 23, 1996.

U.S. Congress. Hearings on Ballistic Missile Defense and the ABM Treaty, House Armed Services Committee, Subcommittees on Military Research & Development and Military Procurement, Mar. 21, 1996.

———. Hearings, House Budget Committee, Feb. 27, 2003.

———. Hearings, Senate Armed Services Committee, Jan. 31, 1992.

———. Hearings, Senate Armed Services Committee, Feb. 25, 2003.

———. Hearings, Senate Foreign Relations Committee, Feb. 7, 2002.

———. House of Representatives. "Republican Contract with America," 1994.

U.S. Defense Dept. Defense Advanced Research Projects Agency, Defense Nuclear Agency. *Summary Report of the Long Range Research and Development Planning Program.* DNA-75–03055. Feb. 7, 1975. Declassified Dec. 31, 1983.

———. Director, Office of Operational Test & Evaluation. *Report in Support of the National Missile Defense Deployment Readiness Review* (Coyle Report). Aug. 10, 2000.

———. Inspector General. *Report on Review of the Pre-Iraqi War Activities of the Office of the Under Secretary of Defense for Policy.* Report No. 07-INTEL-04, Feb. 9, 2007. Declassified Apr. 2007.

———. Office of Net Assessment. Andrew W. Marshall, Memorandum for the Record, "Some Thoughts on Military Revolutions—Second Version." Aug. 23, 1993. (Provided to author.)

———. Office of the Secretary of Defense. *The Quadrennial Defense Review Report.* Sept. 30, 2001.

———. Secretary of Defense Richard Cheney. Speech, Washington Institute for Near East Policy, Mar. 29, 1991.

———. Secretary of Defense Donald Rumsfeld. Press conference, Nov. 29, 2005.

U.S. State Dept. "Chairman's Summary: Preparatory Meetings for Forum for the Future," Sept. 24, 2004.

———. *Foreign Relations of the United States, 1969–1976. Volume 2: Organizational Management of U.S. Foreign Policy.* Washington, D.C.: U.S. Government Printing Office, 2006.

————. Joint Statement of the 4th Round of the Six-Party Talks, Beijing, Sept. 19, 2005.

————. Press conference, Amb. Robert Gallucci, Oct. 25, 1994.

————. Press conference, Secretary Colin Powell and Prince Faisal, Riyadh, Mar. 19, 2004.

————. Press conference, Secretary Condoleezza Rice, Cairo, Jan. 15, 2007.

————. Press conference, Secretary Condoleezza Rice, July 21, 2006.

————. Speech, Secretary Condoleezza Rice, American University, Cairo, Feb. 25, 2005.

White House. *National Security Presidential Directive No. 23* (NSPD-23), Dec. 16, 2002.

————. *National Security Strategy of the United States of America*, March 2006.

————. President George W. Bush. Commencement address, West Point, May 27, 2006.

————. President George W. Bush. Conversation with young German business leaders, Feb. 23, 2005.

————. President George W. Bush. Inaugural address, Jan. 20, 2001.

————. President George W. Bush. Inaugural address, Jan. 20, 2005.

————. President George W. Bush. Press conference, Vienna, June 22, 2006.

————. President George W. Bush, Press conference, Crawford, Tex., Aug. 7, 2006.

————. President George W. Bush. Press conference, Aug. 21, 2006.

————. President George W. Bush. Speech, American Enterprise Institute, Feb. 26, 2003.

————. President George W. Bush. Speech, National Endowment for Democracy, Nov. 6, 2003.

————. President George W. Bush. Speech, Ridley, Pa., Apr. 17, 2004.

————. President George W. Bush. Speech, Rose Garden, June 24, 2002.

————. President George W. Bush. State of the Union address, Jan. 28, 2003.

————. Vice President Dick Cheney. Press availability with Nursultan Nazarbayev, Kazakhstan, May 5, 2006.

————. Vice President Dick Cheney. Remarks at Vilinius conference, May 4, 2006.

Commission Reports, Contractors' Studies, Monographs, Dissertations, Speeches

BDM Corp. *History of Strategic Air and Ballistic Missile Defense.* Army College of Military History, 1975. (Declassified by National Security Archive, George Washington University.)

Biddle, Stephen. *Afghanistan and the Future of Warfare: Implications for Army and Defense Policy*. Carlisle Barracks, Pa.: U.S. Army War College, Nov. 2002.

Boyd, John. *Patterns of Conflict*. Briefing, 1986. (http://www.d-n-i.net/boyd/pdf/poc.pdf).

Bush, Gov. George W. "A Distinctly American Internationalism," speech, Ronald Reagan Presidential Library, Simi Valley, Calif., Nov. 19, 1999.

———. "A Period of Consequences,"speech, The Citadel, Sept. 23, 1999.

Commission on Integrated Long-Term Strategy. *Discriminate Deterrence* (Wohlstetter-Ikle Report), Jan. 1988.

Commission on Presidential Debates. "The Second Gore-Bush Presidential Debate," transcript, Oct. 11, 2000.

Commission to Assess the Ballistic Missile Threat to the United States (Rumsfeld Commission). *Executive Summary of the Report of the Commission to Assess the Ballistic Missile Threat to the United States*, July 15, 1998.

Deptula, Brig. Gen. David A. *Effects-Based Operations: Change in the Nature of Warfare*. Arlington, Va.: Aerospace Education Foundation, 2001.

Frisbee, Lieut. Col. Sean M. *Weaponizing the Predator UAV*. Maxwell Air Force Base, Ala.: School for Advanced Air and Space Studies, Air University Press, June 2004.

Fulkenberry, Maj. Barbara J. *Global Reach—Global Power: Air Force Strategic Vision, Past and Future*. Maxwell Air Force Base, Ala.: Air University Press, Feb. 1996.

Garwin, Richard L. "Scientist, Citizen, and Government—Ethics in Action (Or Ethics Inaction)," speech, May 4, 1993 (www.fas.org/rlg/930504-imsa.htmsa.htm).

Hecker, Siegfried S. "Report on North Korea Nuclear Program." Stanford University/Korea Economic Institute of America, Nov. 15, 2006.

Krepinevich, Andrew F. Jr. *The Military-Technical Revolution: A Preliminary Assessment*. Foreword by Andrew Marshall. Wash., D.C.: Center for Strategic and Budgetary Assessments, 2002. Originally published as classified report by U.S. Defense Dept., Office of Net Assessment, 1992.

National Defense Panel. *Transforming Defense*. Dec. 1997.

Payne, Fred A. "A Discussion of Nike-Zeus Decisions," lecture, Brookings Institution, Oct. 1, 1964. (Provided to author.)

Project for a New American Century. *Rebuilding America's Defenses: Strategy, Forces, and Resources for a New Century*. Sept. 2000.

Sharansky, Natan. "Democracy for Peace," speech, American Enter-
    prise Institute World Forum, Beaver Creek, Colo., June 20, 2002.
———. Resignation letter to Prime Minister Ariel Sharon, May 2, 2005. Re-
    printed http://www.onejerusalem.org/newsletters/sharanskyletter.htm.
Van Atta, Richard H., et. al. *Transformation and Transition: DARPA's
    Role in Fostering an Emerging Revolution in Military Affairs, Vol.
    1—Overall Assessment.* IDA Paper P-3698. Alexandria, Va.: Insti-
    tute for Defense Analysis, Apr. 2003.
Wolf, Charles Jr., and Brian Rosen. "Public Diplomacy: How to Think about
    It and Improve It." Occasional Paper, RAND Corp., 2004.

Archives

GlobalSecurity.org.
Nuclear History File, Electronic Briefing Book, National Security Archive.
    George Washington University, Washington, D.C.
U.S. Army. Combined Arms Command Archive. "CGSC-Departments-
    School of Advanced Military Studies" folder. Ft. Leavenworth, Kan.
U.S. Military Academy. West Point Home Page, "Palmer McGrew Stor-
    ies." http://www.west-point.org/users/usma1958/22097/3tactics.html.
University of California at Santa Barbara. The American Presidency Project.
University of Denver Archival Library. Josef Korbel Papers.

Books

Acheson, Dean. *Present at the Creation: My Years in the State Depart-
    ment.* New York: W.W. Norton & Co., 1969.
Anderson, Martin. *Revolution: The Reagan Legacy.* Stanford, Calif.:
    Hoover Institution Press, 1990.
Boot, Max. *War Made New: Technology, Warfare, and the Course of
    History, 1500 to Today.* New York: Gotham, 2006.
Bremer, L. Paul. *My Year in Iraq.* New York: Simon & Schuster, 2006.
Brzezinski, Zbigniew. *The Choice: Global Domination or Global Lead-
    ership.* New York: Basic Books, 2004.
———. *Second Chance: Three Presidents and the Crisis of American
    Superpower.* New York: Basic Books, 2007.
Chandrasekaran, Rajiv. *Imperial Life in the Emerald City: Inside Iraq's
    Green Zone.* New York: Knopf, 2006.
Clark, Wesley. *Waging Modern War: Bosnia, Kosovo, and the Future of
    Combat.* New York: Public Affairs, 2001.

————. *Winning Modern Wars: Iraq, Terrorism, and the American Empire*. New York: Public Affairs, 2003.

Cockburn, Andrew. *Rumsfeld: His Rise, Fall and Catastrophic Legacy*. New York: Scribner's, 2007.

Cockburn, Patrick. *The Occupation: War and Resistance in Iraq*. New York: Verso, 2006.

Coram, Robert. *Boyd: The Fighter Pilot Who Changed the Art of War*. New York: Little, Brown & Co., 2005.

DeYoung, Karen. *Soldier: The Life of Colin Powell*. New York: Knopf, 2006.

Dobbins, James. *America's Role in Nation-Building: From Germany to Iraq*. Santa Monica & Washington, D.C.: RAND Corp., 2003.

Drew, Elizabeth. *On the Edge: The Clinton Presidency*. New York: Touchstone, 1995.

Fallows, James. *Blind into Baghdad: America's War in Iraq*. New York: Vintage, 2006.

FitzGerald, Frances. *Way Out There in the Blue: Reagan, Star Wars, and the End of the Cold War*. New York: Simon & Schuster, 2000.

Fromkin, David. *A Peace to End All Peace: The Fall of the Ottoman Empire and the Creation of the Modern Middle East*. New York: Henry Holt & Co., 1989.

Fukuyama, Francis. *America at the Crossroads: Democracy, Power, and the Neoconservative Legacy*. New Haven, Conn.: Yale University Press, 2006.

Gordon, Michael R., and Bernard E. Trainor. *Cobra II: The Inside Story of the Invasion and Occupation of Iraq*. New York: Pantheon, 2006.

————. *The Generals' War: The Inside Story of the Conflict in the Gulf*. New York: Little, Brown & Co., 1995.

Hashim, Ahmed S. *Insurgency and Counter-insurgency in Iraq*. Ithaca, N.Y.: Cornell University Press, 2006.

Hersh, Seymour M. *Chain of Command: The Road from 9/11 to Abu Ghraib*. New York: HarperCollins, 2004.

Isikoff, Michael, and David Corn. *Hubris: The Inside Story of Spin, Scandal, and the Selling of the Iraq War*. New York: Crown, 2006.

Kaplan, Fred. *The Wizards of Armageddon*. New York: Simon & Schuster, 1983.

Kaplan, Robert. *Balkan Ghosts: A Journey Through History*. New York: St. Martin's Press, 1993.

Keany, Thomas, and Eliot A. Cohen. *Revolution in Warfare? Air Power in the Persian Gulf*. Annapolis, Md.: Naval Institute Press, 1995.

Kennedy, Robert F. *Thirteen Days: A Memoir of the Cuban Missile Crisis*. New York: W.W. Norton & Co., 1973.

Lawrence, T. E. *Seven Pillars of Wisdom*. New York: Doubleday, 1935.

Lettow, Paul. *Ronald Reagan and His Quest to Abolish Nuclear Weapons*. New York: Random House, 2005.

Lieven, Anatol, and John Hulsman. *Ethical Realism: A Vision for America's Role in the World*. New York: Pantheon, 2006.

Mann, James. *Rise of the Vulcans: The History of Bush's War Cabinet*. New York: Viking, 2004.

Mansfield, Edward, and Jack Snyder. *Electing to Fight: Why Emerging Democracies Go to War*. Cambridge, Mass.: MIT Press, 2005.

Morgenthau, Hans. *Politics Among Nations: The Struggle for Power and Peace*. New York: McGraw Hill, 1948.

Nagl, John A. *Learning to Eat Soup with a Knife: Counterinsurgency Lessons from Malaya and Vietnam*. Chicago & London: University of Chicago Press, 2002.

Nasr, Vali. *The Shia Revival: How Conflicts Within Islam Will Shape the Future*. New York: W.W. Norton & Co., 2006.

Naylor, Sean. *Not a Good Day to Die: The Untold Story of Operation Anaconda*. New York: Berkley Books, 2005.

Packer, George. *The Assassins' Gate: America in Iraq*. New York: Farrar, Strauss & Giroux, 2006.

Ricks, Thomas E. *Fiasco: The American Military Adventure in Iraq*. New York: Penguin Press, 2006.

Rieff, David. *At the Point of a Gun: Democratic Dreams and Armed Intervention*. New York: Simon & Schuster, 2005.

Risen, James. *State of War: The Secret History of the CIA and the Bush Administration*. New York: Free Press, 2006.

Sells, Michael. *The Bridge Betrayed: Religion and Genocide in Bosnia*. Berkeley: University of California Press, 1996.

Sharansky, Natan. *The Case for Democracy: The Power of Freedom to Overthrow Tyranny and Terror*. New York: Public Affairs, 2004.

Smith, Perry Anderson. *The Air Force Plans for Peace, 1943–45*. Baltimore: Johns Hopkins University Press, 1970.

Snyder, Scott. *Negotiating on the Edge: North Korean Negotiating Behavior*. Washington, D.C.: United States Institute of Peace Press, 1999.

Suskind, Ron. *The Price of Loyalty: George W. Bush, the White House, and the Education of Paul O'Neill*. New York: Simon & Schuster, 2004.

Swain, Richard M. *Lucky War: Third Army in Desert Storm*. Ft. Leavenworth, Kan.: U.S. Army Command & General Staff College Press, 1994.

Tuchman, Barbara. *The Guns of August*. New York: Random House, 1962.

Ullman, Harlan, and James Wade. *Shock and Awe: Achieving Rapid Dominance*. Philadelphia: Pavilion Press, 1998.

U.S. Army and Marine Corps. *Counterinsurgency Field Manual*. Forewords by Gen. David H. Petraeus, Lieut. Gen. James F. Amos, Lieut. Col. John A. Nagl, Sarah Sewall. Chicago & London: University of Chicago Press, 2007.

Waltz, Kenneth. *Man, the State, and War*. New York: Columbia University Press, 1965.

Watts, Barry D. *Six Decades of Guided Munitions and Battle Networks: Progress and Prospects*. Washington, D.C.: Center for Strategic and Budgetary Assessments, 2007.

Wit, Joel, Daniel Poneman, and Robert Gallucci. *Going Critical: The First North Korean Nuclear Crisis*. Washington, D.C.: Brookings Institution Press, 2004.

Woodward, Bob. *Bush at War*. New York: Simon & Schuster, 2002.

———. *Plan of Attack*. New York: Simon & Schuster, 2004.

———. *State of Denial: Bush at War, Part III*. New York: Simon & Schuster, 2006.

Zakaria, Fareed. *The Future of Freedom: Illiberal Democracy at Home and Abroad*. New York: W.W. Norton & Co., 2003.

Magazine and Newspaper Articles

Abramowitz, Michael. "Truman's Trials Resonate for Bush." *Washington Post*, Dec. 15, 2006.

"Advanced Studies." *Soldier*, July 1986.

Arkin, William M. "Spiraling Ahead." *Armed Forces Journal*, Feb. 2006.

Auster, Bruce, and Kevin Whitelaw. "Pentagon Comes Up with a Provocative Plan to Face Down North Korea." *U.S. News & World Report*, July 21, 2003.

Baker, Gerald. "Not Dead But Missing in Action." *Financial Times*, Nov. 21, 2001.

Bethe, Hans, and Richard Garwin. "Anti-Ballistic-Missile Systems." *Scientific American*, May 1968.

Biddle, Stephen. "Afghanistan and the Future of Warfare." *Foreign Affairs*, Mar/Apr. 2003.

Cannon, Carl M. "Soul of a Conservative." *National Journal*, May 14, 2005.

Chirac, Jacques. Interview. *New York Times*, Sept. 8, 2002.

Colombani, Jean-Marie. "Nous sommes tous americaines." *Le Monde*, Sept. 12, 2001.

Conason, Joe. "Bush Must Explain Why Washington Slept." *Salon*, Apr. 14, 2004.

Dobbs, Michael. "Back in Political Forefront: Iran-Contra Figure Plays Key Role on Middle East." *Washington Post*, May 27, 2003.

———. "Josef Korbel's Enduring Foreign Policy Legacy." *Washington Post*, Dec. 28, 2000.

Edwards, Rob. "Krypton Clue to North Korean Nuclear Progress." *New Scientist*, July 2003.

"Excerpts: Bush to Remain 'Committed' to War on Terrorism." *Washington Times*, Jan. 12, 2005.

Fineman, Howard. "I Sniff Some Politics." *Newsweek*, May 27, 2002.

Gellman, Barton. "A Strategy's Cautious Evolution." *Washington Post*, Jan. 20, 2002.

Goldberg, Jeffrey. "The Believer." *The New Yorker*, Feb. 13/20, 2006.

Hersh, Seymour M. "The Iraq Hawks." *The New Yorker*, Dec. 24, 2001.

Kaiser, Robert. "Senate Staffer Richard Perle: Behind-Scenes Power Over Arms Policy." *Washington Post*, June 26, 1977.

Kaplan, Fred. "The Army, Faced with Its Limits." *New York Times*, Jan. 1, 2006.

———. "The Art of Camouflage: David Kay Comes Clean, Almost." *Slate*, Jan. 26, 2004.

———. "Elections Aren't Enough." *Slate*, Dec. 15, 2005.

———. "High-Tech US Arsenal Proves Its Worth." *Boston Globe*, Dec. 9, 2001.

———. "Rolling Blunder." *Washington Monthly*, May 2004.

———. "Ron and Mikhail's Excellent Adventure." *Slate*, June 9, 2004.

———. "Shoot-Down: The Pentagon Trashes Bush's Missile Defense Plan." *Slate*, Feb. 21, 2003.

———. "War without Reason." *Slate*, Oct. 8, 2004.

Keller, Bill. "Sunshine Warrior." *New York Times*, Sept. 22, 2002.

Kennan, George ("X"). "The Sources of Soviet Conduct." *Foreign Affairs*, July 1947.

Miller, Greg. "Showdown with Iraq: Democracy Domino Theory 'Not Credible.'" *Los Angeles Times*, Mar. 14, 2003.

Mufson, Steven. "Bush to Pick Up Clinton Talks on North Korea." *Washington Post*, Mar. 7, 2003.

Nelson Report. Mar. 1, 2007.

Packer, George. "Dreaming of Democracy." *New York Times Magazine*, Mar. 2, 2003.

Rennie, David. "Rumsfeld Calls for Regime Change in North Korea." *London Telegraph*, Apr. 22, 2003.

Rice, Condoleezza. "Campaign 2000: Promoting the National Interest." *Foreign Affairs*, Jan/Feb 2000.

———. "The Promise of Democratic Peace: Why Promoting Freedom Is the Only Realistic Path to Security." *Washington Post*, Dec. 11, 2005.

Risen, James. "Ex-Inspector Says CIA Missed Disarray in Iraq Arms Program." *New York Times*, Jan. 26, 2004.

Rodenbeck, Max. "War within War." *New York Review of Books*, Sept. 21, 2006.

Rosenberg, Joel. "Two Great Dissidents." *National Review*, Nov. 13, 2004.

Schiff, Ze'ev. "A Strategic Mistake." *Ha'aretz*, July 20, 2006.

Schmitt, Eric, and Thom Shankar. "Threat and Response: A CIA Rival, Pentagon Sets Up Intelligence Unit." *New York Times*, Oct. 24, 2002.

Tyler, Patrick. "US Strategy Plan Calls for Insuring No Rival Develops in a One-Superpower World." *New York Times*, Mar. 8, 1992.

Wass de Czege, Huba. "How to Change an Army." *Military Review*, Nov. 1984.

———. "Wargaming Insights." *Army*, Mar. 2003.

Werrell, Kenneth. "Did USAF Technology Fail in Vietnam?" *Airpower Journal*, Spring 1998.

Wohlstetter, Albert. "The Delicate Balance of Terror." *Foreign Affairs*, Jan. 1959.

Wright, Robin. "Top Focus Before 9/11 Wasn't on Terrorism." *Washington Post*, Apr. 1, 2004.

Zakaria, Fareed. "Why Do They Hate Us?" *Newsweek*, Oct. 15, 2001.

Zubok, Vladislav M. "Gorbachev's Nuclear Learning: How the Soviet Leader Became a Nuclear Abolitionist." *Boston Review*, Apr-May 2000.

Television and Radio Broadcasts

BBC News. "Poll Suggests World Hostile to US." June 16, 2003.

CBS. Interview with Condoleezza Rice. *60 Minutes*. Nov. 29, 2004.

CNN. Interview with John Bolton. Feb. 12, 2007.

———. Interview with Colin Powell. Mar. 14, 2003.

History News Network. Panel discussion with Natan Sharansky from Feb. 23, 2005. Aired Aug. 22, 2005.

NPR. Josef Korbel lecture from June 1964. *All Things Considered*, Oct. 4, 2006.

PBS. "Missile Wars." *Frontline*. Oct. 10, 2002.

Index